Speeches

By

Black Americans

Speeches

By

Black Americans

Edited and Compiled

by

Daniel J. O'Neill
Youngstown State University

Dickenson Publishing Company, Inc.
Encino, California and Belmont, California

Acknowledgments

James Forten and Russell Perrott, "An Appeal Against the Colonization Movement." Reprinted from James Forten and Russell Perrott, "An Address to the Humane and Benevolent Inhabitants of the City and County of Philadelphia," from Carter Godwin Woodson (Ed.), *Negro Orators and Their Orations* (Washington, D.C.: The Association for the Study of Negro Life and History, 1925), New York: Russell & Russell, 1969. Reprinted by permission of Russell & Russell, Publishers.

Henry Highland Garnet, "An Address to the Slaves of the United States." Reprinted from Carter Godwin Woodson (Ed.), *Negro Orators and Their Orations* (Washington, D.C.: The Association for the Study of Negro Life and History, 1925), New York: Russell & Russell, 1969. Reprinted by permission of Russell & Russell, Publishers.

Frederick Douglass, "Reception Speech in England." Reprinted from Frederick Douglass, *My Bondage and My Freedom,* Arno Press Edition, 1968. Reprinted by permission of Arno Press, Inc.

Frederick Douglass, "Fourth of July Oration." Reprinted from Frederick Douglass, "What to the Slaves Is the Fourth of July?" and "The Internal Slave Trade," from *My Bondage and My Freedom,* Arno Press Edition, 1968. Reprinted by permission of Arno Press, Inc.

Frederick Douglass, "Men of Color, To Arms!" Reprinted from *The Life and Times of Frederick Douglass,* Hartford, 1887.

Robert Brown Elliott, "Speech on the Civil Rights Bill." Reprinted from the *Congressional Record,* Part II, 43rd Congress, 1st Session, pp. 407-410.

Roy Wilkins, "Sail Our NAACP Ship—Keynote Address." Reprinted by permission of Roy Wilkins.

Whitney M. Young, Jr., "Can the City Survive?" Reprinted by permission of Whitney M. Young, Jr., and the Robert Morris Associates. (Speech delivered at the 54th Annual Fall Conference of the Robert Morris Associates, 1968.)

Adam Clayton Powell, Jr., "Can There Any Good Thing Come Out of Nazareth?" Reprinted by permission of Adam Clayton Powell, Jr. Lines from Keith E. Baird, *Nemesis,* reprinted by permission of Freedomways Associates, New York.

Carl T. Rowan, "New Frontiers in Racial Relations." Reprinted by permission of Lester Lewis Associates, Inc., agent for the author.

Floyd McKissick, "The Student and the Ghetto." Reprinted by permission of Floyd McKissick.

Eldridge Cleaver, "Meditation on the Assassination of Martin Luther King, Jr." Reprinted from Eldridge Cleaver, "The Death of Martin Luther King: Requiem for Nonviolence" (pp. 73-79), from *Post-Prison Writings and Speeches,* edited by Robert Scheer. Copyright © 1967, 1968 by Eldridge Cleaver. Reprinted by permission of Random House, Inc.

James Forman, "Black Manifesto." Reprinted by permission of James Forman and the National Black Economic Development Conference.

James Farmer and Malcolm X, "Debate on the Solution to America's Race Problem." Reprinted from James Farmer and Malcolm X, "Separation or Integration: A Debate," *Dialogue Magazine,* II, 3 (May, 1962), pp. 14-18. Reprinted by permission of W. Jack Lewis, Director, Cornell United Religious Work.

Contents

Preface

Speeches by Black Americans helps to fill the need for a book with an historical development of Negro and black oratory. Covering the last century and one half, this collection of significant texts by black speakers can be used in a course on the history of American public address, in a contemporary public address course, perhaps as a supplementary text in a speech skills course, or even as a text in a black studies curriculum.

The primary focus of this book is an historical tracing of black views toward the race problem by way of significant speeches. Many different types of speech situations and rhetorical strategies are represented which can be used by students as illustrative models or as documents for critical, historical, and rhetorical analysis. Collateral readings together with study questions and problems follow each speech and can be used by students and instructor to stimulate further analysis of speaker and speeches. Hopefully, the reader will think of additional questions which need to be asked.

The book is divided into two parts, "The Heritage" and "The Contemporary Scene." Part I contains representative texts of historically significant speakers. Selected speakers and speeches are summarized in a brief introduction to this section. Part II contains a sampling of speeches delivered by black leaders of the post-World War II era. Again, speakers and their speeches are briefly introduced to the reader.

Biographical and textual notes precede each speech. A major effort was made to present authentic texts. The earliest possible editions of a speech were sought and compared with later editions to determine which version seemed more reliable. Fortunately, many contemporary texts have been electrically recorded, while still other contemporary texts were forwarded to me by the speakers themselves.

The editor wishes to acknowledge the help of all who participated in the preparation of this book: librarians, typists, editors, reviewers, and speakers. Special acknowledgment goes to Karen Haller for her assistance in the preparation of the manuscript, and to my wife, Paula, for her patience and encouragement.

D. J. O.

One feels his two-ness—an American, a Negro, two souls, two thoughts, two unreconciled strivings, two warring ideals in one dark body. . . .

—W. E. B. Du Bois, *The Souls of Black Folk*

Introduction

There is both an historical and a rhetorical rationale for the study of black speakers. One can study black speakers for their influence in the shaping of history and for the light they shed on human events. Speeches by blacks in America are important because they define and strengthen the ideals of black people and help to shape the black experience in American society.

Historically, blacks in America have relied heavily upon the spoken word to communicate their thoughts and feelings about the problems facing them as a racial minority. The emphasis that black people have placed on the spoken word may be traced to the earliest slave experiences of Negroes in America; to the important role played by the Negro preacher of the plantation church; to the fear of reprisal for protesting in writing the inhumane black laws of the colonial and antebellum period of American history; to the fact that the mass of blacks in America were illiterate for centuries; and to the power of the spoken word to influence and effect social change in the minds of both white men and black men.

Also, one can study black speakers to test the validity of the theory of rhetorical communication that we have developed over the years. It would be foolish to accept uncritically the proscriptions of speech textbooks without carefully comparing that theory with the actual speech behavior of various groups of speakers, past and present. So we study speeches rhetorically in order to validate our current conceptions about the way speaking should be done. Failure to observe and critically evaluate the speeches of black Americans might well lead to the charge that contemporary rhetoricians are constructing rhetorical theory amenable only to middle-class whites.

Moreover, scholars have contributed literally hundreds of works dealing with the black experience in American society. The Selected Bibliography at the end of the book represents only the seminal works in the field of black oratory and black history. Surely it is time, given the vast amount of bibliographical information relating to the black American experience, to give serious individual attention to the Negro contribution in American public address. No longer can Booker T. Washington's apologia at the Cotton States Exposition in Atlanta, Georgia, to a predominantly white audience, be represented as the only contribution of rhetorical significance produced by the black orator. The eloquence of Frederick Douglass, W. E. B. Du Bois, A. Philip Randolph, Martin Luther King, Jr., and numerous other black rhetors, past and present, demand our most serious scholarly attention. The myth of rhetorical inferiority, together with the myths of biological and social inferiority, are destroyed by an objective analysis of the evidence.

ONE

The Heritage

Introduction

Antebellum Speakers

According to historian Carter G. Woodson in *Negro Orators and Their Orations,* the earliest protest of black Americans occurred among free Negroes who had obtained their freedom from indentured servitude or from slavery and who thereafter attacked the institution of slavery whenever possible. It seems that during the seventeenth and eighteenth centuries, free expression of ideas was not an established principle of the nation, and thus Negroes tended to speak out under assumed names. Woodson pointed to improved educational opportunities and the abolition of slavery in the Northern states as important factors in the development of more forceful and open attacks against slavery. During the early nineteenth century, Negro church leaders, such as Peter Williams, Richard Allen, and Theodore S. Wright, before sympathetic Northern audiences, took the initiative and denounced all forms of prejudice against men of color.

Beginning in 1817, groups of free Negroes met in local and state conventions to protest the formation of the American Colonization Society, whose purpose was to send free Negroes back to Africa. Anticolonization agitation by Negroes increased during the 1820's when the Colonization Society purchased Liberia and began a nationwide colonization movement. The first selection in this anthology is characteristic of early Negro protest to the colonization movement. In an address to the humane citizens of Philadelphia, James Forten argued:

. . . let not a purpose be assisted which will stay the cause of the entire abolition of slavery in the United States, and which may defeat it altogether; which proffers to those who do not ask for them what it calls benefits, but which they consider injuries; and which must insure to the multitudes whose prayers can only reach you through us, misery, and sufferings, and perpetual slavery.[1]

Legal restraints, another impetus to protest, were imposed upon free

[1]See Forten's "An Appeal Against the Colonization Movement."

Negroes by Northern states. The "Black Laws" generated a steady stream of agitation which resulted in the so-called Negro Convention Movement. According to historian August Meier in his book, *Negro Thought in America, 1880-1915*, the Negro Convention Movement was the most representative vehicle of thought among articulate blacks during the antebellum and Reconstruction eras. The first such convention occurred in 1830 as a reaction to legal restrictions and a bloody race riot in Cincinnati, Ohio. "Fearing that legislators and mobsters in the East would follow the pattern set by Ohio, Negro leaders decided to plan concerted action on a nationwide scale to stem the tide of repression. . . ."[2] National conventions were held regularly each year from 1830 to 1835, and irregularly thereafter as the occasion warranted through Reconstruction. "More than any other source, the conventions provide illuminating insight into the thinking of articulate Negroes in regard to the problems facing the race."[3]

Conventions and mass meetings passed resolutions, issued addresses to the public, and sent petitions to governors and legislatures. In campaigning for the franchise, for equal treatment in the courts, for guarantees of civil liberties, and in the Old Northwest, for the abolition of the Black Laws, Negroes emphasized that they were simply asking for basic citizenship rights. First and foremost, therefore, they appealed to the democratic principles upon which the nation was founded. They advanced other arguments as well to support their claims. They denied the existence of innate racial differences, stressed the presence of a thrifty and industrious class of Negroes, and on occasion even enumerated at length the substantial property holdings that free Negroes had acquired under unfavorable conditions. They returned again and again to the theme that Negroes were native Americans, loyal to the nation that oppressed them.[4]

Perhaps the most significant speech to come out of a national Negro convention was the one delivered at the 1843 convention at Buffalo, New York, by Henry Highland Garnet. In this speech, Garnet called for the slaves to rebel.

Brethren arise, arise! Strike for your lives and liberties. Now is the day and the hour. Let every slave throughout the land do this, and the days of slavery are numbered. You cannot be more oppressed than you have been—you cannot suffer greater cruelties than you have already. Rather die freemen than live to be slaves. Remember that you are FOUR MILLIONS! . . . Let your motto be resistance! resistance! RESISTANCE![5]

It is significant to note that the delegates to the Buffalo convention

[2]Philip S. Foner, *The Life and Writing of Frederick Douglass* (New York, 1950), II, p. 20.

[3]Reprinted by permission from August Meier and Elliott M. Rudwick, *From Plantation to Ghetto* (New York: Hill Wang Company, 1966), p. 99.

[4]*Ibid.*, pp. 70-71.

[5]See Garnet's "An Address to the Slaves of the United States."

failed to endorse Garnet's position by a single vote. But the use of violence to eliminate slavery became more widely discussed by Negroes during the later 1840's. Interestingly, Garnet's speech of a similar nature delivered in 1847 at the next convention aroused far less heated disapproval among Negroes.

Black speakers also played an active role in the abolitionist movement. Leon F. Litwack argues that Negro abolitionists protested slavery in a variety of ways.

In addition to legislative petitions, meetings commemorating the abolition of the African slave trade or the end of slavery in a particular state afforded opportunities for such prominent Negro leaders as Peter Williams, Nathaniel Paul, William Hamilton, and Joseph Sidney to voice their sentiments on public issues. The organization of independent churches, Free African societies, Masonic lodges, and anticolonization meetings further intensified a growing race consciousness and helped to arouse the Negro community in several areas to a more vigorous defense of its civil rights.[6]

By 1830 there were fifty Negro antislavery groups in Northern cities.

The most eloquent and influential antebellum agitator was Frederick Douglass, a runaway slave who learned to read and write while in bondage. During the summer of 1841, Douglass attended an antislavery convention in Nantucket, where he was invited to say a few words.

I trembled in every limb. I am not sure that my embarrassment was not the most effective part of my speech, if speech it could be called. At any rate, this is about the only part of my performance that I now distinctly remember. The audience sympathized with me at once, and from having been remarkably quiet, became much excited.[7]

In the 1840's Douglass toured Europe to escape prosecution as a runaway slave, lecturing on slavery in England, Ireland, and Scotland until his freedom was purchased.

As an abolitionist lecturer he was employed by the Massachusetts Antislavery Society, the Rhode Island Antislavery Society, and the American Antislavery Society. Moreover, he was a prominent speaker at numerous national Negro conventions, and after the Civil War he lectured extensively on the Lyceum circuit.

Attesting to Douglass' initial eloquence, William Lloyd Garrison wrote:

A beloved friend from New Bedford prevailed on Mr. Douglass to address the convention: He came forward to the platform with a hesitancy and embarrassment, necessarily the attendants of a sensitive mind in such a novel position. After apologizing for his ignorance, and reminding the audience that slavery

[6]Melvin Drummer, ed., *Black History: A Reappraisal* (Garden City, N.Y., 1968), p. 207.

[7]Frederick Douglass, *The Life and Times of Frederick Douglass* (New York, 1941), p. 239.

was a poor school for the human intellect and heart, he proceeded to narrate some of the facts in his own history as a slave, and in the course of his speech gave utterance to many noble thoughts and thrilling reflections. As soon as he had taken his seat, filled with hope and admiration, I rose, and declared that Patrick Henry, of revolutionary fame, never made a speech more eloquent in the cause of liberty, than the one we had just listened to from the lips of that hunted fugitive.[8]

Three speeches have been chosen for inclusion in this anthology as representative of Douglass' eloquence and ideology. First, the speech at Moorfields, England, is reprinted as an example of black abolitionist speaking before foreign audiences. In the 1840's and 1850's, some abolitionists toured the British Isles to promote the antislavery cause and raise funds for the abolitionist movement. "Englishmen crowded into meeting halls to see and hear leading American Negroes tell of the plight of their people and their own experiences as slaves or freemen."[9] Second, Douglass' "Fourth of July Oration" in Rochester, New York (1852), is included as illustrative of numerous Fourth of July speeches delivered by free Negro leaders who utilized the celebration day as a day of fasting and prayer when Negroes would ask for divine intervention to break the shackles of slavery. Third, the editor has included Frederick Douglass' "Men of Color, to Arms!" which was delivered on the eve of the Civil War. Negroes were almost unanimous in their demand for black troops in the War Between the States, and this speech reflects that sentiment.

Reconstruction

Negro conventions of the 1860's and early 1870's, the Reconstruction conventions, were primarily concerned with obtaining political and civil rights. The importance of education was a frequent theme. To a somewhat lesser degree in the Reconstruction conventions, Negroes advocated an economic program based upon thrift, industry, and the acquisition of wealth as a means of achieving assimilation into American society.

During Reconstruction, segregated Negro churches and mutual help fraternities in the black communities articulated a philosophy of achieving full citizenship through economic, political, and moral uplift of the entire community.[10]

The prevailing vocalized expression of thought during Reconstruction was characterized by a broad program for advancement based upon the equalitarian

[8]Frederick Douglass, *Narrative of the Life of Frederick Douglass* (Boston, 1845), pp. x-xi.

[9]Drummer, p. 211.

[10]Reprinted by permission of August Meier, *Negro Thought in America, 1880-1915* (Ann Arbor: The University of Michigan Press, 1966), pp. 121-138.

traditions in American culture. Negroes focused their attention upon becoming full-fledged citizens. The franchise, education, guarantees for civil rights, the acquisition of property and wealth, and the cultivation of morality were all designed to elevate Negroes and achieve their integration into American society.[11]

Articulate blacks also participated in Reconstruction constitutional conventions and in state and federal legislatures after the Civil War.

Negroes served for some time in the United States Senate: Hiram R. Revals, 1870-71 (an unexpired term), and B. K. Bruce, 1875-81 (a full term). Both were elected from Mississippi. Twenty-one Negroes served in the House of Representatives, from the 43rd through the 56th Congress, 1868-95. They were elected from eight states: Alabama, Florida, Georgia, Louisiana, Mississippi, North Carolina, South Carolina, and Virginia. Eleven served single full terms (two years); six served two full terms each, two served three terms, and one, Joseph H. Rainey of South Carolina, served five terms. The largest number of representatives, seven, came from South Carolina followed by four from North Carolina; Georgia, Mississippi, and Florida elected one each.[12]

An adequate analysis of the influence of black political figures has not yet been written, although some historians contend that Negroes took a leading role in giving authorization to public education in state constitutions and that Negro congressmen played a role in the ratification of the Fourteenth and Fifteenth Amendments.

Since Negro politicians tended to dominate the Reconstruction era both in and out of Congress, the editor has selected perhaps the most famous of the Reconstruction speeches by a Negro congressman—Robert Brown Elliott's speech, "On the Bill to Enforce the Provisions of the Fourteenth Amendment to the Constitution," which he delivered in April, 1871.

The Age of Booker T. Washington

The generation following the collapse of the Reconstruction era in 1877 was a period of increasing prejudice, violence, and discrimination toward black citizens. Through complicated registration and voting procedures, Negro political influence was effectively curtailed in the Southern states. A system of laws evolved known as "Jim Crow" laws, which established legal separation of the races in all public facilities. In the South, legal separation of schools was provided for in the 1870's and 1880's. Railroad coach segregation was instituted in the 1880's and 1890's.[13] Moreover, a climate of increasing violence became the pattern

[11]*Ibid.,* p. 15.

[12]John P. David, ed., *The American Negro Reference Book* (Englewood Cliffs, N.J.: Prentice-Hall, 1969), p. 420.

[13]Meir, *Negro Thought,* pp. 162-164.

in race relations during the post-Reconstruction era. Lynching reached a peak in the 1880's and 1890's, averaging about 150 per year during those two decades.

Booker T. Washington's famous speech at the Cotton States Exposition (Atlanta, Georgia, 1895) can be understood only against this background of political disenfranchisement, racial separation, and increasing violence. The speech reflects a shift in Negro thought from political to economic action and from immediate integration and protest to self-help. According to historian August Meier, Social Darwinists of late nineteenth-century America greatly influenced Negro thinking. Washington's Exposition address is perhaps the fullest articulation of the black American's adoption of the popular notion of a gospel of wealth as it applied to the racial situation. The speech clearly illustrates the change in emphasis from broad civil rights to a narrower emphasis on wealth and frugality.

The Atlanta Exposition speech attracted nationwide attention and made Washington the spokesman for the black race. Northern white philanthropists, such as Andrew Carnegie, offered to underwrite any project Washington proposed. Leaders in government, education, and industry extolled the Tuskegeean's virtues. Because of the cardinal importance of the Atlanta Exposition address in catapulting Booker T. Washington to a position of vast influence, the editor has chosen to present this speech together with Washington's remarks about events preceding the speech and his reflections on the effect of the address. These excerpts are taken from Washington's famous autobiography, *Up from Slavery* (New York, 1901).

Not all Negroes agreed with the sentiments that Washington expressed in 1895. Foremost among Washington's critics was Harvard-educated W. E. B. Du Bois, who held that Washington's accommodating philosophy had led to practical acceptance of the alleged inferiority of the Negro. In 1905 Du Bois helped found the Niagara Movement, which developed a program of public agitation for Negro rights.

The Niagara men told whites that they should not be lulled into thinking that "the Negro-American assents to inferiority, is submissive under oppression and apologetic before insult. . . . We do not hesitate to complain, and to complain loudly and insistently."[14]

White Progressives and Christian Socialists who were dissatisfied with Washington's gradual policy joined with Du Bois and other disenchanted Negroes of the Niagara Movement at the National Negro Convention at New York in 1909 and formed the National Association for the Advancement of Colored People, dedicated to providing a strong central

[14]*Ibid.,* p. 184.

defense committee to advance Negro interests. "In their speeches at the conference, radical leaders like Ida Wells-Barnett and Du Bois stressed the importance of the ballot."[15] Du Bois' remarks at the National Negro Convention are included in this anthology.

Urban Protest

In the decades preceding World War I, many Negroes migrated from Southern rural areas to the cities of the North in an attempt to improve their economic condition. Northern industry encouraged poverty-stricken Negroes to leave the South and fill the need for unskilled and semi-skilled labor.

These Negro migrants entered an urban environment where racial lines were more and more tightly drawn. They were crowded into ghettos and given mostly unskilled jobs, incurring the animosity of whites. Numerous race riots occurred. In the summer of 1919, for example, over twenty riots were reported. The black urban masses of the twenties thus tended to suffer economic privation when demobilization occurred after World War I.[16]

The one man who really reached the frustrated and disillusioned masses in the ghettos was Marcus Garvey, who founded the Universal Negro Improvement Association (UNIA). The Garvey or Back-to-Africa Movement provided a compensatory escape for Negroes caught in the hopelessness of the ghetto. Garvey was an articulate and passionate speaker who stressed race pride and glorified the African past. "On a more practical level he urged Negroes to support Negro businesses, and the UNIA itself organized a chain of groceries, restaurants, laundries, a hotel, a doll factory, and a printing plant."[17]

Garvey denounced white Americans, who he claimed were descendants of Satan. He urged his followers to build an independent nation in Africa where they could choose their own leaders. By the mid 1920's, the Back-to-Africa Movement had over a million followers among lower-class blacks from cities throughout the nation. Only Garvey's conviction for fraud in 1923 and deportation to Jamaica two years later caused the collapse of the movement. The Garvey movement was replaced by store-front churches and cult groups, such as Father Divine and Daddy Grace, who attempted to create a life of meaning out of meaninglessness for poor blacks during the 1920's and 1930's.

Many followers of the nationalist Garvey ended up in the ostentatiously interracial cult of Father Divine, whose "Heavens" did not really multiply until

[15]*Ibid.,* p. 185.

[16]*Ibid.,* pp. 192-196.

[17]*Ibid.,* p. 200.

the economic Depression of the 1930's. Undoubtedly these religious cults provided an alternative for what might otherwise have been a highly explosive nationalist movement.[18]

The last two speeches included in the Heritage section of this anthology are A. Philip Randolph's address to the delegates to the March on Washington Movement Convention in 1942 and Thurgood Marshall's address to the NAACP Wartime Conference in 1944.

The purpose of the March on Washington Movement Convention was to plan an enormous march by Negro citizens to protest discrimination in the nation's defense industry. Randolph, who was the President of the Brotherhood of Sleeping Car Porters, said that the government would not help blacks until it saw "ten, twenty, fifty thousand Negroes on the White House lawn."[19] As the result of the threat of a mass protest march, President Roosevelt signed the famous Executive Order No. 8802, which banned discrimination in defense plants and government agencies because of race, creed, color, or national origin.

It was the first time since Lincoln had signed the Emancipation Proclamation that a President had acted to protect the civil rights of black men. The March-on-Washington threat had shown the value, in Randolph's words, of a "non-violent demonstration of Negro mass power" as a tactic of protest.[20]

In his speech to the NAACP Wartime Conference, Thurgood Marshall, one-time special counsel to the NAACP, explained that organization's legal approach and its underlying philosophy.

Thus it seems clear that although it is necessary and vital to all of us that we continue our program for additional legislation to guarantee and enforce certain of our rights, at the same time we must continue with ever-increasing vigor to enforce those few statutes, both federal and state, which are now on the statute books.[21]

The speeches of Marshall and Randolph anticipate the direction which the civil rights movement was to take in the 1950's and 1960's. The success of the NAACP's legal approach shortly after World War II and the early 1950's soon gave way to Randolph's notion of direct action protest. Thus, these two speeches should be read as portents.

[18]*Ibid.,* p. 204.
[19]Bradford Chambers, *Chronicles of Black Protest* (New York, 1968), p. 175.
[20]*Ibid.*
[21]See Marshall's "The Legal Attack to Secure Civil Rights."

James Forten
and
Russell Perrott

James Forten established a prosperous business in Philadelphia by perfecting a device in the handling of sails. Together with Robert Purvis and Russell Perrott, Forten argued against restrictions to free speech in that city.

A meeting of "people of color" in Philadelphia was called on August 10, 1817, to protest the colonization movement. James Forten served as chairman and Russell Perrott served as secretary.

The issue of emigration to Africa was the first issue on which articulate free Negroes expressed their sentiments openly. In 1816 the American Colonization Society was organized, proposing to solve the race problem by resettling freed Negroes in Africa. The Colonization program appealed to such diverse elements as slaveholders, some gradual emancipationists, and a few philanthropists. Agents of the Society toured the country advocating a new solution to the race problem. It is not surprising that Northern Negroes feared that they would be uprooted from their local communities and sent to Africa.

Together they presented the following address, expressing the dominant view of not only the Negroes of Philadelphia, but most blacks throughout the nation, concerning the policy of returning free Negroes to Africa. They argued that colonization would irreparably divide freemen from slaves. "The cords, which now connect them with us will be stretched by the distance to which their ends will be carried until they break; and all the sources of happiness, which affection and connection, and blood bestow, will be ours or theirs no more." Moreoever, Forten and Perrott contended that emancipated slaves would be subjected to untold miseries if they were sent to Africa without any preparation for independence. "Without arts, without habits of industry, and unaccustomed to provide by their own exertions and foresight for their wants, the colony will soon become the abode of

13

*every vice and the home of every misery." Finally, the authors argued
that the institution of slavery would be perpetuated by a tame and submissive
group of bondmen: "And the tame and submissive will be retained, and
subjected to increased rigour."*

   *The thoughts expressed in the following address were directed toward
a large general audience of white citizens of Philadelphia. Historian Carter
Woodson pointed out that the race problem was national rather than
sectional during the early nineteenth century. Negroes who migrated to
the North were confronted with legal restrictions regarding their movement
from place to place, their rights to public transportation, and their rights
to trial by jury, just to mention a few discriminatory practices. Nevertheless,
Philadelphia had developed a strong tradition for dissent, traceable to
Quaker piety. The larger audience would have been generally hostile to
the position of the black community of Philadelphia, but some of the
Christian and antislavery elements of the white community may have been
well disposed to the position on colonization as expressed by Forten and
Perrott.*

An Appeal Against the Colonization Movement
August 10, 1817

   The free people of colour, assembled together, under circumstances
of deep interest to their happiness and welfare, humbly and respectfully
lay before you this expression of their feelings and apprehensions.

   Relieved from the miseries of slavery, many of us by your aid; possessing the benefits which industry and integrity in this prosperous country
assure to all its inhabitants; enjoying the rich blessings of religion, by
opportunities of worshiping the only true God, under the light of Christianity, each of us according to his understanding; and having afforded
to us and to our children the means of education and improvement;
we have no wish to separate from our present homes, for any purpose
whatever. Contented with our present situation and condition we are
not desirous of increasing their prosperity, but by honest efforts and
by the use of those opportunities for their improvement, which the
Constitution and laws allow to all. It is therefore with painful solicitude,
and sorrowing regret, we have seen a plan for colonizing the free people
of colour of the United States on the coast of Africa, brought forward
under the auspices and sanction of gentlemen whose names give value
to all they recommend, and who certainly are among the wisest, the

best, and the most benevolent of men, in this great nation.

If the plan of colonizing is intended for our benefit and those who now promote it will never seek our injury, we humbly and respectfully urge that it is not asked for by us; nor will it be required by any circumstances, in our present or future condition, as long as we shall be permitted to share the protection of the excellent laws, and just government which we now enjoy, in common with every individual of the community.

We therefore, a portion of those, who are objects of this plan, and among those whose happiness, with that of others of our colour, it is intended to promote, with humble and grateful acknowledgments to those who have devised it, renounce, and disclaim every connection with it, and respectfully but firmly declare our determination not to participate in any part of it.

If this plan of colonization now proposed is intended to provide a refuge and a dwelling for a portion of our brethren who are now held in slavery in the South, we have other and stronger objections to it, and we entreat your consideration of them.

The ultimate and final abolition of slavery in the United States is, under the guidance and protection of a just God, progressing. Every year witnesses the release of numbers of the victims of oppression, and affords new and safe assurances that the freedom of all will in the end be accomplished. As they are thus by degrees relieved from bondage, our brethren have opportunities for instruction and improvement; and thus they become in some measure fitted for their liberty. Every year, many of us have restored to us by the gradual, but certain, march of the cause of abolition, parents, from whom we have been long separated—wives and children, whom we had left in servitude—and brothers, in blood as well as in early sufferings, from whom we had been long parted.

But if the emancipations of our kindred shall, when the plan of colonization shall go into effect, be attended with transportation to a distant land, and shall be granted on no other condition, the consolation for our past sufferings and of those of our colour, who are in slavery, which has hitherto been, and under the present situation of things, would continue to be afforded to us and to them, will cease forever. The cords which now connect them with us will be stretched by the distance to which their ends will be carried until they break; and all the sources of happiness, which affection and connection and blood bestow, will be ours or theirs no more.

Nor do we view the colonization of those who may become emancipated by its operation among our Southern brethren, as capable of producing their happiness. Unprepared by education, and a knowledge of the truths of our blessed religion, for their new situation, those who will thus become colonists will themselves be surrounded by every suffering which can afflict the members of the human family.

Without arts, without habits of industry, and unaccustomed to provide by their own exertions and foresight for their wants, the colony will soon become the abode of every vice and the home of every misery. Soon will the light of Christianity, which now dawns among that section of our species, be shut out by the clouds of ignorance, and their day of life be closed, without the illuminations of the Gospel.

To those of our brethren who shall be left behind, there will be assured perpetual slavery and augmented sufferings. Diminished in numbers the slave population of the Southern states, which by its magnitude alarms its proprietors, will be easily secured. Those among their bondmen, who feel that they should be free, by rights which all mankind have from God and from nature, and who thus may become dangerous to the quiet of their masters, will be sent to the colony, and the tame and submissive will be retained, and subjected to increased rigour. Year after year will witness these means to assure safety and submission among their slaves; and the Southern masters will colonize only those whom it may be dangerous to keep among them. The bondage of a large portion of our brethren will thus be rendered perpetual.

Should the anticipations of misery and want among the colonists, which with great deference we have submitted to your better judgment, be realized; to emancipate and transport to the colony will be held forth by slaveholders as the worst and heaviest of punishments, and they will be threatened and successfully used to enforce increased submission to their wishes and subjection to their commands.

Nor ought the sufferings and sorrows, which must be produced by an exercise of the right to transport and colonize such only of their slaves as may be selected by the slaveholders, escape the attention and consideration of those whom with all humility we now address. Parents will be torn from their children—husbands from their wives—brothers from brothers—and all the heart-rending agonies which were endured by our forefathers when they were dragged into bondage from Africa will be again renewed, and with increased anguish. The shores of America will like the sands of Africa be watered by the tears of those who will be left behind. Those who shall be carried away will roam childless, widowed, and alone, over the burning plains of Guinea.

Disclaiming, as we emphatically do, a wish or desire to interpose our opinions and feelings between all plans of colonization and the judgment of those whose wisdom as far exceeds ours as their situations are exalted above ours; *We humbly,* respectfully, and fervently entreat and beseech your disapprobation of the plan of colonization now offered by "the American society for colonizing the free people of colour of the United States." Here, in the city of Philadelphia, where the voice of the suffering sons of Africa was first heard; where was first commenced the work of abolition, on which Heaven hath smiled, for it could have had success only from the Great Maker, let not a purpose be assisted which will stay the cause of the entire abolition of slavery in the United States, and which may defeat it altogether; which proffers to those who do not ask for them what it calls benefits, but which they consider injuries; and which must insure to the multitudes whose prayers can only reach you through us, *misery, and sufferings, and perpetual slavery.*

Collateral Reading

Aptheker, Herbert, ed., *A Documentary History of the Negro People in the United States.* 2 vols. New York, 1951.

Bardoph, Richard, *The Negro Vanguard.* New York, 1961.

Billington, Roy Allen, "James Forten: Forgotten Abolitionist," *Negro History Bulletin,* XII (November, 1949), 1-6.

Brawley, Benjamin, *A Short History of the Negro in America.* New York, 1931.

Meier, August and Elliott M. Rudwick, *From Plantation to Ghetto.* New York, 1966.

Study Questions and Problems

1. Analyze the language of this address. How would you describe the tone of this appeal? Evaluate the language as to choice of words, clarity, appropriateness, and impressiveness. How do you account for this particular style?

2. How do you account for the change from hostility to approval of colonization which occurred in the 1850's?

3. Study the historical evolution of the colonization movement. Can you relate this early nineteenth-century movement to any twentieth-century separatist movement?

4. Read Martin Delany's views on colonization in Howard Brotz, ed., *Negro Social and Political Thought, 1850-1920* (New York, 1957), and contrast these with Forten's views.

5. Study the background of the founding of Liberia as a colony for the return of former slaves to Africa. What role did Paul Cuffe play in the colonization movement?

Henry Highland Garnet

Henry Highland Garnet was born into slavery in Kent County, Maryland, on December 23, 1815, a descendant of an African chieftain and warrior. The Garnet family escaped from their owner, Colonel William Spencer, and eventually settled in New York City, where Garnet attended the African Free School. As a youth he joined the First Presbyterian Church, which was the pastorate of the famous Negro pulpit orator, Rev. Theodore S. Wright. Garnet was graduated with honors from Oneida Institute at Whitesboro, New York, in 1839. Then he studied theology while he was teaching at the first public school for blacks in Troy, New York. In 1842 he became a licensed preacher and received the first pastorate at the Liberty Street Presbyterian Church in Troy.

As a preacher and abolitionist agitator, Garnet had numerous occasions to speak from pulpit and rostrum. According to all accounts, he had a

wonderful ability for holding audiences spell-bound; his pure English, deep thought and manly dignity in anti-slavery movements were often in demand. He was active and progressive in everything. His speeches were made with such powerful effect that their force could never be put in print. He was a man of strong feeling and a true heart, and in speaking reached the inner nature of men. Many of his speeches can never die, and it is a shame that they cannot be gathered up and preserved as English classics.[1]

Garnet lectured in both the United States and Great Britain in the cause of antislavery.

Garnet's "An Address to the Slaves" is reminiscent of Patrick Henry's "Liberty or Death" speech, highly volatile and hortatory in its attempt to agitate the slaves of America to rebel. "If you must bleed, let it all come at once—rather die freemen than live to be the slaves." Garnet's thesis, simply stated, was that the time had come for the slaves themselves to overthrow their oppressors. "Brethren, the time has come when you must act for yourselves. It is an old and true saying that, 'if hereditary bondmen would be free, they must themselves strike the blow.' "

[1]William J. Simmons, *Men of Mark* (New York, 1968), pp. 658-659.

To Garnet, slavery was an intolerable evil and a contradiction to Christian doctrine. Garnet effectively recalled examples of past heroes and martyrs who sought to gain freedom from slavery, including Denmark Vesey, Nat Turner, Joseph Cinque, and Madison Washington.

Noble men! Those who have fallen in freedom's conflict, their memories will be cherished by the true-hearted and the God-fearing in all future generations; those who are living, their names are surrounded by a halo of glory.

Finally, the speech concludes with a magnificent appeal for action.

Brethren, arise, arise! Strike for your lives and liberties. Now is the day and the hour. Let every slave throughout the land do this, and the days of slavery are numbered. You cannot be more oppressed than you have been—you cannot suffer greater cruelties than you have already. Rather die freemen than live to be slaves. *Remember that you are FOUR MILLIONS!*

This speech, then, is an excellent example of agitational rhetoric. Garnet's appeal was delivered to an immediate audience of delegates attending the National Convention of Colored Citizens held in Buffalo, New York, on August 21-24, 1843. We know that Garnet's call to rebellion almost swayed the small number of delegates in attendance to adopt a resolution calling for the slaves to rebel. The resolution was defeated by one vote, with Frederick Douglass leading the opposition to the motion. The speech later had some propagandistic effect when published in pamphlet form by John Brown.

An Address to the Slaves of the United States

August 21-24, 1843

BRETHREN AND FELLOW CITIZENS: Your brethren of the North, East and West have been accustomed to meet together in National Conventions, to sympathize with each other, and to weep over your unhappy condition. In these meetings we have addressed all classes of the free, but we have never, until this time, sent a word of consolation and advice to you. We have been contented in sitting still and mourning over your sorrows, earnestly hoping that before this day your sacred liberties would have been restored. But, we have hoped in vain. Years have rolled on, and tens of thousands have been borne on streams of blood and tears to the shores of eternity. While you have been oppressed, we have also been partakers with you; nor can we be free while you are enslaved. We, therefore, write to you as being bound with you.

Many of you are bound to us not only by the ties of a common humanity, but we are connected by the more tender relations of parents, wives, husbands, and sisters, and friends. As such we most affectionately address you.

Slavery has fixed a deep gulf between you and us, and while it shuts out from you the relief and consolation which your friends would willingly render, it afflicts and persecutes you with a fierceness which we might not expect to see in the fiends of hell. But still the Almighty Father of mercies has left to us a glimmering ray of hope, which shines out like a lone star in a cloudy sky. Mankind are becoming wiser, and better—the oppressor's power is fading, and you, every day, are becoming better informed, and more numerous. Your grievances, brethren, are many. We shall not attempt, in this short address, to present to the world all the dark catalogue of the nation's sins, which have been committed upon an innocent people. Nor is it indeed necessary, for you feel them from day to day, and all the civilized world looks upon them with amazement.

Two hundred and twenty-seven years ago the first of our injured race were brought to the shores of America. They came not with glad spirits to select their homes in the New World. They came not with their own consent, to find an unmolested enjoyment of the blessings of this fruitful soil. The first dealings they had with men calling themselves Christians exhibited to them the worst features of corrupt and sordid hearts, and convinced them that no cruelty is too great, no villainy and no robbery too abhorrent for even enlightened men to perform, when influenced by avarice and lust. Neither did they come flying upon the wings of Liberty to a land of freedom. But they came with broken hearts, from their beloved native land, and were doomed to unrequited toil and deep degradation. Nor did the evil of their bondage end at their emancipation by death. Succeeding generations inherited their chains, and millions have come from eternity into time, and have returned again to the world of spirits, cursed and ruined by American slavery.

The propagators of the system, or their immediate successors, very soon discovered its growing evil, and its tremendous wickedness, and secret promises were made to destroy it. The gross inconsistency of a people holding slaves, who had themselves "ferried o'er the wave" for freedom's sake, was too apparent to be entirely overlooked. The voice of Freedom cried, "Emancipate your slaves." Humanity supplicated with tears for the deliverance of the children of Africa. Wisdom urged her solemn plea. The bleeding captive pled his innocence, and pointed to

Christianity, who stood weeping at the cross. Jehovah frowned upon the nefarious institution, and thunderbolts, red with vengeance, struggled to leap forth to blast the guilty wretches who maintained it. But all was vain. Slavery had stretched its dark wings of death over the land, the Church stood silently by—the priests prophesied falsely, and the people loved to have it so. Its throne is established, and now it reigns triumphant.

Nearly three millions of your fellow-citizens are prohibited by law and public opinion (which in this country is stronger than law) from reading the Book of Life. Your intellect has been destroyed as much as possible, and every ray of light they have attempted to shut out from your minds. The oppressors themselves have become involved in the ruin. They have become weak, sensual, and rapacious—they have cursed you—they have cursed themselves—they have cursed the earth which they have trod.

The colonies threw the blame upon England. They said that the mother country entailed the evil upon them, and they would rid themselves of it if they could. The world thought they were sincere, and the philanthropic pitied them. But time soon tested their sincerity. In a few years the colonists grew strong, and severed themselves from the British Government. Their independence was declared, and they took their station among the sovereign powers of the earth. The declaration was a glorious document. Sages admired it, and the patriotic of every nation reverenced the Godlike sentiments which it contained. When the power of Government returned to their hands, did they emancipate the slaves? No; they rather added new links to our chains. Were they ignorant of the principles of Liberty? Certainly they were not. The sentiments of their revolutionary orators fell in burning eloquence upon their hearts, and with one voice they cried, LIBERTY OR DEATH. Oh, what a sentence was that! It ran from soul to soul like electric fire, and nerved the arms of thousands to fight in the holy cause of Freedom. Among the diversity of opinions that are entertained in regard to physical resistance, there are but a few found to gainsay the stern declaration. We are among those who do not.

Slavery! How much misery is comprehended in that single word. What mind is there that does not shrink from its direful effects? Unless the image of God be obliterated from the soul, all men cherish the love of liberty. The nice, discerning political economist does not regard the sacred right more than the untutored African who roams in the wilds of Congo. Nor has the one more right to the full enjoyment of his freedom than the other. In every man's mind the good seeds of liberty are planted, and he who brings his fellow down so low, as to make him contented with a condition of slavery, commits the highest crime against God and man. Brethren, your oppressors aim to do this. They endeavor to make you as much like brutes as possible. When they have blinded the eyes of your mind—when they have embittered the sweet waters of life—when they have shut out the light which shines from the word of God—then, and not till then, has American slavery done its perfect work.

To such degradation it is sinful in the extreme for you to make voluntary submission. The divine commandments you are in duty bound to reverence and obey. If you do not obey them, you will surely meet with the displeasure of the Almighty. He requires you to love Him supremely, and your neighbor as yourself—to keep the Sabbath day holy—to search the Scriptures—and bring up your children with respect for His laws, and to worship no other God but Him. But slavery sets all these at nought, and hurls defiance in the face of Jehovah. The forlorn condition in which you are placed does not destroy your obligation to God. You are not certain of heaven, because you allow yourselves to remain in a state of slavery, where you cannot obey the commandments of the Sovereign of the universe. If the ignorance of slavery is a passport to heaven, then it is a blessing, and no curse, and you should rather desire its perpetuity than its abolition. God will not receive slavery, nor ignorance, nor any other state of mind, for love and obedience to Him. Your condition does not absolve you from your moral obligation. The diabolical injustice by which your liberties are cloven down, *neither God nor angels, or just men, command you to suffer for a single moment. Therefore, it is your solemn and imperative duty to use every means, moral, intellectual, and physical, that promises success.* If a band of heathen men should attempt to enslave a race of Christians, and to place their children under the influence of some false religion, surely Heaven would frown upon the men who would not resist such aggression, even to death. If, on the other hand, a band of Christians should attempt to enslave a race of heathen men, and to entail slavery upon them, and to keep them in heathenism in the midst of Christianity, the God of heaven would smile upon every effort which the injured might make to disenthrall themselves.

Brethren, it is as wrong for your lordly oppressors to keep you in slavery as it was for the man thief to steal our ancestors from the coast of Africa. You should therefore now use the same manner of resistance as would have been just in our ancestors when the bloody footprints of the first remorseless soul-thief was placed upon the shores of our fatherland. The humblest peasant is as free in the sight of God as the proudest monarch that ever swayed a sceptre. Liberty is a spirit sent out from God, and like its great Author, is no respecter of persons.

Brethren, the time has come when you must act for yourselves. It is an old and true saying that, "if hereditary bondmen would be free, they must themselves strike the blow." You can plead your own cause, and do the work of emancipation better than any others. The nations of the Old World are moving in the great cause of universal freedom, and some of them at least will, ere long, do you justice. The combined powers of Europe have placed their broad seal of disapprobation upon the African slave trade. But in the slaveholding parts of the United States the trade is as brisk as ever. They buy and sell you as though you were brute beasts. The North has done much—her opinion of slavery in the abstract is known. But in regard to the South, we adopt the opinion of the *New York Evangelist*—"We have advanced so far, that the cause apparently waits for a more effectual door to be thrown open than has been yet." We are about to point you to that more effectual door. Look around you, and behold the bosoms of your loving wives heaving with untold agonies! Hear the cries of your poor children! Remember the stripes your fathers bore. Think of the torture and disgrace of your noble mothers. Think of your wretched sisters, loving virtue and purity, as they are driven into concubinage and are exposed to the unbridled lusts of incarnate devils. Think of the undying glory that hangs around the ancient name of Africa—and forget not that you are native-born American citizens, and as such you are justly entitled to all the rights that are granted to the freest. Think how many tears you have poured out upon the soil which you have cultivated with unrequited toil and enriched with your blood; and then go to your lordly enslavers and tell them plainly, that you *are determined to be free.* Appeal to their sense of justice, and tell them that they have no more right to oppress you than you have to enslave them. Entreat them to remove the grievous burdens which they have imposed upon you, and to remunerate you for your labor. Promise them renewed diligence in the cultivation of the soil, if they will render to you an equivalent for your services. Point them to the increase of happiness and prosperity in the British West Indies since the Act of Emancipation. Tell them in language which they cannot misunderstand of the exceeding sinfulness of slavery, and of a future judgment, and of the righteous retributions of an indignant God. Inform them that all you desire is FREEDOM, and that nothing else will suffice.. Do this, and forever after cease to toil for the heartless tyrants, who give you no other reward but stripes and abuse. If they then commence work of death, they, and not you, will be responsible for the consequences. You had far better all die—*die immediately,* than live slaves, and entail your wretchedness upon your posterity. If you would be free in this generation, here is your only hope. However much you and all of us may desire it, there is not much hope of redemption without the shedding of blood. If you must bleed, let it all come at once—*rather die freemen than live to be the slaves.* It is impossible, like the children of Israel, to make a grand exodus from the land of bondage. The Pharaohs are on both sides of the blood-red waters! You cannot move *en masse* to the dominions of the British Queen—nor can you pass through Florida and overrun Texas, and at last find peace in Mexico. The propagators of American slavery are spending their blood and treasure that they may plant the black flag in the heart of Mexico and riot in the halls of the Montezumas. In language of the Reverend Robert Hall, when addressing the volunteers of Bristol, who were rushing forth to repel the invasion of Napoleon, who threatened to lay waste the fair homes of England, "Religion is too much interested in your behalf not to shed over you her most gracious influences."

You will not be compelled to spend much time in order to become inured to hardships. From the first movement that you breathed the air of heaven, you have been accustomed to nothing else but hardships. The heroes of the American Revolution were never put upon harder fare than a peck of corn and few herrings per week. You have not become enervated by the luxuries of life. Your sternest energies have been beaten out upon the anvil of severe trial. Slavery has done this to make you subservient to its own purposes; but it has done more than this, it has prepared you for any emergency. If you receive good treatment, it is what you can hardly expect; if you meet with pain, sorrow, and even death, these are the common lot of the slaves.

Fellowmen! patient sufferers! behold your dearest rights crushed to the earth! See your sons murdered, and your wives, mothers, and sisters doomed to prostitution. In the name of the merciful God, and by all that life is worth, let it no longer be a debatable question, whether it is better to choose *liberty* or *death.*

In 1822, Denmark Vesey, of South Carolina, formed a plan for the liberation of his fellowmen. In the whole history of human efforts to overthrow slavery, a more complicated and tremendous plan was never formed. He was betrayed by the treachery of his own people, and died a martyr to freedom. Many a brave hero fell, but history, faithful to her high trust, will transcribe his name on the same monument with Moses, Hampden, Tell, Bruce, and Wallace, Toussaint L'Ouverture, Lafayette, and Washington. That tremendous movement shook the whole empire of slavery. The guilty soul-thieves were overwhelmed with fear. It is a matter of fact that at this time and in consequence of the threatened revolution, the slave states talked strongly of emancipation. But they blew but one blast of the trumpet of freedom, and then laid it aside.

As these men became quiet, the slaveholders ceased to talk about emancipation: and now behold your condition today! Angels sigh over it, and humanity has long since exhausted her tears in weeping on your account!

The patriotic Nathaniel Turner followed Denmark Vesey. He was goaded to desperation by wrong and injustice. By despotism, his name has been recorded on the list of infamy, and future generations will remember him among the noble and brave.

Next arose the immortal Joseph Cinque, the hero of the Amistad. He was a native African, and by the help of God he emancipated a whole ship-load of his fellowmen on the high seas. And he now sings of liberty on the sunny hills of Africa and beneath his native palm trees, where he hears the lion roar and feels himself as free as the king of the forest.

Next arose Madison Washington, that bright star of freedom, and took his station in the constellation of true heroism. He was a slave on board the brig *Creole,* of Richmond, bound to New Orleans, that great slave mart, with a hundred and four others. Nineteen struck for liberty or death. But one life was taken, and the whole were emancipated, and the vessel was carried into Nassau, New Providence.

Noble men! Those who have fallen in freedom's conflict, their memories will be cherished by the true-hearted and the God-fearing in all future generations; those who are living, their names are surrounded by a halo of glory.

Brethren, arise, arise! Strike for your lives and liberties. Now is the day and the hour. Let every slave throughout the land do this, and the days of slavery are numbered. You cannot be more oppressed than you have been—you cannot suffer greater cruelties than you have already. *Rather die freemen than live to be slaves.* Remember that you are FOUR MILLIONS!

It is in your power so to torment the God-cursed slaveholders that they will be glad to let you go free. If the scale was turned, and black men were the masters and white men the slaves, every destructive agent and element would be employed to lay the oppressor low. Danger and death would hang over their heads day and night. Yes, the tyrants would meet with plagues more terrible than those of Pharaoh. But you are a patient people. You act as though you were made for the special use of these devils. You act as though your daughters were born to pamper the lusts of your masters and overseers. And worse than all, you tamely submit while your lords tear your wives from your embraces and defile them before your eyes. In the name of God, we ask, are you men? Where is the blood of your fathers? Has it all run out of your veins? Awake, awake; millions of voices are calling you! Your dead fathers speak to you from their graves. Heaven, as with a voice of thunder, calls on you to arise from the dust.

Let your motto be resistance! *resistance!* RESISTANCE! No oppressed people have ever secured their liberty without resistance. What kind of resistance you had better make you must decide by the circumstances that surround you, and according to the suggestion of expediency. Brethren, adieu! Trust in the living God. Labor for the peace of the human race, and remember that you are FOUR MILLIONS!

Collateral Reading

Brewer, William M., "Henry Highland Garnet," *Journal of Negro History,* XII (January, 1928), 36-52.

Kennicott, Patrick C., "Negro Antislavery Speakers in America." Unpublished Ph.D. dissertation, Florida State University, 1967.

Simmons, William J., *Men of Mark.* New York, 1968.

Whittaker, Helen B., "The Negro in the Abolition Movement, 1830-1850." Unpublished Master's thesis, Howard University, 1935.

Study Questions and Problems

1. Which contemporary speakers employ a style of rhetoric similar to that of Henry Highland Garnet?

2. Contrast Garnet's speech with the appeal made by Forten. Which do you think was more effective? Why?

3. Compare Garnet's address with Patrick Henry's "Liberty or Death" speech. What similarities do you find?

4. What effect did Garnet's speech have on Frederick Douglass' position with regard to the abolition of slavery?

5. How would you determine the effectiveness of this speech? By its results? By the standards of good speech? By the "truth" contained in this speech? Discuss the criteria involved in determining the effectiveness of a speech.

Frederick Douglass

Frederick Douglass was born a slave in Tuckahoe, Maryland about 1817. His mother was employed on another plantation, where the master was alleged to be Douglass' father. At the age of ten, Douglass was sent to Baltimore to work as a house servant. There the mistress of the household taught him to read until her husband interfered and stopped the instruction.

At the age of nineteen he escaped bondage and eventually settled in New Bedford, Massachusetts. He became involved in the antislavery movement, initially speaking at meetings before Negro audiences. In 1842 Douglass became an agent of the American Antislavery Society. He lectured throughout the Northern states. He soon became so skilled as an orator that friends feared that his audiences would not believe that he was a slave. Thus, he wrote his autobiography, Narrative of the Life of Frederick Douglass. Unfortunately, the popularity of the book brought slave agents North to capture him. Threatened with recapture, he escaped by sailing to England in 1846, where he conducted a two-year antislavery lecture tour of Great Britain. Douglass' freedom was finally purchased by funds contributed by a friend, and he then returned to America and settled in Rochester, New York, where he edited the North Star, an abolitionist newspaper.

During the years preceding the Civil War, Douglass grew estranged from the white abolitionists and became increasingly more violent in his appeals for an end to slavery. Some historians believe that he may even have played a role in the planning of John Brown's raid on Harper's Ferry, although the evidence is inconclusive. During the Civil War, he, together with other black leaders, urged that black men be enlisted as soldiers in the Union Army. After the war, he assumed many political offices and advocated constitutional reform to grant equal citizenship rights regardless of race or color.

Reception Speech

The "Reception Speech," according to one authority, is noted for its "originality of thought, beauty and force of expression and impassioned *eloquence." Douglass began by telling his British audience that his purpose was to inform them of the institution of slavery in the United States. He defined slavery as "the granting of that power by which one man exercises and enforces a right of property in the body and soul of another." He then proceeded to an extended discussion of the physical evils of slavery, in which he skillfully developed through description, illustration, and personal anecdote all the horrors and torments which could be inflicted upon the slave.*

Finally, Douglass concluded by stating that his purpose in speaking to the British public was to expose the slaveholder and to make him accountable to world public opinion:

I want him to feel that he has no sympathy in England, Scotland, or Ireland; that he has none in Canada, none in Mexico, none among the poor wild Indians; that the voice of the civilized, aye, and savage world, is against him. I would have condemnation blaze down upon him in every direction, till, stunned and overwhelmed with shame and confusion, he is compelled to let go the grasp he holds upon the persons of his victims, and restore them to their long-lost rights.

We may assume that Douglass' audience was congenial rather than hostile, for from all historical accounts, Frederick Douglass was well received in England, Scotland, and Ireland. Also, the text of his speech suggests that he thought many members of his audience were uninformed about slavery as it was practiced in the United States. Moreoover, we know from history that slave traffic had been legally abolished by Parliament nearly forty years before. Finally, we know that Douglass was in touch with English reformers such as John Bright. Those who advocated reform in Britain probably attended Douglass' lectures. Thus, the audience was generally uninformed about slavery, congenial, and oriented toward reform.

Fourth of July Oration

Douglass used the occasion of the United States celebration of independence to appeal to the sense of liberty and fairness with regard to the question of slavery. He began by describing the conditions which led to the signing of the Declaration of Independence. In praise of the founding fathers, Douglass stated, "They were peace men; but they preferred revolution to peaceful submission to bondage."

Frederick Douglass then contrasted the great significance of an independence celebration with the present status of black men in America. "This Fourth of July is yours, *not* mine. *You* may *rejoice, I* must *mourn." Then came a vivid description of the racial injustice which prevailed throughout the Union. "What, to the American slave is your Fourth of July? I answer, a day that reveals to him, more than all other days in the year, the gross injustice and cruelty to which he is the constant victim."*

As is characteristic of Douglass' speeches, the descriptions of racial injustice are vivid personal recollections of the institution of slavery coupled with factual information about racial practices common in America during the middle nineteenth century. Of particular interest to the reader may be Douglass' direct indictment of religious groups which refrained from making a pronouncement on slavery and those religious groups which endorsed slavery on biblical grounds.

Douglass concluded this forceful attack upon slavery with a ringing declaration of the ethical consequences for the nation if slavery were allowed to persist.

Men of Color, To Arms!

This speech is brief and to the point. It is a simple admonition to join in the struggle against the Southern slave states. "I urge you to fly to arms, and smite with death the power that would bury the government and your liberty in the same hopeless grave." After some twenty years of agitation by Douglass, little remained to be said; it was a time for action.

Reception Speech in England

I feel exceedingly glad of the opportunity now afforded me of presenting the claims of my brethren in bonds in the United States, to so many in London and from various parts of Britain, who have assembled here on the present occasion. I have nothing to commend me to your consideration in the way of learning, nothing in the way of education, to entitle me to your attention; and you are aware that slavery is a very bad school for rearing teachers of morality and religion. Twenty-one years of my life have been spent in slavery—personal slavery—surrounded by degrading influences, such as can exist nowhere beyond the pale of slavery; and it will not be strange, if under such circumstances, I should betray, in what I have to say to you, a deficiency of that refinement which is seldom or never found, except among persons that have experienced superior advantages to those which I have enjoyed. But I will take it for granted that you know something about the degrading influences of slavery, and that you will not expect great things from me this evening, but simply such facts as I may be able to advance immediately in connection with my own experience of slavery.

Now, what is this system of slavery? This is the subject of my lecture this evening—what is the character of this institution? I am about to answer the inquiry, what is American slavery? I do this the more readily, since I have found persons in this country who have identified the term slavery with that which I think it is not, and in some instances, I have feared, in so doing, have rather (unwittingly, I know) detracted much from the horror with which the term slavery is contemplated. It is common in this country to distinguish every bad thing by the name of slavery. Intemperance is slavery; to be deprived of the right to vote is slavery, says one; to have to work hard is slavery, says another; and I do not know but that if we should let them go on, they would say that to eat when we are hungry, to walk when we desire to have exercise, or to minister to our necessities, or have necessities at all, is slavery.

Frederick Douglass   *Frederic Lewis Photo*

I do not wish for a moment to detract from the horror with which the
evil of intemperance is contemplated—not at all; nor do I wish to throw
the slightest obstruction in the way of any political freedom that any
class of persons in this country may desire to obtain. But I am here
to say that I think the term slavery is sometimes abused by identifying
it with that which it is not. Slavery in the United States is the granting
of that power by which one man exercises and enforces a right of property
in the body and soul of another. The condition of a slave is simply
that of the brute beast. He is a piece of property—a marketable com-
modity, in the language of the law, to be bought or sold at the will
and caprice of the master who claims him to be his property; he is
spoken of, thought of, and treated as property. His own good, his conscience, his intellect, his affections, are all set aside by the master. The
will and the wishes of the master are the law of the slave. He is as
much a piece of property as a horse. If he is fed, he is fed because
he is property. If he is clothed, it is with a view to the increase of his
value as property. Whatever of comfort is necessary to him for his body
or soul that is inconsistent with his being property, is carefully wrested
from him, not only by public opinion, but by the law of the country.
He is carefully deprived of everything that tends in the slightest degree
to detract from his value as property. He is deprived of education. God
has given him an intellect; the slaveholder declares it shall not be
cultivated. If his moral perception leads him in a course contrary to
his value as property, the slaveholder declares he shall not exercise it.
The marriage institution cannot exist among slaves, and one-sixth of
the population of democratic America is denied its privileges by the
law of the land. What is to be thought of a nation boasting of its liberty,
boasting of its humanity, boasting of its Christianity, boasting of its
love of justice and purity, and yet having within its own borders three
millions of persons denied by law the right of marriage?—what must
be the condition of that people? I need not lift up the veil by giving
you any experience of my own. Everyone that can put two ideas together,
must see the most fearful results from such a state of things as I have
just mentioned. If any of these three millions find for themselves com-
panions, and prove themselves honest, upright, virtuous persons to each
other, yet in these cases—few as I am bound to confess they are—the
virtuous live in constant apprehension of being torn asunder by the
merciless men-stealers that claim them as their property. This is American
slavery; no marriage—no education—the light of the gospel shut out from
the dark mind of the bondman—and he forbidden by law to learn to
read. If a mother shall teach her children to read, the law in Louisiana
proclaims that she may be hanged by the neck. If the father attempt

to give his son a knowledge of letters, he may be punished by the whip in one instance, and in another be killed, at the discretion of the court. Three millions of people shut out from the light of knowledge! It is easy for you to conceive the evil that must result from such a state of things.

I now come to the physical evils of slavery. I do not wish to dwell at length upon these, but it seems right to speak of them, not so much to influence your minds on this question, as to let the slaveholders of America know that the curtain which conceals their crimes is being lifted abroad; that we are opening the dark cell, and leading the people into the horrible recesses of what they are pleased to call their domestic institution. We want them to know that a knowledge of their whippings, their scourgings, their brandings, their chainings, is not confined to their plantations, but that some Negro of theirs has broken loose from his chains—has burst through the dark incrustation of slavery, and is now exposing their deeds of deep damnation to the gaze of the Christian people of England.

The slaveholders resort to all kinds of cruelty. If I were disposed, I have matter enough to interest you on this question for five or six evenings, but I will not dwell at length upon these cruelties. Suffice it to say, that all the peculiar modes of torture that were resorted to in the West India islands are resorted to, I believe, even more frequently, in the United States of America. Starvation, the bloody whip, the chain, the gag, the thumb-screw, cat-hauling, the cat-o'-nine-tails, the dungeon, the bloodhound, are all in requisition to keep the slave in his condition as a slave in the United States. If anyone has a doubt upon this point, I would ask him to read the chapter on slavery in Dickens's *Notes on America*. If any man has a doubt upon it, I have here the "testimony of a thousand witnesses," which I can give at any length, all going to prove the truth of my statement. The bloodhound is regularly trained in the United States, and advertisements are to be found in the Southern papers of the Union, from persons advertising themselves as bloodhound trainers, and offering to hunt down slaves at fifteen dollars apiece, recommending their hounds as the fleetest in the neighborhood, never known to fail. Advertisements are from time to time inserted, stating that slaves have escaped with iron collars about their necks, with bands of iron about their feet, marked with the lash, branded with red-hot irons, the initials of their master's name burned into their flesh; and the masters advertise the fact of their being thus branded with their own signature, thereby proving to the world, that, however damning it may appear to non-slaveholders, such practices are not regarded discreditable among the slaveholders themselves. Why, I believe if a

man should brand his horse in this country—burn the initials of his
name into any of his cattle, and publish the ferocious deed here—that
the united execrations of Christians in Britain would descend upon him.
Yet in the United States, human beings are thus branded. As Whittier
says—

> . . . Our countrymen in chains,
>   The whip on woman's shrinking flesh,
> Our soil yet reddening with the stains
>   Caught from her scourgings warm and fresh.

The slave-dealer boldly publishes his infamous acts to the world. Of
all things that have been said of slavery to which exception has been
taken by slaveholders, this, the charge of cruelty, stands foremost, and
yet there is no charge capable of clearer demonstration than that of
the most barbarous inhumanity on the part of the slaveholders toward
their slaves. And all this is necessary; it *is* necessary to resort to these
cruelties, in order to *make the slave a slave,* and to *keep him a slave.*
Why, my experience all goes to prove the truth of what you will call
a marvelous proposition, that the better you treat a slave, the more
you destroy his value *as a slave,* and enhance the probability of his
eluding the grasp of the slaveholder; the more kindly you treat him,
the more wretched you make him, while you keep him in the condition
of a slave. My experience, I say, confirms the truth of this proposition.
When I was treated exceedingly ill; when my back was being scourged
daily; when I was whipped within an inch of my life—*life* was all I
cared for. "Spare my life," was my continual prayer. When I was looking
for the blow about to be inflicted upon my head, I was not thinking
of my liberty; it was my life. But, as soon as the blow was not to be
feared, then came the longing for liberty. If a slave had a bad master,
his ambition is to get a better; when he gets a better, he aspires to
have the best; and when he gets the best, he aspires to be his own
master. But the slave must be brutalized to keep him as a slave. The
slaveholder feels this necessity. I admit this necessity. If it be right to
hold slaves at all, it is right to hold them in the only way in which
they can be held; and this can be done only by shutting out the light
of education from their minds, and brutalizing their persons. The whip,
the chain, the gag, the thumb-screw, the bloodhound, the stocks, and
all the other bloody paraphernalia of the slave system, are indispensably
necessary to the relation of master and slave. The slave must be subjected
to these, or he ceases to be a slave. Let him know that the whip is
burned; that the fetters have been turned to some useful and profitable
employment; that the chain is no longer for his limbs; that the blood-

hound is no longer to be put upon his track; that his master's authority over him is no longer to be enforced by taking his life—and immediately he walks out from the house of bondage and asserts his freedom as a man. The slaveholder finds it necessary to have these implements to keep the slave in bondage; finds it necessary to be able to say, "Unless you do so and so; unless you do as I bid you—I will take away your life!"

Some of the most awful scenes of cruelty are constantly taking place in the middle states of the Union. We have in those states what are called the slave-breeding states. Allow me to speak plainly. Although it is harrowing to your feelings, it is necessary that the facts of the case should be stated. We have in the United States slave-breeding states. The very state from which the minister from our court to yours comes, is one of these states—Maryland, where men, women, and children are reared for the market, just as horses, sheep, and swine are raised for the market. Slave-rearing is there looked upon as a legitimate trade; the law sanctions it, public opinion upholds it, the church does not condemn it. It goes on in all its bloody horrors, sustained by the auctioneer's block. If you would see the cruelties of this system, hear the following narrative. Not long since the following scene occurred. A slave-woman and a slave-man had united themselves as man and wife in the absence of any law to protect them as man and wife. They had lived together by the permission, not by right, of their master, and they had reared a family. The master found it expedient, and for his interest, to sell them. He did not ask them their wishes in regard to the matter at all; they were not consulted. The man and woman were brought to the auctioneer's block, under the sound of the hammer. The cry was raised, "Here goes; who bids cash?" Think of it—a man and wife to be sold! The woman was placed on the auctioneer's block; her limbs, as is customary, were brutally exposed to the purchasers, who examined her with all the freedom with which they would examine a horse. There stood the husband, powerless; no right to his wife; the master's right preëminent. She was sold. He was next brought to the auctioneer's block. His eyes followed his wife in the distance; and he looked beseechingly, imploringly, to the man that had bought his wife, to buy him also. But he was at length bid off to another person. He was about to be separated forever from her he loved. No word of his, no work of his, could save him from this separation. He asked permission of his new master to go and take the hand of his wife at parting. It was denied him. In the agony of his soul he rushed from the man who had just bought him, that he might take a farewell of his wife; but his way was obstructed, he was struck over the head with a loaded whip, and was held for a moment; but his agony was too great. When he was let go, he fell a corpse at the feet of his master. His heart was broken. Such scenes are the every-day fruits of American slavery. Some two years since, the Hon. Seth M. Gates, an antislavery gentleman of the state of New York, a representative in the congress of the United States, told me he saw with his own eyes the following circumstance. In the national District of Columbia, over which the star-spangled emblem is constantly waving, where orators are ever holding forth on the subject of American liberty, American democracy, American republicanism, there are two slave prisons. When going across a bridge, leading to one of these prisons, he saw a young woman run out, bare-footed and bare-headed, and with very little clothing on. She was running with all speed to the bridge he was approaching. His eye was fixed upon her, and he stopped to see what was the matter. He had not paused long before he saw three men run out after her. He now knew what the nature of the case was; a slave escaping from her chains—a young woman, a sister—escaping from the bondage in which she had been held. She made her way to the bridge, but had not reached it ere from the Virginia side there came two slaveholders. As soon as they saw them, her pursuers called out, "Stop her!" True to their Virginian instincts, they came to the rescue of their brother kidnappers, across the bridge. The poor girl now saw that there was no chance for her. It was a trying time. She knew if she went back, she must be a slave forever—she must be dragged down to the scenes of pollution which the slaveholders continually provide for most of the poor, sinking, wretched young women, whom they call their property. She formed her resolution; and just as those who were about to take her, were going to put hands upon her, to drag her back, she leaped over the balustrades of the bridge, and down she went to rise no more. She chose death, rather than to go back into the hands of those Christian slaveholders from whom she had escaped.

Can it be possible that such things as these exist in the United States? Are not these the exceptions? Are any such scenes as this general? Are not such deeds condemned by the law and denounced by public opinion? Let me read to you a few of the laws of the slaveholding states of America. I think no better exposure of slavery can be made than is made by the laws of the states in which slavery exists. I prefer reading the laws to making any statement in confirmation of what I have said myself; for the slaveholders cannot object to this testimony, since it is the calm, the cool, the deliberate enactment of their wisest heads, of their most clear-sighted, their own constituted representatives. "If more than seven slaves together are found in any road without a white person, twenty lashes apiece; for visiting a plantation without a written pass, ten lashes;

for letting loose a boat from where it is made fast, thirty-nine lashes for the first offense; and for the second, shall have cut off from his head one ear; for keeping or carrying a club, thirty-nine lashes; for having any article for sale, without a ticket from his master, ten lashes; for traveling in any other than the most usual and accustomed road, when going alone to any place, forty lashes; for traveling in the night without a pass, forty lashes." I am afraid you do not understand the awful character of these lashes. You must bring it before your mind. A human being in a perfect state of nudity, tied hand and foot to a stake, and a strong man standing behind with a heavy whip, knotted at the end, each blow cutting into the flesh, and leaving the warm blood dripping to the feet; and for these trifles. "For being found in another person's Negro-quarters, forty lashes; for hunting with dogs in the woods, thirty lashes; for being on horseback without the written permission of his master, twenty-five lashes; for riding or going abroad in the night, or riding horses in the daytime, without leave, a slave may be whipped, cropped, or branded in the cheek with the letter R, or otherwise punished, such punishment not extending to life, or so as to render him unfit for labor." The laws referred to may be found by consulting Brevard's Digest; Haywood's Manual; Virginia Revised Code; Prince's Digest; Missouri Laws; Mississippi Revised Code. A man, for going to visit his brethren, without the permission of his master—and in many instances he may not have that permission; his master, from caprice or other reasons, may not be willing to allow it—may be caught on his way, dragged to a post, the branding-iron heated, and the name of his master or the letter R branded into his cheek or on his forehead. They treat slaves thus, on the principle that they must punish for light offenses, in order to prevent the commission of larger ones. I wish you to mark that in the single state of Virginia there are seventy-one crimes for which a colored man may be executed; while there are only three of these crimes, which, when committed by a white man, will subject him to that punishment. There are many of these crimes which if the white man did not commit, he would be regarded as a scoundrel and a coward. In the state of Maryland, there is a law to this effect: that if a slave shall strike his master, he may be hanged, his head severed from his body, his body quartered, and his head and quarters set up in the most prominent places in the neighborhood. If a colored woman, in the defense of her own virtue, in defense of her own person, should shield herself from the brutal attacks of her tyrannical master, or make the slightest resistance, she may be killed on the spot. No law whatever will bring the guilty man to justice for the crime.

But you will ask me, can these things be possible in a land professing

Christianity? Yes, they are so; and this is not the worst. No; a darker feature is yet to be presented than the mere existence of these facts. I have to inform you that the religion of the Southern states, at this time, is the great supporter, the great sanctioner of the bloody atrocities to which I have referred. While America is printing tracts and Bibles; sending missionaries abroad to convert the heathen; expending her money in various ways for the promotion of the gospel in foreign lands— the slave not only lies forgotten, uncared for, but is trampled under foot by the very churches of the land. What have we in America? Why, we have slavery made part of the religion of the land. Yes, the pulpit there stands up as the great defender of this cursed *institution,* as it is called. Ministers of religion come forward and torture the hallowed pages of inspired wisdom to sanction the bloody deed. They stand forth as the foremost, the strongest defenders of this "institution." As a proof of this, I need not do more than state the general fact, that slavery has existed under the droppings of the sanctuary of the South for the last two hundred years, and there has not been any war between the *religion* and the *slavery* of the South. Whips, chains, gags, and thumb-screws have all lain under the droppings of the sanctuary, and instead of [wresting them from] the limbs of the bondman, those droppings have served to preserve them in all their strength. Instead of preaching the gospel against this tyranny, rebuke, and wrong, ministers of religion have sought, by all and every means, to throw in the background what-ever in the Bible could be construed into opposition to slavery, and to bring forward that which they could torture into its support. This I conceive to be the darkest feature of slavery, and the most difficult to attack, because it is identified with religion, and exposes those who denounce it to the charge of infidelity. Yes, those with whom I have been laboring, namely, the old organization antislavery society of America, have been again and again stigmatized as infidels, and for what reason? Why, solely in consequence of the faithfulness of their attacks upon the slaveholding religion of the Southern states, and the Northern religion that sympathizes with it. I have found it difficult to speak on this matter without persons coming forward and saying, "Doug-lass, are you not afraid of injuring the cause of Christ? You do not desire to do so, we know; but are you not undermining religion?" This has been said to me again and again, even since I came to this country, but I cannot be induced to leave off these exposures. I love the religion of our blessed Savior. I love that religion that comes from above, in the "wisdom of God," which is first pure, then peaceable, gentle, and easy to be entreated, full of mercy and good fruits, without partiality and without hypocrisy. I love that religion that sends its votaries to bind up the wounds of him that has fallen among thieves. I love that religion that makes it the duty of its disciples to visit the fatherless and the widow in their affliction. I love that religion that is based upon the glorious principle, of love to God and love to man; which makes its followers do unto others as they themselves would be done by. If you demand liberty to yourself, it says, grant it to your neighbors. If you claim a right to think for yourself, it says, allow your neighbors the same right. If you claim to act for yourself, it says, allow your neighbors the same right. It is because I love this religion that I hate the slaveholding, the woman-whipping, the mind-darkening, the soul-destroying religion that exists in the Southern states of America. It is because I regard the one as good, and pure, and holy, that I cannot but regard the other as bad, corrupt, and wicked. Loving the one I must hate the other; holding to the one I must reject the other.

I may be asked why I am so anxious to bring this subject before the British public—why I do not confine my efforts to the United States? My answer is, first, that slavery is the common enemy of mankind, and all mankind should be made acquainted with its abominable character. My next answer is, that the slave is a man, and, as such, is entitled to your sympathy as a brother. All the feelings, all the susceptibilities, all the capacities, which you have, he has. He is a part of the human family. He has been the prey—the common prey—of Christendom for the last three hundred years, and it is but right, it is but just, it is but proper, that his wrongs should be known throughout the world. I have another reason for bringing this matter before the British public, and it is this: slavery is a system of wrong, so blinding to all around, so hardening to the heart, so corrupting to the morals, so deleterious to religion, so sapping to all the principles of justice in its immediate vicinity, that the community surrounding it lacks the moral stamina necessary to its removal. It is a system of such gigantic evil, so strong, so overwhelming in its power, that no one nation is equal to its removal. It requires the humanity of Christianity, the morality of the world to remove it. Hence, I call upon the people of Britain to look at this matter, and to exert the influence I am about to show they possess, for the removal of slavery from America. I can appeal to them, as strongly by their regard for the slaveholder as for the slave, to labor in this cause. I am here, because you have an influence on America that no other nation can have. You have been drawn together by the power of steam to a marvelous extent; the distance between London and Boston is now reduced to some twelve or fourteen days, so that the denunciations against slavery, uttered in London this week, may be heard in a fortnight in the streets of Boston, and reverberating amidst the hills of Massachusetts.

There is nothing said here against slavery that will not be recorded in the United States. I am here, also, because the slaveholders do not want me to be here; they would rather that I were not here. I have adopted a maxim laid down by Napoleon, never to occupy ground which the enemy would like me to occupy. The slaveholders would much rather have me, if I will denounce slavery, denounce it in the Northern states, where their friends and supporters are, who will stand by and mob me for denouncing it. They feel something as the man felt, when he uttered his prayer in which he made out a most horrible case for himself, and one of his neighbors touched him and said, "My friend, I always had the opinion of you that you have now expressed for yourself—that you are a very great sinner." Coming from himself, it was all very well, but coming from a stranger it was rather cutting. The slaveholders felt that when slavery was denounced among themselves, it was not so bad; but let one of the slaves get loose, let him summon the people of Britain, and make known to them the conduct of the slaveholders toward their slaves, and it cuts them to the quick, and produces a sensation such as would be produced by nothing else. The power I exert now is something like the power that is exerted by the man at the end of the lever; my influence now is just in proportion to the distance that I am from the United States. My exposure of slavery abroad will tell more upon the hearts and consciences of slaveholders, than if I was attacking them in America; for almost every paper that I now receive from the United States, comes teeming with statements about this fugitive Negro, calling him a "glib-tongued scoundrel," and saying that he is running out against the institutions and people of America. I deny the charge that I am saying a word against the institutions of America, or the people, as such. What I have to say is against slavery and slaveholders. I feel at liberty to speak on this subject. I have on my back the marks of the lash; I have four sisters and one brother now under the galling chain. I feel it my duty to cry aloud and spare not. I am not averse to having the good opinion of my fellow-creatures. I am not averse to being kindly regarded by all men; but I am bound, even at the hazard of making a large class of religionists in this country hate me, oppose me, and malign me as they have done—I am bound by the prayers, and tears, and entreaties of three millions of kneeling bondmen, to have no compromise with men who are in any shape or form connected with the slaveholders of America. I expose slavery in this country, because to expose it is to kill it. Slavery is one of those monsters of darkness to whom the light of truth is death. Expose slavery, and it dies. Light is to slavery what the heat of the sun is to the root of a tree; it must die under it. All the slaveholder asks of me is silence. He does not ask me to go abroad and preach *in favor* of slavery; he does not ask any one to do that. He would not say that slavery is a good thing, but the best under the circumstances. The slaveholders want total darkness on the subject. They want the hatchway shut down, that the monster may crawl in his den of darkness, crushing human hopes and happiness, destroying the bondman at will, and having no one to reprove or rebuke him. Slavery shrinks from the light; it hateth the light, neither cometh to the light, lest its deeds should be reproved. To tear off the mask from this abominable system, to expose it to the light of heaven, aye, to the heat of the sun, that it may burn and wither it out of existence, is my object in coming to this country. I want the slaveholder surrounded, as by a wall of anti-slavery fire, so that he may see the condemnation of himself and his system glaring down in letters of light. I want him to feel that he has no sympathy in England, Scotland, or Ireland; that he has none in Canada, none in Mexico, none among the poor wild Indians; that the voice of the civilized, aye, and savage world is against him. I would have condemnation blaze down upon him in every direction, till, stunned and overwhelmed with shame and confusion, he is compelled to let go the grasp he holds upon the persons of his victims, and restore them to their long-lost rights.

Fourth of July Oration

July 5, 1852

FELLOW-CITIZENS—Pardon me, and allow me to ask, why am I called upon to speak here today? What have I, or those I represent, to do with your national independence? Are the great principles of political freedom and of natural justice, embodied in that Declaration of Independence, extended to us? And am I, therefore, called upon to bring our humble offering to the national altar, and to confess the benefits, and express devout gratitude for the blessings, resulting from your independence to us?

Would to God, both for your sakes and ours, that an affirmative answer could be truthfully returned to these questions! Then would my task be light, and my burden easy and delightful. For who is there so cold that a nation's sympathy could not warm him? Who so obdurate and dead to the claims of gratitude, that would not thankfully acknowledge such priceless benefits? Who so stolid and selfish, that would not give his voice to swell the hallelujahs of a nation's jubilee, when the chains of servitude had been torn from his limbs? I am not that man. In a case like that, the dumb might eloquently speak, and the "lame man leap as an hart."

But, such is not the state of the case. I say it with a sad sense of the disparity between us. I am not included within the pale of this glorious anniversary! Your high independence only reveals the immeasurable distance between us. The blessings in which you this day rejoice, are not enjoyed in common. The rich inheritance of justice, liberty, prosperity, and independence, bequeathed by your fathers, is shared by you, not by me. The sunlight that brought life and healing to you, has brought stripes and death to me. This Fourth of July is *yours*, not *mine*. *You* may rejoice, *I* must mourn. To drag a man in fetters into the grand illuminated temple of liberty, and call upon him to join you in joyous anthems, were inhuman mockery and sacrilegious irony. Do you mean, citizens, to mock me, by asking me to speak today? If so, there is a parallel to your conduct. And let me warn you that it is dangerous to copy the example of a nation whose crimes, towering up to heaven, were thrown down by the breath of the Almighty, burying that nation in irrecoverable ruin! I can today take up the plaintive lament of a peeled and woe-smitten people.

"By the rivers of Babylon, there we sat down. Yea! we wept when we remembered Zion. We hanged our harps upon the willows in the midst thereof. For there, they that carried us away captive, required of us a song; and they who wasted us required of us mirth, saying, 'Sing us one of the songs of Zion.' How can we sing the Lord's song in a strange land? If I forget thee, O Jerusalem, let my right hand forget her cunning. If I do not remember thee, let my tongue cleave to the roof of my mouth."

Fellow-citizens, above your national, tumultuous joy, I hear the mournful wail of millions, whose chains, heavy and grievous yesterday, are today rendered more intolerable by the jubilant shouts that reach them. If I do forget, if I do not faithfully remember those bleeding children of sorrow this day, "may my right hand forget her cunning, and may my tongue cleave to the roof of my mouth!" To forget them, to pass lightly over their wrongs, and to chime in with the popular theme, would be treason most scandalous and shocking, and would make me a reproach before God and the world. My subject, then, fellow-citizens, is *American Slavery*. I shall see this day and its popular characteristics from the slave's point of view. Standing there, identified with the American bondman, making his wrongs mine, I do not hesitate to declare, with all my soul, that the character and conduct of this nation never

looked blacker to me than on this Fourth of July. Whether we turn
to the declarations of the past, or to the professions of the present, the
conduct of the nation seems equally hideous and revolting. America
is false to the past, false to the present, and solemnly binds herself to
be false to the future. Standing with God and the crushed and bleeding
slave on this occasion, I will, in the name of humanity which is outraged,
in the name of liberty which is fettered, in the name of the constitution
and the Bible, which are disregarded and trampled upon, dare to call
in question and to denounce, with all the emphasis I can command,
everything that serves to perpetuate slavery—the great sin and shame
of America! "I will not equivocate; I will not excuse"; I will use the
severest language I can command; and yet not one word shall escape
me that any man, whose judgment is not blinded by prejudice, or who
is not at heart a slaveholder, shall not confess to be right and just.

But I fancy I hear someone of my audience say, it is just in this
circumstance that you and your brother abolitionists fail to make a
favorable impression on the public mind. Would you argue more, and
denounce less, would you persuade more and rebuke less, your cause
would be much more likely to succeed. But, I submit, where all is plain
there is nothing to be argued. What point in the antislavery creed would
you have me argue? On what branch of the subject do the people of
this country need light? Must I undertake to prove that the slave is
a man? That point is conceded already. Nobody doubts it. The slaveholders themselves acknowledge it in the enactment of laws for their
government. They acknowledge it when they punish disobedience on
the part of the slave. There are seventy-two crimes in the state of Virginia,
which, if committed by a black man (no matter how ignorant he be),
subject him to the punishment of death; while only two of these same
crimes will subject a white man to the like punishment. What is this
but the acknowledgment that the slave is a moral, intellectual, and
responsible being. The manhood of the slave is conceded. It is admitted
in the fact that Southern statute books are covered with enactments
forbidding, under severe fines and penalties, the teaching of the slave
to read or write. When you can point to any such laws, in reference
to the beasts of the field, then I may consent to argue the manhood
of the slave. When the dogs in your streets, when the fowls of the air,
when the cattle on your hills, when the fish of the sea, and the reptiles
that crawl, shall be unable to distinguish the slave from a brute, then
will I argue with you that the slave is a man!

For the present, it is enough to affirm the equal manhood of the
Negro race. Is it not astonishing that, while we are plowing, planting,
and reaping, using all kinds of mechanical tools, erecting houses, con-

structing bridges, building ships, working in metals of brass, iron, copper, silver, and gold; that, while we are reading, writing, and cyphering, acting as clerks, merchants, and secretaries, having among us lawyers, doctors, ministers, poets, authors, editors, orators, and teachers; that, while we are engaged in all manner of enterprises common to other men—digging gold in California, capturing the whale in the Pacific, feeding sheep and cattle on the hillside, living, moving, acting, thinking, planning, living in families as husbands, wives, and children, and, above all, confessing and worshiping the Christian's God, and looking hopefully for life and immortality beyond the grave—we are called upon to prove that we are men!

Would you have me argue that man is entitled to liberty? that he is the rightful owner of his own body? You have already declared it. Must I argue the wrongfulness of slavery? Is that a question for republicans? Is it to be settled by the rules of logic and argumentation, as a matter beset with great difficulty, involving a doubtful application of the principle of justice, hard to be understood? How should I look today in the presence of Americans, dividing and subdividing a discourse, to show that men have a natural right to freedom, speaking of it relatively and positively, negatively and affirmatively? To do so, would be to make myself ridiculous, and to offer an insult to your understanding. There is not a man beneath the canopy of heaven that does not know that slavery is wrong *for him.*

What! Am I to argue that it is wrong to make men brutes, to rob them of their liberty, to work them without wages, to keep them ignorant of their relations to their fellow-men, to beat them with sticks, to flay their flesh with the lash, to load their limbs with irons, to hunt them with dogs, to sell them at auction, to sunder their families, to knock out their teeth, to burn their flesh, to starve them into obedience and submission to their masters? Must I argue that a system, thus marked with blood and stained with pollution, is wrong? No; I will not. I have better employment for my time and strength than such arguments would imply.

What, then, remains to be argued? Is it that slavery is not divine; that God did not establish it; that our doctors of divinity are mistaken? There is blasphemy in the thought. That which is inhuman cannot be divine. Who can reason on such a proposition! They that can, may; I cannot. The time for such argument is past.

At a time like this, scorching irony, not convincing argument, is needed. Oh! Had I the ability, and could I reach the nation's ear, I would today pour out a fiery stream of biting ridicule, blasting reproach, withering sarcasm, and stern rebuke. For it is not light that is needed, but fire;

it is not the gentle shower, but thunder. We need the storm, the whirlwind, and the earthquake. The feeling of the nation must be quickened; the conscience of the nation must be roused; the propriety of the nation must be startled; the hypocrisy of the nation must be exposed; and its crimes against God and man must be proclaimed and denounced.

What to the American slave is your Fourth of July? I answer, a day that reveals to him, more than all other days in the year, the gross injustice and cruelty to which he is the constant victim. To him, your celebration is a sham; your boasted liberty, an unholy license; your national greatness, swelling vanity; your sounds of rejoicing are empty and heartless; your denunciations of tyrants, brass-fronted impudence; your shouts of liberty and equality, hollow mockery; your prayers and hymns, your sermons and thanksgivings, with all your religious parade and solemnity, are to him mere bombast, fraud, deception, impiety, and hypocrisy—a thin veil to cover up crimes which would disgrace a nation of savages. There is not a nation on the earth guilty of practices more shocking and bloody, than are the people of these United States, at this very hour.

Go where you may, search where you will, roam through all the monarchies and despotisms of the old world, travel through South America, search out every abuse, and when you have found the last, lay your facts by the side of the every-day practices of this nation, and you will say with me, that, for revolting barbarity and shameless hypocrisy, America reigns without a rival.

Take the American slave trade, which, we are told by the papers, is especially prosperous just now. Ex-senator Benton tells us that the price of men was never higher than now. He mentions the fact to show that slavery is in no danger. This trade is one of the peculiarities of American institutions. It is carried on in all the large towns and cities in one-half of this confederacy; and millions are pocketed every year by dealers in this horrid traffic. In several states this trade is a chief source of wealth. It is called (in contradistinction to the foreign slave trade) *"the internal slave trade."* It is, probably, called so, too, in order to divert from it the horror with which the foreign slave trade is contemplated. That trade has long since been denounced by this government as piracy. It has been denounced with burning words, from the high places of the nation, as an execrable traffic. To arrest it, to put an end to it, this nation keeps a squadron, at immense cost, on the coast of Africa. Everywhere in this country, it is safe to speak of this foreign slave trade as a most inhuman traffic, opposed alike to the laws of God and of man. The duty to extirpate and destroy it is admitted even by our *doctors of divinity.* In order to put an end to it, some of these last have consented that their colored brethren (nominally free) should leave this country, and establish themselves on the western coast of Africa. It is, however, a notable fact, that, while so much execration is poured out by Americans, upon those engaged in the foreign slave trade, the men engaged in the slave trade between the states pass without condemnation, and their business is deemed honorable.

Behold the practical operation of this internal slave trade—the American slave trade sustained by American politics and American religion! Here you will see men and women reared like swine for the market. You know what is a swine-drover? I will show you a man-drover. They inhabit all our southern states. They perambulate the country, and crowd the highways of the nation with droves of human stock. You will see one of these human-flesh jobbers, armed with pistol, whip and bowie-knife, driving a company of a hundred men, women and children, from the Potomac to the slave market at New Orleans. Those wretched people are to be sold singly, or in lots, to suit purchasers. They are food for the cottonfield and the deadly sugar-mill. Mark the sad procession as it moves wearily along, and the inhuman wretch who drives them. Hear his savage yells and his blood-chilling oaths, as he hurries on his affrighted captives. There, see the old man, with locks thinned and gray. Cast one glance, if you please, upon that young mother, whose shoulders are bare to the scorching sun, her briny tears falling on the brow of the babe in her arms. See, too, that girl of thirteen, weeping, yes, weeping, as she thinks of the mother from whom she has been torn. The drove moves tardily. Heat and sorrow have nearly consumed their strength. Suddenly you hear a quick snap, like the discharge of a rifle; the fetters clank, and the chain rattles simultaneously; your ears are saluted with a scream that seems to have torn its way to the center of your soul. The crack you heard was the sound of the slave whip; the scream you heard was from the woman you saw with the babe. Her speed had faltered under the weight of her child and her chains; that gash on her shoulder tells her to move on. Follow this drove to New Orleans. Attend the auction; see men examined like horses; see the forms of women rudely and brutally exposed to the shocking gaze of American slave-buyers. See this drove sold and separated forever; and never forget the deep, sad sobs that arose from that scattered multitude. Tell me, citizens, where, under the sun, can you witness a spectacle more fiendish and shocking. Yet this is but a glance at the American slave trade, as it exists at this moment, in the ruling part of the United States.

I was born amid such sights and scenes. To me the American slave trade is a terrible reality. When a child, my soul was often pierced with a sense of its horrors. I lived on Philpot Street, Fell's Point, Baltimore, and have watched from the wharves the slave ships in the basin, anchored from the shore, with their cargoes of human flesh, waiting for favorable winds to waft them down the Chesapeake. There was, at that time, a grand slave mart kept at the head of Pratt Street, by Austin Woldfolk. His agents were sent into every town and county in Maryland, announcing their arrival through the papers, and on flaming hand-bills, headed, "Cash for Negroes." These men were generally well dressed, and very captivating in their manners; ever ready to drink, to treat, and to gamble. The fate of many a slave has depended upon the turn of a single card; and many a child has been snatched from the arms of its mother by bargains arranged in a state of brutal drunkenness.

The flesh-mongers gather up their victims by dozens, and drive them, chained, to the general depot at Baltimore. When a sufficient number have been collected here, a ship is chartered, for the purpose of conveying the forlorn crew to Mobile or to New Orleans. From the slave-prison to the ship, they are usually driven in the darkness of night; for since the antislavery agitation a certain caution is observed.

In the deep, still darkness of midnight, I have been often aroused by the dead, heavy footsteps and the piteous cries of the chained gangs that passed our door. The anguish of my boyish heart was intense; and I was often consoled, when speaking to my mistress in the morning, to hear her say that the custom was very wicked; that she hated to hear the rattle of the chains, and the heart-rending cries. I was glad to find one who sympathized with me in my horror.

Fellow-citizens, this murderous traffic is today in active operation in this boasted republic. In the solitude of my spirit, I see clouds of dust raised on the highways of the South; I see the bleeding footsteps; I hear the doleful wail of fettered humanity, on the way to the slave markets, where the victims are to be sold like horses, sheep and swine, knocked off to the highest bidder. There I see the tenderest ties ruthlessly broken, to gratify the lust, caprice, and rapacity of the buyers and sellers of men. My soul sickens at the sight.

> Is this the land your fathers loved?
> The freedom which they toiled to win?
> Is this the earth whereon they moved?
> Are these the graves they slumber in?

But a still more inhuman, disgraceful, and scandalous state of things remains to be presented. By an act of the American congress, not yet two years old, slavery has been nationalized in its most horrible and revolting form. By that act, Mason and Dixon's line has been obliterated; New York has become as Virginia; and the power to hold, hunt, and sell men, women and children as slaves remains no longer a mere state institution, but is now an institution of the whole United States. The power is co-extensive with the star-spangled banner and American Christianity. Where these go, may also go the merciless slave-hunter. Where these are, man is not sacred. He is a bird for the sportsman's gun. By that most foul and fiendish of all human decrees, the liberty and person of every man are put in peril. Your broad republican domain is a hunting-ground for *men.* Not for thieves and robbers, enemies of society, merely, but for men guilty of no crime. Your law-makers have commanded all good citizens to engage in this hellish sport. Your president, your secretary of state, your lords, nobles, and ecclesiastics, enforce as a duty you owe to your free and glorious country and to your God, that you do this accursed thing. Not fewer than forty Americans have within the past two years been hunted down, and without a moment's warning, hurried away in chains, and consigned to slavery and excruciating torture. Some of these have had wives and children dependent on them for bread; but of this no account was made. The right of the hunter to his prey, stands superior to the right of marriage, and to *all* rights in this republic, the rights of God included! For black men there are neither law, justice, humanity, nor religion. The fugitive slave law makes *mercy to them a crime;* and bribes the judge who tries them. An American judge *gets ten dollars for every victim he consigns* to slavery, and five, when he fails to do so. The oath of any two villains is sufficient, under this hell-black enactment, to send the most pious and exemplary black man into the remorseless jaws of slavery! His own testimony is nothing. He can bring no witnesses for himself. The minister of American justice is bound by the law to hear but *one side;* and that side is the side of the oppressor. Let this damning fact be perpetually told. Let it be thundered around the world, that, in tyrant-killing, king-hating, people-loving, democratic, Christian America, the seats of justice are filled with judges, who hold their office under an open and palpable *bribe,* and are bound, in deciding in the case of a man's liberty, *to hear only his accusers!*

In glaring violation of justice, in shameless disregard of the forms of administering law, in cunning arrangement to entrap the defenseless, and in diabolical intent, this fugitive slave law stands alone in the annals of tyrannical legislation. I doubt if there be another nation on the globe having the brass and the baseness to put such a law on the statute-book. If any man in this assembly thinks differently from me in this matter, and feels able to disprove my statements, I will gladly confront him at any suitable time and place he may select.

Men of Color, to Arms!

March 2, 1863

When first the rebel cannon shattered the walls of Sumter and drove away its starving garrison, I predicted that the war then and there inaugurated would not be fought out entirely by white men. Every month's experience during these dreary years has confirmed that opinion. A war undertaken and brazenly carried on for the perpetual enslavement of colored men calls logically and loudly for colored men to help suppress it. Only a moderate share of sagacity was needed to see that the arm of the slave was the best defense against the arm of the slaveholder. Hence with every reverse to the national arms, with every exulting shout of victory raised by the slaveholding rebels, I have implored the imperiled nation to unchain against her foes her powerful black hand. Slowly and reluctantly that appeal is beginning to be heeded. Stop not now to complain that it was not heeded sooner. It may or it may not have been best that it should not. This is not the time to discuss that question. Leave it to the future. When the war is over, the country is saved, peace is established, and the black man's rights are secured, as they will be, history with an impartial hand will dispose of that and sundry other questions. Action! Action! Not criticism, is the plain duty of this hour. Words are now useful only as they stimulate to blows. The office of speech now is only to point out when, where, and how to strike to the best advantage. There is no time to delay. The tide is at its flood that leads on to fortune. From East to West, from North to South, the sky is written all over, "Now or never." Liberty won by white men would lose half its luster. "Who would be free themselves must strike the blow." "Better even die free, than to live slaves." This is the sentiment of every brave colored man amongst us. There are weak and cowardly men in all nations. We have them amongst us. They tell you this is the "white man's war"; that you will be no "better off after than before the war"; that the getting of you into the army is to "sacrifice you on the first opportunity." Believe them not; cowards themselves, they do not wish to have their cowardice shamed by your brave example. Leave them to their timidity, or to whatever motive may hold them back. I have not thought lightly of the words I am now addressing you. The counsel I give comes of close observation of the great struggle now in progress, and of the deep conviction that this is your hour and mine. In good earnest then, and after the best deliberation, I now for the first time during this war feel at liberty to call and counsel you to arms. By every consideration which binds you to your enslaved fellow-countrymen, and the peace and welfare of your country; by every aspiration which you cherish for the freedom and equality of yourselves and your children; by all the ties of blood and identity which make us one with the brave black men now fighting our battles in Louisiana and in South Carolina, I urge you to fly to arms, and smite with death the power that would bury the government and your liberty in the same hopeless grave. I wish I could tell you that the state of New York calls you to this high honor. For the moment her constituted authorities are silent on the subject. They will speak by and by, and doubtless on the right side; but we are not compelled to wait for her. We can get at the throat of treason and slavery through the state of Massachusetts. She was first in the War of Independence; first to break the chains of her slaves; first to make the black man equal before the law; first to admit colored children to her common schools, and she was first to answer with her blood the alarm cry of the nation, when its capital was menaced by rebels. You know her patriotic governor, and you know Charles Sumner. I need not add more.

Massachusetts now welcomes you to arms as soldiers. She has but a small colored population from which to recruit. She has full leave of the general government to send one regiment to the war, and she has undertaken to do it. Go quickly and help fill up the first colored regiment from the North. I am authorized to assure you that you will receive the same wages, the same rations, the same equipments, the same protection, the same treatment, and the same bounty, secured to the white soldiers. You will be led by able and skillful officers, men who will take especial pride in your efficiency and success. They will be quick to accord to you all the honor you shall merit by your valor, and see that your rights and feelings are respected by other soldiers. I have assured myself on these points, and can speak with authority. More than twenty years of unswerving devotion to our common cause may give me some humble claim to be trusted at this momentous crisis. I will not argue. To do so implies hesitation and doubt, and you do not hesitate. You do not doubt. The day dawns; the morning star is bright upon the horizon! The iron gate of our prison stands half open. One gallant rush from the North will fling it wide open, while four millions of our brothers and sisters shall march out into liberty. The chance is now given you to end in a day the bondage of centuries, and to rise in one bound from social degradation to the plane of common equality with all other varieties of men. Remember Denmark Vesey of Charleston; remember Nathaniel Turner of Southampton; remember

Shields Green and Copeland, who followed noble John Brown, and fell as glorious martyrs for the cause of the slave. Remember that in a contest with oppression, the Almighty has no attribute which can take sides with oppressors. The case is before you. This is our golden opportunity. Let us accept it, and forever wipe out the dark reproaches unsparingly hurled against us by our enemies. Let us win for ourselves the gratitude of our country, and the best blessings of our posterity through all time. The nucleus of this first regiment is now in camp at Readville, a short distance from Boston. I will undertake to forward to Boston all persons adjudged fit to be mustered into the regiment, who shall apply to me at any time within the next two weeks.

Collateral Reading

Douglass, Frederick, *Narrative of the Life of Frederick Douglass, An American Slave.* Boston, 1845.

——————, *The Life and Times of Frederick Douglass.* Hartford, 1887.

Foner, Philip S., ed., *The Life and Writings of Frederick Douglass.* 4 vols. New York, 1930-1955.

Frazer, E. Franklin, *The Negro in the United States.* New York, 1957.

Woodson, Carter, *Negro Orators and Their Orations.* Washington, D.C., 1927.

Study Questions and Problems

1. Did Frederick Douglass adapt his speech at Moorfields, England, to his audience? What passages in the text of this speech suggest that he understood (or misunderstood) the nature of his audience?

2. Read Frederick Douglass' autobiography, *Narrative of the Life of Frederick Douglass,* in order to understand his early life.

3. What techniques of persuasion appear to be used consistently by Douglass in the three speeches included in this anthology?

4. Determine the central ideas of each of the three speeches.

5. What kinds of developing materials did Frederick Douglass use to amplify his ideas?

6. How did Douglass gain the interest of his audience in his "Fourth of July" speech?

7. Do you think that Douglass' personal experiences added to his credibility as a speaker? Justify your conclusion.

8. What is the purpose of the speech "Men of Color, to Arms!"—to create, change, or intensify an attitude?

9. Why is the "Men of Color, to Arms!" speech so brief? What explanation can you suggest? Did Douglass effectively develop his topic in this short speech? Justify your position.

Robert Brown Elliott

Robert Brown Elliott was born in Boston, Massachusetts, in 1842. He received his education in private schools in the United States and abroad, eventually graduating from Eton College in England.

Elliott's political career began when he was elected to the Constitutional Convention of South Carolina after the Civil War. He was elected to the state legislature in 1868 and to Congress in 1870 and 1872. In addition, he held several appointive offices at the state and local levels.

The ability to speak well was of great value to Elliott. While in Congress, he engaged in a famous debate with Rep. Beck from Kentucky, Rep. Harris from Virginia, and Congressman Alexander Stephens from Georgia on the so-called Civil Rights Bill, or "Bill to Enforce the Provisions of the Fourteenth Amendment to the Constitution," which sought to guarantee equal privileges to all classes of Americans.

Elliott's speech is an excellent example of refutative legislative debate speaking. He effectively refutes the major contentions of Beck, Harris, and Stephens, who opposed the Civil Rights Bill.

Elliott began by describing the contributions of black people in defense of the nation during the American Revolution and the War of 1812. He then quoted General Jackson's comment about an unreliable Kentucky regiment in the Battle of New Orleans in order to discredit Beck's exaggerated claims of the odium of the Negro and the chivalry of his state.

He then answered Stephens' charge that Congress had no power to pass such a law by submitting into evidence Leiber on Civil Liberty, *Alexander Hamilton's* History of the American Republic, *and the French Constitution of June, 1793.*

Next, Elliott answered Beck's charge that the Supreme Court barred the Civil Rights Bill in its decision in the so-called Slaughterhouse Cases:

Mr. Speaker, I venture to say here in the presence of the gentleman from Kentucky, and the gentleman from Georgia, and in the presence of the whole country, that there is not a line or word, not a thought or dictum even, in the decision of the Supreme Court in the great Slaughterhouse Cases which casts *a shadow of doubt on the right of Congress to pass the pending bill, or to adopt such other legislation as it may judge proper and necessary to secure perfect equality before the law to every citizen of the Republic.*

Elliott used the Supreme Court's written opinion as his main source of evidence for disproving Beck's claim.

Elliott also attacked Beck's charge that literacy tests such as Massachusetts had enacted would be abridged by the Civil Rights bill. Here Elliott argued with the help of statistical evidence that Massachusetts did not discriminate on the basis of race with its literacy test.

He concluded his refutation of Beck's contentions by observing the following: "Mr. Speaker, I have neither the time nor the inclination to notice the many illogical and forced conclusions, the numerous transfers of terms, or the vulgar insinuations which further incumber the argument of the gentleman from Kentucky."

Both Stephens and Harris were swiftly refuted, the former by scathing invective and the latter by silence. In rebuttal to remarks made earlier by Congressman Stephens, Elliott stated:

While the honorable gentleman contented himself with harmless speculation in his study, or in the columns of a newspaper, we might well smile at the impotence of his efforts to turn back the advancing tide of opinion and progress; but, when he comes again upon this national arena, and throws himself with all his power and influence across the path which leads to the full enfranchisement of my race, I meet him only as an adversary; nor shall age or any other consideration restrain me from saying that he now offers his Government, which he has done his utmost to destroy, a very poor return for its magnanimous treatment, to come here and seek to continue, by the assertion of doctrines obnoxious to the true principles of our Government, the burdens and oppressions which rest upon five millions of his countrymen who never failed to lift their earnest prayers for the success of this Government when the gentleman was seeking to break up the Union of these States and to blot the American Republic from the galaxy of nations.

Equally scathing was Elliott's treatment of Harris. He referred to Harris' remarks as a "diatribe" meant (according to Harris' own words) for white men only. Rather than take issue with such obvious racial slurs, Elliott wisely chose to damn his opponent with contemptuous silence.

I shall have no word of reply. Let him feel that a Negro was not only too magnanimous to smite him in his weakness, but was even charitable enough to grant him the mercy of his silence.

Speech on the Civil Rights Bill

April, 1873

While I am sincerely grateful for this high mark of courtesy that has been accorded to me by this House, it is a matter of regret to me that it is necessary at this day that I should rise in the presence of an American Congress to advocate a bill which simply asserts equal rights and equal public privileges for all classes of American citizens. I regret, sir, that the dark hue of my skin may lend a color to the imputation that I am controlled by motives personal to myself in my advocacy of this great measure of national justice. Sir, the motive that impels me is restricted by no such narrow boundary, but is as broad as your Constitution. I advocate it, sir, because it is right. The bill, however, not only appeals to your justice, but it demands a response from your gratitude.

In the events that led to the achievement of American Independence the Negro was not an inactive or unconcerned spectator. He bore his part bravely upon many battlefields, although uncheered by that certain hope of political elevation which victory would secure to the white man. The tall granite shaft, which a grateful state has reared above its sons who fell in defending Fort Griswold against the attack of Benedict Arnold, bears the name of Jordan, Freeman, and other brave men of the African race who there cemented with their blood the cornerstone of the Republic. In the state which I have the honor in part to represent, the rifle of the black man rang out against the troops of the British crown in the darkest days of the American Revolution. Said General Greene, who has been justly termed the Washington of the North, in a letter written by him to Alexander Hamilton, on the 10th day of January, 1781, from the vicinity of Camden, South Carolina:

> There is no such thing as national character or national sentiment. The inhabitants are numerous, but they would be rather formidable abroad than at home. There is a great spirit of enterprise among the black people, and those that come out as volunteers are not a little formidable to the enemy.

At the battle of New Orleans, under the immortal Jackson, a colored regiment held the extreme right of the American line unflinchingly, and drove back the British column that pressed upon them, at the point of the bayonet. So marked was their valor on that occasion that it evoked from their great commander the warmest encomiums, as will be seen from his dispatch announcing the brilliant victory.

As the gentleman from Kentucky [Mr. Beck], who seems to be the leading exponent on this floor of the party that is arrayed against the principle of this bill, has been pleased, in season and out of season, to cast odium upon the Negro and to vaunt the chivalry of his state, I may be pardoned for calling attention to another portion of the same dispatch. Referring to the various regiments under his command, and their conduct on that field which terminated the second war of American Independence, General Jackson says:

At the very moment when the entire discomfiture of the enemy was looked for with a confidence amounting to certainty, the Kentucky reenforcements, in whom so much reliance had been placed, ingloriously fled.

In quoting this indisputable piece of history, I do so only by way of admonition and not to question the well-attested gallantry of the true Kentuckian, and to suggest to the gentleman that it would be well that he should not flaunt his heraldry so proudly while he bears this bar sinister on the military escutcheon of his State—a State which answered the call of the Republic in 1861, when treason thundered at the very gates of the capital, by coldly declaring her neutrality in the impending struggle. The Negro, true to that patriotism and love of country that have ever characterized and marked his history on this continent, came to the aid of the Government in its efforts to maintain the Constitution. To that Government he now appeals; that Constitution he now invokes for protection against outrage and unjust prejudices founded upon caste.

But, sir, we are told by the distinguished gentleman from Georgia [Mr. Stephens] that Congress has no power under the Constitution to pass such a law, and that the passage of such an act is in direct contravention of the rights of the states. I cannot assent to any such proposition. The Constitution of a free government ought always to be construed in favor of human rights. Indeed, the Thirteenth, Fourteenth, and Fifteenth Amendments, in positive words, invest Congress with the power to protect the citizen in his civil and political rights. Now, sir, what are civil rights? Rights natural, modified by civil society. Mr. Lieber says:

By civil liberty is meant, not only the absence of individual restraint, but liberty within the social system and political organism—a combination of principles and laws which acknowledge, protect, and favor the dignity of man. . . . Civil liberty is the result of man's twofold character as an individual and social being, so soon as both are equally respected.—*Lieber on Civil Liberty,* page 25.

Alexander Hamilton, the right-hand man of Washington in the perilous days of the then infant Republic, the great interpreter and expounder of the Constitution, says:

Natural liberty is a gift of the beneficent Creator to the whole human race; civil liberty is founded on it; civil liberty is only natural liberty modified and secured by civil society.—*Hamilton's History of the American Republic,* vol. 1, page 70.

In the French Constitution of June, 1793, we find this grand and noble declaration:

Government is instituted to insure to man the free use of his natural and inalienable rights. These rights are equality, liberty, security, property. All men are equal by nature and before the law. . . . Law is the same for all, be it protective or penal. Freedom is the power by which man can do what does not interfere with the rights of another; its basis is nature, its standard is justice, its protection is law, its moral boundary is the maxim: "Do not unto others what you do not wish they should do unto you."

Are we then, sir, with the amendments to our Constitution staring us in the face; with these grand truths of history before our eyes; with innumerable wrongs daily inflicted upon five million citizens demanding redress, to commit this question to the diversity of state legislation? In the words of Hamilton—

Is it the interest of the Government to sacrifice individual rights to the preservation of the rights of an artificial being, called States? There can be no truer principle than this, that every individual of the community at large has an equal right to the protection of Government. Can this be a free Government if partial distinctions are tolerated or maintained?

The rights contended for in this bill are among "the sacred rights of mankind, which are not to be rummaged for among old parchments or musty records; they are written as with a sunbeam, in the whole volume of human nature, by the hand of the Divinity itself, and can never be erased or obscured by mortal power."

But the Slaughterhouse Cases!—the Slaughterhouse Cases!

The honorable gentleman from Kentucky, always swift to sustain the failing and dishonored cause of proscription, rushes forward and flaunts in our faces the decision of the Supreme Court of the United States in the Slaughterhouse Cases, and in that act he has been willingly aided by the gentleman from Georgia. Hitherto, in the contests which have marked the progress of the cause of equal civil rights, our opponents have appealed sometimes to custom, sometimes to prejudice, more often to pride of race, but they have never sought to shield themselves behind the Supreme Court. But now, for the first time, we are told that we are barred by a decision of that court, from which there is no appeal. If this be true we must stay our hands. The cause of equal civil rights must pause at the command of a power whose edicts must be obeyed till the fundamental law of our country is changed.

Has the honorable gentleman from Kentucky considered well the claim he now advances? If it were not disrespectful I would ask, has he ever read the decision which he now tells us is an insuperable barrier to the adoption of this great measure of justice?

In the consideration of this subject, has not the judgment of the gentleman from Georgia been warped by the ghost of the dead doctrines of state-rights? Has he been altogether free from prejudices engendered by long training in that school of politics that well-nigh destroyed this Government?

Mr. Speaker, I venture to say here in the presence of the gentleman from Kentucky, and the gentleman from Georgia, and in the presence of the whole country, that there is not a line or word, not a thought or dictum even, in the decision of the Supreme Court in the great Slaughterhouse Cases which casts a shadow of doubt on the right of Congress to pass the pending bill, or to adopt such other legislation as it may judge proper and necessary to secure perfect equality before the law to every citizen of the Republic. Sir, I protest against the dishonor now cast upon our Supreme Court by both the gentleman from Kentucky and the gentleman from Georgia. In other days, when the whole country was bowing beneath the yoke of slavery, when press, pulpit, platform, Congress, and courts felt the fatal power of the slave oligarchy, I remember a decision of that court which no American now reads without shame and humiliation. But those days are past. The Supreme Court of today is a tribunal as true to freedom as any department of this Government, and I am honored with the opportunity of repelling a deep disgrace which the gentleman from Kentucky, backed and sustained as he is by the gentleman from Georgia, seeks to put upon it.

What were these Slaughterhouse Cases? The gentleman should be aware that a decision of any court should be examined in the light of the exact question which is brought before it for decision. That is all that gives authority to any decision.

The State of Louisiana, by act of her Legislature, had conferred on certain persons the exclusive right to maintain stock-landings and slaughterhouses within the city of New Orleans, or the parishes of Orleans, Jefferson, and Saint Bernard, in that State. The corporation which was thereby chartered were invested with the sole and exclusive privilege of conducting and carrying on the livestock, landing, and slaughterhouse business within the limits designated.

The supreme court of Louisiana sustained the validity of the act conferring these exclusive privileges, and the plaintiffs in error brought the case before the Supreme Court of the United States for review. The plaintiffs in error contended that the act in question was void, because, first, it established a monopoly which was in derogation of common right and in contravention of the common law; and, second, that the grant of such exclusive privileges was in violation of the Thirteenth and Fourteenth Amendments of the Constitution of the United States.

It thus appears from a simple statement of the case that the question which was before the court was not whether a State law which denied to a particular portion of her citizens the rights conferred on her citizens generally, on account of race, color, or previous condition of servitude, was unconstitutional because in conflict with the recent amendments, but whether an act which conferred on certain citizens exclusive privileges for police purposes was in conflict therewith, because imposing an involuntary servitude forbidden by the Thirteenth Amendment, or abridging the rights and immunities of citizens of the United States, or denying the equal protection of the laws, prohibited by the Fourteenth Amendment.

On the part of the defendants in error it was maintained that the act was the exercise of the ordinary and unquestionable power of the State to make regulation for the health and comfort of society—the exercise of the police power of the State, defined by Chancellor Kent to be "the right to interdict unwholesome trades, slaughterhouses, operations offensive to the senses, the deposit of powder, the application of steam-power to propel cars, the building with combustible materials, and the burial of the dead in the midst of dense masses of population, on the general and rational principle that every person ought so to use his own property as not to injure his neighbors, and that private interests must be made subservient to the general interests of the community."

The decision of the Supreme Court is to be found in the 16th volume of Wallace's Reports, and was delivered by Associate Justice Miller. The court held, first, that the act in question is a legitimate and warrantable exercise of the police power of the State in regulating the business of stock-landing and slaughtering in the city of New Orleans and the territory immediately contiguous. Having held this, the court proceeds to discuss the question whether the conferring of exclusive privileges, such as those conferred by the act in question, is the imposing of an involuntary servitude, the abridging of the rights and immunities of citizens of the United States, or the denial to any person within the jurisdiction of the State of the equal protection of the laws.

That the act is not the imposition of an involuntary servitude the court hold to be clear, and they next proceed to examine the remaining questions arising under the Fourteenth Amendment. Upon this question the court held that the leading and comprehensive purpose of the Thirteenth, Fourteenth, and Fifteenth Amendments was to secure the complete freedom of the race, which, by the events of the war, had been wrested from the unwilling grasp of their owners. I know no finer or more just picture, albeit painted in the neutral tints of true judicial impartiality, of the motives and events which led to these amendments. Has the gentleman from Kentucky read these passages which I now quote? Or has the gentleman from Georgia considered well the force of the language therein used? Says the court on page 70:

The process of restoring to their proper relations with the Federal Government and with the other states those which had sided with the rebellion, undertaken under the proclamation of President Johnson in 1865, and before the assembling of Congress, developed the fact that, notwithstanding the formal recognition by those states of the abolition of slavery, the condition of the slave race would, without further protection of the Federal Government, be almost as bad as it was before. Among the first acts of legislation adopted by several of the states in the legislative bodies which claimed to be in their normal relations with the Federal Government, were laws which imposed upon the colored race onerous disabilities and burdens, and curtailed their rights in the pursuit of life, liberty, and property to such an extent that their freedom was of little value, while they had lost the protection which they had received from their former owners from motives both of interest and humanity.

They were in some states forbidden to appear in the towns in any other character than menial servants. They were required to reside on and cultivate the soil, without the right to purchase or own it. They were excluded from any occupations of gain, and were not permitted to give testimony in the courts in any case where a white man was a party. It was said that their lives were at the mercy of bad men, either because the laws for their protection were insufficient or were not enforced.

These circumstances, whatever of falsehood or misconception may have been mingled with their presentation, forced upon the statesmen who had conducted the Federal Government in safety through the crisis of the rebellion, and who supported that by the Thirteenth Article of Amendment they had secured the result of their labors, the conviction that something more was necessary in the way of constitutional protection to the unfortunate race who had suffered so much. They accordingly passed through Congress the proposition for the Fourteenth Amendment, and they declined to treat as restored to their full participation in the Government of the Union the states which had been in insurrection until they ratified that article by a formal vote of their legislative bodies.

Before we proceed to examine more critically the provisions of this amendment on which the plaintiffs in error rely, let us complete and dismiss the history of the recent amendments, as that history relates to the general purpose which pervades them all. A few years' experience satisfied the thoughtful men who had been the authors of the other two amendments that, notwithstanding the restraints of those articles on the States and the laws passed under the additional powers granted to Congress, these were inadequate for the protection of life, liberty, and property, without which freedom to the slave was no boon. They were in all those States denied the right of suffrage. The laws were administered by the white man alone. It was urged that a race of men distinctively marked as was the Negro, living in the midst of another and dominant race, could never be fully secured in their person and their property without the right of suffrage.

Hence the Fifteenth Amendment, which declares that "the right of a citizen of the United States to vote shall not be denied or abridged by any State on account of race, color, or previous condition of servitude." The Negro having, by the Fourteenth Amendment, been declared to be a citizen of the United States, is thus made a voter in every State of the Union.

We repeat, then, in the light of this recapitulation of events almost too recent to be called history, but which are familiar to us all, and on the most casual examination of the language of these amendments, no one can fail to be impressed with the one pervading purpose found in them all, lying at the foundation of each, and without which none of them would have been even suggested: we mean the freedom of the slave race, the security and firm establishment of that freedom, and the protection of the newly-made freeman and citizen from the oppressions of those who had formerly exercised unlimited dominion over him. It is true that only the Fifteenth Amendment in terms mentions the Negro by speaking of his color and his slavery. But it is just as true that each of the other articles was addressed to the grievances of that race, and designed to remedy them, as the Fifteenth.

These amendments, one and all, are thus declared to have as their all-pervading design and end the security to the recently enslaved race, not only their nominal freedom, but their complete protection from those who had formerly exercised unlimited dominion over them. It is in this broad light that all these amendments must be read, the purpose to secure the perfect equality before the law of all citizens of the United States. What you give to one class you must give to all; what you deny to one class you shall deny to all, unless in the exercise of the common and universal police power of the State you find it needful to confer exclusive privileges on certain citizens, to be held and exercised still for the common good of all.

Such are the doctrines of the Slaughterhouse Cases—doctrines worthy of the Republic, worthy of the age, worthy of the great tribunal which thus loftily and impressively enunciates them. Do they—I put it to any man, be he lawyer or not; I put it to the gentleman from Georgia—do they give color even to the claim that this Congress may not now legislate against a plain discrimination made by state laws or state customs against that very race for whose complete freedom and protection these great amendments were elaborated and adopted? Is it pretended, I ask the honorable gentleman from Kentucky or the honorable gentleman from Georgia—is it pretended anywhere that the evils of which we complain, our exclusion from the public inn, from the saloon and table of the steamboat, from the sleeping-coach on the railway, from the right of sepulture in the public burial-ground, are an exercise of the police power of the state? Is such oppression and injustice nothing but the exercise by the state of the right to make regulations for the health, comfort and security of all her citizens? Is it merely enacting that one man shall so use his own as not to injure another's? Are the colored race to be assimilated to an unwholesome trade or to combustible materials, to be interdicted, to be shut up within prescribed limits? Let the gentleman from Kentucky or the gentleman from Georgia answer. Let the country know to what extent even the audacious prejudice of the gentleman from Kentucky will drive him, and how far even the gentleman from Georgia will permit himself to be led captive by the unrighteous teachings of a false political faith.

If we are to be likened in legal view to "unwholesome trades," to "large and offensive collections of animals," to "noxious slaughterhouses," to "the offal and stench which attend on certain manufactures," let it be avowed. If that is still the doctrine of the political party to which the gentlemen belong, let it be put upon record. If state laws which deny us the common rights and privileges of other citizens, upon no possible or conceivable ground save one of prejudice, or of "taste," as the gentleman from Texas termed it, and as I suppose the gentlemen will prefer to call it, are to be placed under the protection of a decision which affirms the right of a state to regulate the police of her great cities, then the decision is in conflict with the bill before us. No man will dare maintain such a doctrine. It is as shocking to the legal mind as it is offensive to the heart and conscience of all who love justice or respect manhood. I am astonished that the gentleman from Kentucky or the gentleman from Georgia should have been so grossly misled as to rise here and assert that the decision of the Supreme Court in these cases was a denial to Congress of the power to legislate against discriminations on account of race, color, or previous condition of servitude, because that court has decided that exclusive privileges conferred for the common protection of the lives and health of the whole community are not in violation of the recent amendments. The only ground upon which the grant of exclusive privileges to a portion of the community is ever defended is that the substantial good of all is promoted; that in truth it is for the welfare of the whole community that certain persons should alone pursue certain occupations. It is not the special benefit conferred on the few that moves the legislature, but the ultimate and real benefit of all, even of those who are denied the right to pursue those specified occupations. Does the gentleman from Kentucky say that my good is promoted when I am excluded from the public inn? Is the health or safety of the community promoted? Doubtless his prejudice is gratified. Doubtless his democratic instincts are pleased; but will he or his able coadjutor say that such exclusion is a lawful exercise of the police power of the state, or that it is not a denial to me of the equal protection of the laws? They will not so say.

But each of these gentlemen quote at some length from the decision of the court to show that the court recognizes a difference between citizenship of the United States and citizenship of the states. That is true, and no man here who supports this bill questions or overlooks the difference. There are privileges and immunities which belong to me as a citizen of the United States, and there are other privileges and immunities which belong to me as a citizen of my state. The former are under the protection of the Constitution and laws of the United States, and the latter are under the protection of the constitution and laws of my state. But what of that? Are the rights which I now claim—the right to enjoy the common public conveniences of travel on public highways, of rest and refreshment at public inns, of education in public schools, of burial in public cemeteries—rights which I hold as a citizen of the United States or of my state? Or, to state the question more exactly, is not the denial of such privileges to me a denial to me of the equal protection of the laws? For it is under this clause of the Fourteenth Amendment that we place the present bill, no state shall "deny to any person within its jurisdiction the equal protection of the laws." No matter, therefore, whether his rights are held under the United States or under his particular state, he is equally protected by this amendment. He is always and everywhere entitled to the equal protection of the laws. All discrimination is forbidden; and while the rights of citizens of a state as such are not defined or conferred by the Constitution of the United States, yet all discrimination, all denial of equality before the law, all denial of the equal protection of the laws, whether state or national laws, is forbidden.

The distinction between the two kinds of citizenship is clear, and the Supreme Court have clearly pointed out this distinction, but they have nowhere written a word or line which denies to Congress the power to prevent a denial of equality of rights, whether those rights exist by virtue of citizenship of the United States or of a state. Let honorable members mark well this distinction. There are rights which are conferred on us by the United States. There are other rights conferred on us by the states of which we are individually the citizens. The Fourteenth Amendment does not forbid a state to deny to all its citizens any of those rights which the state itself has conferred, with certain exceptions, which are pointed out in the decision which we are examining. What it does forbid is inequality, is discrimination, or, to use the words of the amendment itself, is the denial "to any person within its jurisdiction the equal protection of the laws." If a state denies to me rights which are common to all her other citizens, she violates this amendment, unless she can show, as was shown in the Slaughterhouse Cases, that she does it in the legitimate exercise of her police power. If she abridges the rights of all her citizens equally, unless those rights are specially guarded by the Constitution of the United States, she does not violate this amendment. This is not to put the rights which I hold by virtue of my citizenship of South Carolina under the protection of the national Government; it is not to blot out or overlook in the slightest particular the distinction between rights held under the United States and rights held under the states; but it seeks to secure equality, to prevent discrimination, to confer as complete and ample protection on the humblest as on the highest.

The gentleman from Kentucky, in the course of the speech to which I am now replying, made a reference to the State of Massachusetts which betrays again the confusion which exists in his mind on this precise point. He tells us that Massachusetts excludes from the ballot-box all who cannot read and write, and points to that fact as the exercise of a right which this bill would abridge or impair. The honorable gentleman from Massachusetts [Mr. Dawes] answered him truly and well, but I submit that he did not make the best reply. Why did he not ask the gentleman from Kentucky if Massachusetts had ever discriminated against any of her citizens on account of color, or race, or previous condition of servitude? When did Massachusetts sully her proud record by placing on her statute-book any law which admitted to the ballot the white man and shut out the black man? She has never done it; she will not do it; she cannot do it so long as we have a Supreme Court which reads the Constitution of our country with the eyes of justice; nor can Massachusetts or Kentucky deny to any man, on account of his race, color, or previous condition of servitude, that perfect equality of protection under the laws so long as Congress shall exercise the power to enforce, by appropriate legislation, the great and unquestionable securities embodied in the Fourteenth Amendment to the Constitution.

But, sir, a few words more as to the suffrage regulation of Massachusetts.

It is true that Massachusetts in 1857, finding that her illiterate population was being constantly augmented by the continual influx of ignorant emigrants, placed in her constitution the least possible limitation consistent with manhood suffrage to stay this tide of foreign ignorance. Its benefit has been fully demonstrated in the intelligent character of the voters of that honored Commonwealth, reflected so conspicuously in the able Representatives she has today upon this floor. But neither is the inference of the gentleman from Kentucky legitimate, nor do the statistics of the census of 1870, drawn from his own state, sustain his astounding assumption. According to the statistics we find the whole white population of that state is 1,098,692; the whole colored population 222,210. Of the whole white population who cannot write we find 201,077; of the whole colored population who cannot write, 126,048; giving us, as will be seen, 96,162 colored persons who can write to 897,615 white persons who can write. Now, the ratio of the colored population to the white is as 1 to 5, and the ratio of the illiterate colored population to the whole colored population is as 1 to 2; the ratio of the illiterate white population is to the whole white population as 1 is to 5. Reducing this, we have only a preponderance of three-tenths in favor of the whites as to literacy, notwithstanding the advantages which they have always enjoyed and do now enjoy of free-school privileges, and this, too, taking solely into account the single item of being unable to write; for with regard to the inability to read, there is no discrimination in the statistics between the white and colored population. There is, moreover, a peculiar felicity in these statistics with regard to the state of Kentucky, quoted so opportunely for me by the honorable gentleman; for I find that the population of that state, both with regard to its white and colored populations, bears the same relative rank in regard to the white and colored populations of the United States; and, therefore, while one Negro would be disfranchised were the limitation of Massachusetts put in force, nearly three white men would at the same time be deprived of the right of suffrage—a consummation which I think would be far more acceptable to the colored people of that state than to the whites.

Now, sir, having spoken as to the intention of the prohibition imposed by Massachusetts, I may be pardoned for a slight inquiry as to the effect of this prohibition. First, it did not in any way abridge or curtail the exercise of the suffrage by any person who at that time enjoyed such right. Nor did it discriminate between the illiterate native and the illiterate foreigner. Being enacted for the good of the entire Commonwealth, like all just laws, its obligations fell equally and impartially upon all its citizens. And as a justification for such a measure, it is a fact too well known almost for mention here that Massachusetts had, from the beginning of her history, recognized the inestimable value of an educated ballot, by not only maintaining a system of free schools, but also enforcing an attendance thereupon, as one of the safeguards for the preservation of a real republican form of government. Recurring then, sir, to the possible contingency alluded to by the gentleman from Kentucky, should the state of Kentucky, having first established a system of common schools whose doors shall swing open freely to all, as contemplated by the provisions of this bill, adopt a provision similar to that of Massachusetts, no one would have cause justly to complain. And if in the coming years the result of such legislation should produce a constituency rivaling that of the old Bay State, no one would be more highly gratified than I.

Mr. Speaker, I have neither the time nor the inclination to notice the many illogical and forced conclusions, the numerous transfers of terms, or the vulgar insinuations which further incumber the argument of the gentleman from Kentucky. Reason and argument are worse than wasted upon those who meet every demand for political and civil liberty by such ribaldry as this—extracted from the speech of the gentleman from Kentucky:

> I suppose there are gentlemen on this floor who would arrest, imprison, and fine a young woman in any state of the South if she were to refuse to marry a Negro man on account of color, race, or previous condition of servitude, in the event of his making her a proposal of marriage, and her refusing on that ground. That would be depriving him of a right he had under the amendment, and Congress would be asked to take it up and say, "This insolent white woman must be taught to know that it is a misdemeanor to deny a man marriage because of race, color, or previous condition of servitude"; and Congress will be urged to say after a while that that sort of thing must be put a stop to, and your conventions of colored men will come here asking you to enforce that right.

Now, sir, recurring to the venerable and distinguished gentleman from Georgia [Mr. Stephens], who has added his remonstrance against the passage of this bill, permit me to say that I share in the feeling of high personal regard for that gentleman which pervades this House. His years, his ability, and his long experience in public affairs entitle him to the measure of consideration which has been accorded to him on this floor. But in this discussion I cannot and I will not forget that the welfare and rights of my whole race in this country are involved. When, therefore, the honorable gentleman from Georgia lends his voice and influence to defeat this measure, I do not shrink from saying that it is not from him that the American House of Representatives should take lessons in matters touching human rights or the joint relations of the state and national governments. While the honorable gentleman contented himself with harmless speculations in his study, or in the columns of a newspaper, we might well smile at the impotence of his efforts to turn back the advancing tide of opinion and progress; but, when he comes again upon this national arena, and throws himself with all his power and influence across the path which leads to the full enfranchisement of my race,

I meet him only as an adversary; nor shall age or any other consideration restrain me from saying that he now offers this Government, which he has done his utmost to destroy, a very poor return for its magnanimous treatment, to come here and seek to continue, by the assertion of doctrines obnoxious to the true principles of our Government, the burdens and oppressions which rest upon five millions of his countrymen who never failed to lift their earnest prayers for the success of this Government when the gentleman was seeking to break up the Union of these States and to blot the American Republic from the galaxy of nations. [Loud applause.]

Sir, it is scarcely twelve years since that gentleman shocked the civilized world by announcing the birth of a government which rested on human slavery as its cornerstone. The progress of events has swept away that *pseudo*-government which rested on greed, pride, and tyranny; and the race whom he then ruthlessly spurned and trampled on are here to meet him in debate, and to demand that the rights which are enjoyed by their former oppressors—who vainly sought to overthrow a Government which they could not prostitute to the base uses of slavery—shall be accorded to those who even in the darkness of slavery kept their allegiance true to freedom and the Union. Sir, the gentleman from Georgia has learned much since 1861; but he is still a laggard. Let him put away entirely the false and fatal theories which have so greatly marred an otherwise enviable record. Let him accept, in its fullness and beneficence, the great doctrine that American citizenship carries with it every civil and political right which manhood can confer. Let him lend his influence, with all his masterly ability, to complete the proud structure of legislation which makes this nation worthy of the great declaration which heralded its birth, and he will have done that which will most nearly redeem his reputation in the eyes of the world, and best vindicate the wisdom of that policy which has permitted him to regain his seat upon this floor.

To the diatribe of the gentleman from Virginia [Mr. Harris], who spoke on yesterday, and who so far transcended the limits of decency and propriety as to announce upon this floor that his remarks were addressed to white men alone, I shall have no word of reply. Let him feel that a Negro was not only too magnanimous to smite him in his weakness, but was even charitable enough to grant him the mercy of his silence. [Laughter and applause on the floor and in the galleries.] I shall, sir, leave to others less charitable the unenviable and fatiguing task of sifting out of that mass of chaff the few grains of sense that may, perchance, deserve notice. Assuring the gentleman that the Negro in this country aims at a higher degree of intellect than that exhibited by him in this debate, I cheerfully commend him to the commiseration of all intelligent men the world over—black men as well as white men.

Sir, equality before the law is now the broad, universal, glorious rule and mandate of the Republic. No state can violate that. Kentucky and Georgia may crowd their statute-books with retrograde and barbarous legislation; they may rejoice in the odious eminence of their consistent hostility to all the great steps of human progress which have marked out national history since slavery tore down the stars and stripes on Fort Sumter; but, if Congress shall do its duty, if Congress shall enforce the great guarantees which the Supreme Court has declared to be the one pervading purpose of all the recent amendments, then their unwise and unenlightened conduct will fall with the same weight upon the gentlemen from those states who now lend their influence to defeat this bill, as upon the poorest slave who once had no rights which the honorable gentlemen were bound to respect.

But, sir, not only does the decision in the Slaughterhouse Cases contain nothing which suggests a doubt of the power of Congress to pass the pending bill, but it contains an express recognition and affirmance of such power. I quote now from page 81 of the volume:

"Nor shall any State deny to any person within its jurisdiction the equal protection of the laws."

In the light of the history of these amendments, and the pervading purpose of them, which we have already discussed, it is not difficult to give a meaning to this clause. The existence of laws in the States where the newly emancipated Negroes resided, which discriminated with gross injustice and hardship against them as a class, was the evil to be remedied by this clause, and by it such laws are forbidden.

If, however, the States did not conform their laws to its requirements, then, by the fifth section of the article of amendment, Congress was authorized to enforce it by suitable legislation. We doubt very much whether any action of a State not directed by way of discrimination against the Negroes as a class, or on account of their race, will ever be held to come within the purview of this provision. It is so clearly a provision for that race and that emergency, that a strong case would be necessary for its application to any other. But as it is a State that is to be dealt with, and not alone the validity of its laws, we may safely leave that matter until Congress shall have exercised its power, or some case of State oppression, by denial of equal justice in its courts, shall have claimed a decision at our hands.

No language could convey a more complete assertion of the power of Congress over the subject embraced in the present bill than is here expressed. If the States do not conform to the requirements of this clause, if they continue to deny to any person within their jurisdiction the equal protection of the laws, or as the Supreme Court had said, "deny equal justice in its courts," then Congress is here said to have power to enforce the constitutional guarantee by appropriate legislation. That is the power which this bill now seeks to put in exercise. It proposes to enforce the constitutional guarantee against inequality and discrimination by appropriate legislation. It does not seek to confer new rights, nor to place rights conferred by State citizenship under the protection of the United States, but simply to prevent and forbid inequality and discrimination on account of race, color, or previous condition of servitude. Never was there a bill more completely within the constitutional power of Congress. Never was there a bill which appealed for support more strongly to that sense of justice and fair-play which has been said, and in the main with justice, to be a characteristic of the Anglo-Saxon race. The Constitution warrants it; the Supreme Court sanctions it; justice demands it.

Sir, I have replied to the extent of my ability to the arguments which have been presented by the opponents of this measure. I have replied also to some of the legal propositions advanced by gentlemen on the other side; and now that I am about to conclude, I am deeply sensible of the imperfect manner in which I have performed the task. Technically, this bill is to decide upon the civil status of the colored American citizen; a point disputed at the very formation of our present Government, when by a short-sighted policy, a policy repugnant to true republican government, one Negro counted as three-fifths of a man. The logical result of this mistake of the framers of the Constitution strengthened the cancer of slavery, which finally spread its poisonous tentacles over the Southern portion of the body-politic. To arrest its growth and save the nation we have passed through the harrowing operation of intestine war, dreaded at all times, resorted to at the last extremity, like the surgeon's knife, but absolutely necessary to extirpate the disease which threatened with the life of the nation the overthrow of civil and political liberty on this continent. In that dire extremity the members of the race which I have the honor in part to represent—the race which pleads for justice at your hands today, forgetful of their inhuman and brutalizing servitude at the South, their degradation and ostracism at the North—flew willingly and gallantly to the support of the national Government. Their sufferings, assistance, privations, and trials in the swamps and in the rice fields, their valor on the land and on the sea, is a part of the ever-glorious record which makes up the history of a nation preserved, and might, should I urge the claim, incline you to respect and guarantee their rights and privileges as citizens of our common Republic. But I remember that valor, devotion, and loyalty are not always rewarded according to their just desserts, and that after the battle some who have borne the brunt of the fray may, through neglect or contempt, be assigned to a subordinate place, while the enemies in war may be preferred to the sufferers.

The results of the war, as seen in Reconstruction, have settled forever the political status of my race. The passage of this bill will determine the civil status, not only of the Negro, but of any other class of citizens who may feel themselves discriminated against. It will form the capstone of that temple of liberty, begun on this continent under discouraging circumstances, carried on in spite of the sneers of monarchists and the cavils of pretended friends of freedom, until at last it stands in all its beautiful symmetry and proportions, a building the grandest which the world has ever seen, realizing the most sanguine expectations and the highest hopes of those who, in the name of equal, impartial, and universal liberty, laid the foundation stones.

The Holy Scriptures tell us of an humble handmaiden who long, faithfully and patiently gleaned in the rich fields of her wealthy kinsman; and we are told further that at last, in spite of her humble antecedents, she found complete favor in his sight. For over two centuries our race has "reaped down your fields." The cries and woes which we have uttered have "entered into the ears of the Lord of Sabaoth," and we are at last politically free. The last vestiture only is needed—civil rights. Having gained this, we may, with hearts overflowing with gratitude, and thankful that our prayer has been granted, repeat the prayer of Ruth: "Entreat me not to leave thee, or to return from following after thee; for whither thou goest, I will go; and where thou lodgest, I will lodge; thy people shall be my people, and thy God my God; where thou diest, will I die, and there will I be buried; the Lord do so to me, and more also, if aught but death part thee and me." [Great applause.]

Collateral Reading

Congressional Record, Part I, 43rd Session, 1873.

Meier, August, *Negro Thought in America, 1880-1915.* Ann Arbor, 1966.

Simmons, William J., *Men of Mark.* New York, 1968.

Woodson, Carter G., *Negro Orators and Their Orations.* Washington, D.C., 1921.

Woodward, C. Van, *Origins of the New South.* Baton Rouge, 1951.

Study Questions and Problems

1. What kinds of proof (ethical, emotional, or logical) prevail in this speech? Identify as many kinds of proof as you can.

2. List Elliott's contentions for enforcement of the Civil Rights Bill. What arguments and evidence are used to support each contention?

3. Elliott's speech is extremely long. Discuss what rhetorical factors one should consider when determining the length of an address.

4. Many political speeches occur in the *Congressional Record.* What hazards does one encounter when using this material as a source of speech texts? What changes have been made in the reporting of speeches in the *Congressional Record?*

5. Read the Reconstruction oratory contained in Woodson's *Negro Orators and Their Orations.*

6. What were the "Jim Crow" laws? Read Woodward's *The Strange Case of Jim Crow* (New York, 1955).

Booker T. Washington

Booker T. Washington was born into slavery in Franklin County, Virginia, around 1856. He rose through diligence and effort to become the principal of Tuskegee Normal and Industrial Institute in Alabama, 1881-1915. As an educator, he gained nationwide fame for his concept of technical education for Negro advancement by separate but equal development.

During Washington's career as a speaker, he probably delivered between two and four thousand speeches. He participated in the debating society at Hampton Institute, where he also took private voice and diction lessons. After graduation he had practical speech experience as a stump speaker arguing for the establishment of the state capitol at Charleston. Later, as a teacher, he made occasional addresses. Thus, when he became principal at Tuskegee, he had already acquired useful experience and training as a public speaker.

Booker T. Washington took great pains to direct his speeches to his specific audience.

I always make it a rule to make special preparation for each separate address. No two audiences are exactly alike. It is my aim to reach and talk to the heart of each individual audience, taking it into my confidence very much as I would a person. When I am speaking to an audience, I care little for how what I am saying is going to sound in the newspapers, or to another audience, or to an individual. At the time, the audience before me absorbs all my sympathy, thought, and energy.

He also took pains to have important speeches, especially to mixed audiences, criticized before delivery. The Atlanta address is the prime example of this characteristic. Copies of the speech were sent to men of both races in the North and South.

Washington's speeches were typified by such traits as sincerity, tact, modesty, and humor. He delivered his speeches in a direct, lively, conversational manner. His speeches tended to be loosely organized expositions using statistical evidence and testimony in support of his arguments when necessary.

Booker T. Washington was severely criticized in later years by W. E. B. Du Bois for his program of vocational education and racial harmony. To Du Bois and other black intellectuals, Washington was an "Uncle Tom" to his race. Perhaps his seemingly apologist program explains why contemporary black leaders find little inspiration in his ideas.

Booker T. Washington gave a "five-minute speech" at the opening of the Cotton States Exposition at Atlanta where he addressed an audience composed of Southern whites, Northern supporters of Negro rights, and the Southern Negroes themselves. It was one of the most prestigious occasions for a black orator in the nineteenth century, and Washington's speech received overwhelming acclaim throughout the nation.

Preceding the text of Washington's Atlanta speech is some introductory background information by Washington about public speaking in general and the particular circumstances surrounding the Atlanta address.

Speech at the Cotton States Exposition
September 18, 1895

Background Information

I have often been asked how I began the practice of public speaking. In answer I would say that I never planned to give any large part of my life to speaking in public. I have always had more of an ambition to *do* things than merely to talk *about* doing them. It seems that when I went North with General Armstrong to speak at the series of public meetings to which I have referred, the President of the National Educational Association, the Hon. Thomas W. Bicknell, was present at one of those meetings and heard me speak. A few days afterward he sent me an invitation to deliver an address at the next meeting of the Educational Association. This meeting was to be held in Madison, Wis. I accepted the invitation. This was, in a sense, the beginning of my public-speaking career.

On the evening that I spoke before the Association there must have been not far from four thousand persons present. Without my knowing it, there were a large number of people present from Alabama, and some from the town of Tuskegee. These white people afterward frankly told me that they went to this meeting expecting to hear the South roundly abused, but were pleasantly surprised to find that there was no word of abuse in my address. On the contrary, the South was given credit for all the praiseworthy things that it had done. A white lady who was a teacher in a college in Tuskegee wrote back to the local paper that she was gratified, as well as surprised, to note the credit which I gave the white people of Tuskegee for their help in getting the school started. This address at Madison was the first that I had delivered that in any large measure dealt with the general problem of the races. Those who heard it seemed to be pleased with what I said and with the general position that I took.

When I first came to Tuskegee, I determined that I would make it my home, that I would take as much pride in the right actions of the people of the town as any white man could do, and that I would, at the same time, deplore the wrong-doing of the people as much as any white man. I determined never to say anything in a public address in the North that I would not be willing to say in the South. I early learned that it is a hard matter to convert an individual by abusing him, and that this is more often accomplished by giving credit for all the praiseworthy actions performed than by calling attention alone to all the evil done.

While pursuing this policy I have not failed, at the proper time and in the proper manner, to call attention, in no uncertain terms, to the wrongs which any part of the South has been guilty of. I have found that there is a large element in the South that is quick to respond to straightforward, honest criticism of any wrong policy. As a rule, the place to criticise the South, when criticism is necessary, is in the South—not in Boston. A Boston man who came to Alabama to criticise Boston would not effect so much good, I think, as one who had his word of criticism to say in Boston.

In this address at Madison I took the ground that the policy to be pursued with reference to the races was, by every honourable means, to bring them together and to encourage the cultivation of friendly relations, instead of doing that which would embitter. I further contended that, in relation to his vote, the Negro should more and more consider the interests of the community in which he lived, rather than seek alone to please someone who lived a thousand miles away from him and from his interests.

In this address I said that the whole future of the Negro rested largely upon the question as to whether or not he should make himself, through his skill, intelligence, and character, of such undeniable value to the community in which he lived that the community could not dispense with his presence. I said that any individual who learned to do something better than anybody else—learned to do a common thing in an uncommon manner—had solved his problem, regardless of the colour of his skin, and that in proportion as the Negro learned to produce what other people wanted and must have, in the same proportion would he be respected.

I spoke of an instance where one of our graduates had produced two hundred and sixty-six bushels of sweet potatoes from an acre of ground, in a community where the average production had been only forty-nine bushels to the acre. He had been able to do this by reason of his knowledge of the chemistry of the soil and by his knowledge of improved methods of agriculture. The white farmers in the neighbourhood respected him, and came to him for ideas regarding the raising of sweet potatoes. These white farmers honoured and respected him because he, by his skill and knowledge, had added something to the wealth and the comfort of the community in which he lived. I explained that my theory of education for the Negro would not, for example, confine him for all time to farm life—to the production of the best and the most sweet potatoes—but that, if he succeeded in this line of industry, he could lay the foundations upon which his children and grandchildren could grow to higher and more important things in life.

Such, in brief, were some of the views I advocated in this first address dealing with the broad question of the relations of the two races, and since that time I have not found any reason for changing my views on any important point.

In my early life I used to cherish a feeling of ill will toward anyone who spoke in bitter terms against the Negro, or who advocated measures that tended to oppress the black man or take from him opportunities for growth in the most complete manner. Now, whenever I hear anyone advocating measures that are meant to curtail the development of another, I pity the individual who would do this. I know that the one who makes this mistake does so because of his own lack of opportunity for the highest kind of growth. I pity him because I know that he is trying to stop the progress of the world, and because I know that in time the development and the ceaseless advance of humanity will make him ashamed of his weak and narrow position. One might as well try to stop the progress of a mighty railroad train by throwing his body across the track, as to try to stop the growth of the world in the direction of giving mankind more intelligence, more culture, more skill, more liberty, and in the direction of extending more sympathy and more brotherly kindness.

The address which I delivered at Madison, before the National Educational Association, gave me a rather wide introduction in the North, and soon after that opportunities began offering themselves for me to address audiences there.

I was anxious, however, that the way might also be opened for me to speak directly to a representative Southern white audience. A partial opportunity of this kind, one that seemed to me might serve as an entering wedge, presented itself in 1893, when the international meeting of Christian Workers was held at Atlanta, Georgia. When this invitation came to me, I had engagements in Boston that seemed to make it impossible for me to speak in Atlanta. Still, after looking over my list of dates and places carefully, I found that I could take a train from Boston that would get me into Atlanta about thirty minutes before my address was to be delivered, and that I could remain in that city about sixty minutes before taking another train for Boston. My invitation to speak in Atlanta stipulated that I was to confine my address to five minutes. The question, then, was whether or not I could put enough into a five-minute address to make it worthwhile for me to make such a trip.

I knew that the audience would be largely composed of the most influential class of white men and women, and that it would be a rare opportunity for me to let them know what we were trying to do at Tuskegee, as well as to speak to them about the relations of the races. So I decided to make the trip. I spoke for five minutes to an audience of two thousand people, composed mostly of Southern and Northern whites. What I said seemed to be received with favour and enthusiasm. The Atlanta papers of the next day commented in friendly terms on my address, and a good deal was said about it in different parts of the country. I felt that I had in some degree accomplished my object—that of getting a hearing from the dominant class of the South.

The demands made upon me for public addresses continued to increase, coming in about equal numbers from my own people and from Northern whites. I gave as much time to these addresses as I could spare from the immediate work at Tuskegee. Most of the addresses in the North were made for the direct purpose of getting funds with which to support the school. Those delivered before the coloured people had for their main object the impressing upon them of the importance of industrial and technical education in addition to academic and religious training.

I now come to that one of the incidents in my life which seems to have excited the greatest amount of interest, and which perhaps went further than anything else in giving me a reputation that in a sense might be called National. I refer to the address which I delivered at the opening of the Atlanta Cotton States and International Exposition, at Atlanta, Georgia, September 18, 1895.

So much has been said and written about this incident, and so many questions have been asked me concerning the address, that perhaps I may be excused for taking up the matter with some detail. The five-minute address in Atlanta, which I came from Boston to deliver, was possibly the prime cause for an opportunity being given me to make the second address there. In the spring of 1895 I received a telegram from prominent citizens in Atlanta asking me to accompany a committee from that city to Washington for the purpose of appearing before a committee of Congress in the interest of securing Government help for the Exposition. The committee was composed of about twenty-five of the most prominent and most influential white men of Georgia. All the members of this committee were white men except Bishop Grant, Bishop Gaines, and myself. The Mayor and several other city and state officials spoke before the committee. They were followed by the two coloured bishops. My name was the last on the list of speakers. I had never before appeared before such a committee, nor had I ever delivered any address in the capital of the Nation. I had many misgivings as to what I ought to say, and as to the impression that my address would make. While I cannot recall in detail what I said, I remember that I tried to impress upon the committee, with all the earnestness and plain-ness of any language that I could command, that if Congress wanted to do something which would assist in ridding the South of the race question and making friends between the two races, it should, in every proper way, encourage the material and intellectual growth of both races. I said that the Atlanta Exposition would present an opportunity for both races to show what advance they had made since freedom, and would at the same time afford encouragement to them to make still greater progress.

I tried to emphasize the fact that while the Negro should not be deprived by unfair means of the franchise, political agitation alone would not save him, and that back of the ballot he must have property, industry, skill, economy, intelligence, and character, and that no race without these elements could permanently succeed. I said that in granting the appro-priation Congress could do something that would prove to be of real and lasting value to both races, and that it was the first great opportunity of the kind that had been presented since the close of the Civil War.

I spoke for fifteen or twenty minutes, and was surprised at the close of my address to receive the hearty congratulations of the Georgia committee and of the members of Congress who were present. The Committee was unanimous in making a favourable report, and in a few days the bill passed Congress. With the passing of this bill the success of the Atlanta Exposition was assured.

Soon after this trip to Washington the directors of the Exposition decided that it would be a fitting recognition of the coloured race to erect a large and attractive building which should be devoted wholly

to showing the progress of the Negro since freedom. It was further decided
to have the building designed and erected wholly by Negro mechanics.
This plan was carried out. In design, beauty, and general finish the
Negro Building was equal to the others on the grounds.

After it was decided to have a separate Negro exhibit, the question
arose as to who should take charge of it. The officials of the Exposition
were anxious that I should assume this responsibility, but I declined
to do so, on the plea that the work at Tuskegee at that time demanded
my time and strength. Largely at my suggestion, Mr. I. Garland Penn,
of Lynchburg, Va., was selected to be at the head of the Negro department. I gave him all the aid that I could. The Negro exhibit, as a whole,
was large and creditable. The two exhibits in this department which
attracted the greatest amount of attention were those from the Hampton
Institute and the Tuskegee Institute. The people who seemed to be the
most surprised, as well as pleased, at what they saw in the Negro Building
were the Southern white people.

As the day for the opening of the Exposition drew near, the Board
of Directors began preparing the programme for the opening exercises.
In the discussion from day to day of the various features of this programme, the question came up as to the advisability of putting a member
of the Negro race on for one of the opening addresses, since the Negroes
had been asked to take such a prominent part in the Exposition. It
was argued, further, that such recognition would mark the good feeling
prevailing between the two races. Of course there were those who were
opposed to any such recognition of the rights of the Negro, but the
Board of Directors, composed of men who represented the best and
most progressive element in the South, had their way, and voted to
invite a black man to speak on the opening day. The next thing was
to decide upon the person who was thus to represent the Negro race.
After the question had been canvassed for several days, the directors
voted unanimously to ask me to deliver one of the opening-day addresses,
and in a few days after that I received the official invitation.

The receiving of this invitation brought to me a sense of responsibility
that it would be hard for anyone not placed in my position to appreciate.
What were my feelings when this invitation came to me? I remembered
that I had been a slave; that my early years had been spent in the
lowest depths of poverty and ignorance, and that I had had little opportunity to prepare me for such a responsibility as this. It was only a few
years before that time that any white man in the audience might have
claimed me as his slave; and it was easily possible that some of my
former owners might be present to hear me speak.

I knew, too, that this was the first time in the entire history of the Negro that a member of my race had been asked to speak from the same platform with white Southern men and women on any important National occasion. I was asked now to speak to an audience composed of the wealth and culture of the white South, the representatives of my former masters. I knew, too, that while the greater part of my audience would be composed of Southern people, yet there would be present a large number of Northern whites, as well as a great many men and women of my own race.

I was determined to say nothing that I did not feel from the bottom of my heart to be true and right. When the invitation came to me, there was not one word of intimation as to what I should say or as to what I should omit. In this I felt that the Board of Directors had paid a tribute to me. They knew that by one sentence I could have blasted, in a large degree, the success of the Exposition. I was also painfully conscious of the fact that, while I must be true to my own race in my utterances, I had it in my power to make such an ill-timed address as would result in preventing any similar invitation being extended to a black man again for years to come. I was equally determined to be true to the North, as well as to the best element of the white South, in what I had to say.

The papers, North and South, had taken up the discussion of my coming speech, and as the time for it drew near this discussion became more and more widespread. Not a few of the Southern white papers were unfriendly to the idea of my speaking. From my own race I received many suggestions as to what I ought to say. I prepared myself as best I could for the address, but as the eighteenth of September drew nearer, the heavier my heart became, and the more I feared that my effort would prove a failure and a disappointment.

The invitation had come at a time when I was very busy with my school work, as it was the beginning of our school year. After preparing my address, I went through it, as I usually do with all those utterances which I consider particularly important, with Mrs. Washington, and she approved of what I intended to say. On the sixteenth of September, the day before I was to start for Atlanta, so many of the Tuskegee teachers expressed a desire to hear my address that I consented to read it to them in a body. When I had done so, and had heard their criticisms and comments, I felt somewhat relieved, since they seemed to think well of what I had to say.

On the morning of September 17, together with Mrs. Washington and my three children, I started for Atlanta. I felt a good deal as I

suppose a man feels when he is on his way to the gallows. In passing
through the town of Tuskegee I met a white farmer who lived some
distance out in the country. In a jesting manner this man said: "Washington, you have spoken before the Northern white people, the Negroes
in the South, and to us country white people in the South; but in Atlanta,
tomorrow, you will have before you the Northern whites, the Southern
whites, and the Negroes all together. I am afraid that you have got
yourself into a tight place." This farmer diagnosed the situation correctly,
but his frank words did not add anything to my comfort.

In the course of the journey from Tuskegee to Atlanta both coloured
and white people came to the train to point me out, and discussed with
perfect freedom, in my hearing, what was going to take place the next
day. We were met by a committee in Atlanta. Almost the first thing
that I heard when I got off the train in that city was an expression
something like this, from an old coloured man nearby: "Dat's de man
of my race what's gwine to make a speech at de Exposition tomorrow.
I'se sho' gwine to hear him."

Atlanta was literally packed, at the time, with people from all parts
of this country, and with representatives of foreign governments, as well
as with military and civic organizations. The afternoon papers had
forecasts of the next day's proceedings in flaring headlines. All this tended
to add to my burden. I did not sleep much that night. The next morning,
before day, I went carefully over what I intended to say. I also kneeled
down and asked God's blessing upon my effort. Right here, perhaps,
I ought to add that I make it a rule never to go before an audience,
on any occasion, without asking the blessing of God upon what I want
to say.

I always make it a rule to make especial preparation for each separate
address. No two audiences are exactly alike. It is my aim to reach and
talk to the heart of each individual audience, taking it into my confidence
very much as I would a person. When I am speaking to an audience,
I care little for how what I am saying is going to sound in the newspapers,
or to another audience, or to an individual. At the time, the audience
before me absorbs all my sympathy, thought, and energy.

Early in the morning a committee called to escort me to my place
in the procession which was to march to the Exposition grounds. In
this procession were prominent coloured citizens in carriages, as well
as several Negro military organizations. I noted that the Exposition
officials seemed to go out of their way to see that all of the coloured
people in the procession were properly placed and properly treated. The
procession was about three hours in reaching the Exposition grounds,

and during all of this time the sun was shining down upon us disagreeably hot. When we reached the grounds, the heat, together with my nervous anxiety, made me feel as if I were about ready to collapse, and to feel that my address was not going to be a success. When I entered the audience-room, I found it packed with humanity from bottom to top, and there were thousands outside who could not get in.

The room was very large, and well suited to public speaking. When I entered the room, there were vigorous cheers from the coloured portion of the audience, and faint cheers from some of the white people. I had been told, while I had been in Atlanta, that while many white people were going to be present to hear me speak, simply out of curiosity, and that others who would be present would be in full sympathy with me, there was a still larger element of the audience which would consist of those who were going to be present for the purpose of hearing me make a fool of myself, or, at least, of hearing me say some foolish thing, so that they could say to the officials who had invited me to speak, "I told you so!"

One of the trustees of the Tuskegee Institute, as well as my personal friend, Mr. William H. Baldwin, Jr., was at the time General Manager of the Southern Railroad, and happened to be in Atlanta on that day. He was so nervous about the kind of reception that I would have, and the effect that my speech would produce, that he could not persuade himself to go into the building, but walked back and forth in the grounds outside until the opening exercises were over.

The Atlanta Exposition, at which I had been asked to make an address as a representative of the Negro race, . . . was opened with a short address from Governor Bullock. After other interesting exercises, including an invocation from Bishop Nelson, of Georgia, a dedicatory ode by Albert Howell, Jr., and addresses by the President of the Exposition and Mrs. Joseph Thompson, the President of the Woman's Board, Governor Bullock introduced me with the words, "We have with us today a representative of Negro enterprise and Negro civilization."

When I arose to speak, there was considerable cheering, especially from the coloured people. As I remember it now, the thing that was uppermost in my mind was the desire to say something that would cement the friendship of the races and bring about hearty cooperation between them. So far as my outward surroundings were concerned, the only thing that I recall distinctly now is that when I got up, I saw thousands of eyes looking intently into my face. The following is the address which I delivered:

MR. PRESIDENT AND GENTLEMEN OF THE BOARD OF DIRECTORS AND
CITIZENS:

One-third of the population of the South is of the Negro race. No
enterprise seeking the material, civil, or moral welfare of this section
can disregard this element of our population and reach the highest
success. I but convey to you, Mr. President and Directors, the sentiment
of the masses of my race when I say that in no way have the value
and manhood of the American Negro been more fittingly and generously
recognized than by the managers of this magnificent Exposition at every
stage of its progress. It is a recognition that will do more to cement
the friendship of the two races than any occurrence since the dawn of
our freedom.

Not only this, but the opportunity here afforded will awaken among
us a new era of industrial progress. Ignorant and inexperienced, it is
not strange that in the first years of our new life we began at the top
instead of at the bottom; that a seat in Congress or the state legislature
was more sought than real estate or industrial skill; that the political
convention or stump speaking had more attractions than starting a dairy
farm or truck garden.

A ship lost at sea for many days suddenly sighted a friendly vessel.
From the mast of the unfortunate vessel was seen a signal, "Water,
water; we die of thirst!" The answer from the friendly vessel at once
came back, "Cast down your bucket where you are." A second time
the signal, "Water, water; send us water!" ran up from the distressed
vessel, and was answered, "Cast down your bucket where you are." The
captain of the distressed vessel, at last heeding the injunction, cast down
his bucket, and it came up full of fresh, sparkling water from the mouth
of the Amazon River. To those of my race who depend on bettering
their condition in a foreign land or who underestimate the importance
of cultivating friendly relations with the Southern white man, who is
their next-door neighbour, I would say: "Cast down your bucket where
you are"—cast it down in making friends in every manly way of the
people of all races by whom we are surrounded.

Cast it down in agriculture, mechanics, in commerce, in domestic
service, and in the professions. And in this connection it is well to bear
in mind that whatever other sins the South may be called to bear, when
it comes to business, pure and simple, it is in the South that the Negro
is given a man's chance in the commercial world, and in nothing is
this Exposition more eloquent than in emphasizing this chance. Our

greatest danger is that in the great leap from slavery to freedom we may overlook the fact that the masses of us are to live by the productions of our hands, and fail to keep in mind that we shall prosper in proportion as we learn to dignify and glorify common labour and put brains and skill into the common occupations of life; shall prosper in proportion as we learn to draw the line between the superficial and the substantial, the ornamental gewgaws of life and the useful. No race can prosper till it learns that there is as much dignity in tilling a field as in writing a poem. It is at the bottom of life we must begin, and not at the top. Nor should we permit our grievances to overshadow our opportunities.

To those of the white race who look to the incoming of those of foreign birth and strange tongue and habits for the prosperity of the South, were I permitted I would repeat what I say to my own race, "Cast down your bucket where you are." Cast it down among the eight millions of Negroes whose habits you know, whose fidelity and love you have tested in days when to have proved treacherous meant the ruin of your firesides. Cast down your bucket among these people who have, without strikes and labour wars, tilled your fields, cleared your forests, built your railroads and cities, and brought forth treasures from the bowels of the earth, and helped make possible this magnificent representation of the progress of the South. Casting down your bucket among my people, helping and encouraging them as you are doing on these grounds, and to education of head, hand, and heart, you will find that they will buy your surplus land, make blossom the waste places in your fields, and run your factories. While doing this, you can be sure in the future, as in the past, that you and your families will be surrounded by the most patient, faithful, law-abiding, and unresentful people that the world has seen. As we have proved our loyalty to you in the past, in nursing your children, watching by the sick-bed of your mothers and fathers, and often following them with tear-dimmed eyes to their graves, so in the future, in our humble way, we shall stand by you with a devotion that no foreigner can approach, ready to lay down our lives, if need be, in defence of yours, interlacing our industrial, commercial, civil, and religious life with yours in a way that shall make the interests of both races one. In all things that are purely social we can be as separate as the fingers, yet one as the hand in all things essential to mutual progress.

There is no defence or security for any of us except in the highest intelligence and development of all. If anywhere there are efforts tending to curtail the fullest growth of the Negro, let these efforts be turned into stimulating, encouraging, and making him the most useful and intelligent citizen. Effort or means so invested will pay a thousand per cent interest. These efforts will be twice blessed—"blessing him that gives and him that takes."

There is no escape through law of man or God from the inevitable:—

> The laws of changeless justice bind
> Oppressor with oppressed;
> And close as sin and suffering joined
> We march to fate abreast.

Nearly sixteen millions of hands will aid you in pulling the load upward, or they will pull against you the load downward. We shall constitute one-third and more of the ignorance and crime of the South, or one-third its intelligence and progress; we shall contribute one-third to the business and industrial prosperity of the South, or we shall prove a veritable body of death, stagnating, depressing, retarding every effort to advance the body politic.

Gentlemen of the Exposition, as we present to you our humble effort at an exhibition of our progress, you must not expect overmuch. Starting thirty years ago with ownership here and there in a few quilts and pumpkins and chickens (gathered from miscellaneous sources), remember the path that has led from these to the inventions and production of agricultural implements, buggies, steam-engines, newspapers, books, statuary, carving, paintings, the management of drug-stores and banks, has not been trodden without contact with thorns and thistles. While we take pride in what we exhibit as a result of our independent efforts, we do not for a moment forget that our part in this exhibition would fall far short of your expectations but for the constant help that has come to our educational life, not only from the Southern states, but especially from Northern philanthropists, who have made their gifts a constant stream of blessing and encouragement.

The wisest among my race understand that the agitation of questions of social equality is the extremest folly, and that progress in the enjoyment of all the privileges that will come to us must be the result of severe and constant struggle rather than of artificial forcing. No race that has anything to contribute to the markets of the world is long in any degree ostracized. It is important and right that all privileges of the law be ours, but it is vastly more important that we be prepared for the exercises of these privileges. The opportunity to earn a dollar in a factory just now is worth infinitely more than the opportunity to spend a dollar in an opera-house.

In conclusion, may I repeat that nothing in thirty years has given us more hope and encouragement, and drawn us so near to you of the white race, as this opportunity offered by the Exposition; and here bending, as it were, over the altar that represents the results of the struggles of your race and mine, both starting practically empty-handed three decades ago, I pledge that in your effort to work out the great and intricate problem which God has laid at the doors of the South, you shall have at all times the patient, sympathetic help of my race; only let this be constantly in mind, that, while from representations in these buildings of the product of field, of forest, of mine, of factory, letters, and art, much good will come, yet far above and beyond material benefits will be that higher good, that, let us pray God, will come, in a blotting out of sectional differences and racial animosities and suspicions, in a determination to administer absolute justice, in a willing obedience among all classes to the mandates of law. This, this, coupled with our material prosperity, will bring into our beloved South a new heaven and a new earth.

Additional Notes by the Speaker

The first thing that I remember, after I had finished speaking, was that Governor Bullock rushed across the platform and took me by the hand, and that others did the same. I received so many and such hearty congratulations that I found it difficult to get out of the building. I did not appreciate to any degree, however, the impression which my address seemed to have made, until the next morning, when I went into the business part of the city. As soon as I was recognized, I was surprised to find myself pointed out and surrounded by a crowd of men who wished to shake hands with me. This was kept up on every street onto which I went, to an extent which embarrassed me so much that I went back to my boarding-place. The next morning I returned to Tuskegee. At the station in Atlanta, and at almost all of the stations at which the train stopped between that city and Tuskegee, I found a crowd of people anxious to shake hands with me.

The papers in all parts of the United States published the address in full, and for months afterward there were complimentary editorial references to it. Mr. Clark Howell, the editor of the Atlanta *Constitution,* telegraphed to a New York paper, among other words, the following, "I do not exaggerate when I say that Professor Booker T. Washington's address yesterday was one of the most notable speeches, both as to character and as to the warmth of its reception, ever delivered to a Southern audience. The address was a revelation. The whole speech is a platform upon which blacks and whites can stand with full justice to each other."

The Boston *Transcript* said editorially: "The speech of Booker T. Washington at the Atlanta Exposition, this week, seems to have dwarfed all the other proceedings and the Exposition itself. The sensation that it has caused in the press has never been equalled."

Collateral Reading

Brigance, William Norwood, ed., *A History and Criticism of American Public Address.* Vol. I. New York, 1960.

Hawkins, Hugh, ed., *Booker T. Washington and His Critics: The Problem of Negro Leadership.* Boston, 1962.

Meier, August, *Negro Thought in America, 1880-1915.* Ann Arbor, 1963.

————, "Toward a Reinterpretation of Booker T. Washington," *Journal of Negro History,* XXIII (May, 1967), 220-227.

Washington, Booker T., *Up From Slavery.* (Available in numerous paperback editions.)

Washington, E. D., ed., *Selected Speeches of Booker T. Washington.* Garden City, N.Y., 1932.

Study Questions and Problems

1. Prepare a 500-word summary of the logic in Washington's thinking.

2. Prepare a 500-word summary of Washington's use of psychological proof in the Exposition address.

3. Prepare a 500-word summary of Washington's ethical appeals in the speech at the Atlanta Exposition.

4. How does Washington's speech reflect the dominant ideas of America of 1895? Study the influence of Social Darwinism on the age in which Booker T. Washington lived.

5. What are your views on Washington's notion of industrial education?

W. E. B. Du Bois

W. E. B. Du Bois was born in Great Barrington, Massachusetts, in 1868. He received a B.A. from Fisk University, Nashville, Tennessee. He studied for two years at the University of Berlin and in 1895 became the first black man to receive a Ph.D. from Harvard. His dissertation entitled "The Suppression of the African Slave Trade" was published by the Harvard Historical Studies.

Du Bois taught in Wilberforce College in Ohio, and at Atlanta University in Georgia. He spent a short time at the University of Pennsylvania where he made a pioneer sociological study entitled The Philadelphia Negro: A Social Study. *Then followed Du Bois'* The Souls of Black Folk. *"It is in this book that he grows to fullness as a writer, fusing into a style that is beautifully lucid the emotional power that later made his* Crisis *editorials unsurpassed by any writing of their kind."*

In 1905 he called a conference of twenty-nine black leaders from fourteen states, and they called the convention the Niagara Movement. A platform of principles was adopted which called for an end to discrimination and recognition of the principle of human brotherhood.

Responding to the impetus of the Niagara Movement, a larger and stronger organization of white and black leaders was formed in 1909, the National Association for the Advancement of Colored People. Du Bois became director of publicity and research in 1910 and edited the NAACP magazine Crisis. *As an editor he wielded tremendous influence for over twenty-four years.*

The speech entitled "Address to the National Negro Convention" is a scholarly lecture which briefly describes the problems of the past for black Americans and, in somewhat greater depth, analyzes the problems of early twentieth-century black Americans. Du Bois enumerated three central propositions which he claimed defined the nature of the racial caste system then in effect in America: (1) that it was a mistake to give Negroes the ballot, (2) that Negroes are essentially an inferior race, and (3) that the only permanent settlement of the race problem will be open and legal recognition of this inferiority. Each proposition is critically evaluated and the myth of racial caste exposed to the light of reason.

The analysis of the claim that Negroes are racially inferior was brilliantly argued by Du Bois. He skillfully questioned the assumption by some Social Darwinists that white European stock represented the strongest racial group. He pointed out slow but real racial progress of black men in the generation since emancipation. He argued that no evidence supported the assertion that white Europeans were the only ones capable of great deeds: "We can point to degenerate individuals and families here and there among all races, but there is not the slightest warrant for assuming that there do not exist among the Chinese and Hindus, the African Bantus and American Indians as lofty possibilities of human culture as any European race has ever exhibited." Finally, he observed that many signs of degeneracy had appeared among members of the white race. "Their birthrate is falling, their average ability is not increasing, their physical stamina is impaired, their social condition is not reassuring, and their religion is a growing mass of transparent and self-confessed hypocrisy."

Du Bois' solution to the race problem in America was to propose selective marriage among the races with self-control and toleration for all races. "We can not ensure the survival of the best blood by the public murder and degradation of unworthy suitors, but we can substitute a civilized human selection of husbands and wives which shall ensure the survival of the fittest. Not the methods of the jungle, not even the careless choices of the drawing room, but the thoughtful selection of the schools and laboratory is the ideal of future marriage."

This great intellectual's concluding remarks were an appeal to determine the facts behind Negro poverty and oppression and an appeal to seek "the truth."

Address to the National Negro Convention
May 31, 1909

Those who complain that the Negro problem is always with us and apparently insoluble must not forget that under this vague and general designation are gathered many social problems and many phases of the same problem; that these problems and phases have passed through a great evolutionary circle and that today especially one may clearly see a repetition, vaster but similar, of the great cycle of the past.

That problem of the past, so far as the black American was concerned, began with caste—a definite place preordained in custom, law and religion where all men of black blood must be thrust. To be sure, this caste idea as applied to blacks was no sudden, full-grown conception, for the enslavement of the workers was an idea which America inherited from Europe and was not synonymous for many years with the enslavement of the blacks, although the blacks were the chief workers. Men came to the idea of exclusive black slavery by gradually enslaving the workers, as was the world's long custom, and then gradually conceiving certain sorts of work and certain colors of men as necessarily connected. It was, when once set up definitely in the Southern slave system, a logically cohering whole which the simplest social philosopher could easily grasp

W. E. B. Du Bois   *Frederic Lewis Photo*

and state. The difficulty was it was too simple to be either just or true. Human nature is not simple and any classification that roughly divides men into good and bad, superior and inferior, slave and free, is and must ever be ludicrously untrue and universally dangerous as a permanent exhaustive classification. So in the Southern slave system the thing that from the first damned it was the free Negro—the Negro legally free, the Negro economically free and the Negro spiritually free.

How was the Negro to be treated and conceived of who was legally free? At first with perfect naturalness he was treated as a man—he voted in Massachusetts and in South Carolina, in New York and Virginia; he intermarried with black and white, he claimed and received his civil rights—all this until the caste of color was so turned as to correspond with the caste of work and enslave not only slaves but black men who were not slaves. Even this system, however, was unable to ensure complete economic dependence on the part of all black men; there were continually artisans, foremen and skilled servants who became economically too valuable to be slaves. In vain were laws hurled at Negro intelligence and responsibility; black men continued to hire their time and to steal some smattering of knowledge, and it was this fact that became the gravest menace to the slave system. But even legal and economic freedom was not so dangerous to slavery as the free spirit which continually cropped out among men fated to be slaves: they thought, they dreamed, they aspired, they resisted. In vain were they beaten, sold South and killed; the ranks were continually filled with others and they either led revolt at home or ran away to the North, and these by showing their human qualities continually gave the lie to the slave assumption. Thus it was the free Negro in these manifold phases of his appearance who hastened the economic crisis which killed slavery and who made it impossible to make the caste of work and the caste of color correspond, and who became at once the promise and excuse of those who forced the critical revolution.

Today in larger cycle and more intricate detail we are passing through certain phases of a similar evolution. Today we have the caste idea—again not a sudden full-grown conception but one being insidiously but consciously and persistently pressed upon the nation. The steps toward it which are being taken are: first, political disfranchisement, then vocational education with the distinct idea of narrowing to the uttermost the vocations in view, and finally a curtailment of civil freedom of travel, association, and entertainment, in systematic effort to instill contempt and kill self-respect.

Here then is the new slavery of black men in America—a new attempt to make degradation of social condition correspond with certain physical characteristics—not to be sure fully realized as yet, and probably unable for reasons of social development ever to become as systematized as the economic and physical slavery of the past—and yet realized to an extent almost unbelievable by those who have not taken the pains to study the facts—to an extent which makes the lives of thinking black men in this land a perpetual martyrdom.

But right here as in the past stands in the path of this idea the figure of this same thinking black man—this new freedman. This freedman again as in the past presents himself as free in varying phases: there is the free black voter of the North and border states whose power is far more tremendous than even he dare think, so that he is afraid to use it; there is the black man who has accomplished economic freedom and who by working himself into the vast industrial development of the nation is today accumulating property at a rate that is simply astounding. And finally there is the small but growing number of black men emerging into spiritual freedom and becoming participators and freemen of the kingdom of culture around which it is so singularly difficult to set metes and bounds, and who in art, science and literature are making their modest but ineffaceable mark.

The question is, what is the significance of this group of men for the future of the caste programme and for the future social development of America? In order to answer this question intelligently, let us retrace our steps and follow more carefully the details of the proposed programme of renewed caste in America. This programme, when one comes to define and state it, is elusive. There are even those who deny its existence as a definite, consciously conceived plan of action. But, certain it is, there is growing unanimity of a peculiar sort on certain matters. And this unanimity is centering about three propositions:

1. That it was a mistake to give Negroes the ballot.
2. That Negroes are essentially an inferior race.
3. That the only permanent settlement of the race problem will be open and legal recognition of this inferiority.

When now a modern nation condemns ten million of its fellows to such a fate, it would be supposed that this conclusion has been reluctantly forced upon them after a careful study and weighing of the facts. This, however, is not the case in the Negro problem. On the contrary, there has been manifest a singular reluctance and indisposition carefully to study the Negro problem. Ask the average American: Why should the ballot have been withheld from the Negro, and he will answer: "Because he wasn't fit for it." But that is not a sufficient answer: first, because few newly enfranchised groups of the most successful democracies have been fit for the ballot when it was first given, and secondly, because

there were Negroes in the United States fit for the ballot in 1870.
Moreover the political philosophy that condemns out of hand the Fifteenth Amendment does not often stop to think that the problem before
the American nation 1865-1870 was not a simple problem of fixing the
qualifications of voters. It was, on the contrary, the immensely more
complicated problem of enforcing a vast social and economic revolution
on a people determined not to submit to it. Whenever a moral reform
is forced on a people from without there ensue complicated and tremendous problems, whether that reform is the correction of the abuse of
alcohol, the abolition of child labor or the emancipation of slaves. The
enforcement of such a reform will strain every nerve of the nation and
the real question is not: Is it a good thing to strain the framework of
the nation, but rather: Is slavery so dangerous a thing that sudden
enfranchisement of the ex-slaves is too great a price to pay for its
abolition?

To be sure, there are those who profess to think that the white South
of its own initiative after the war, with the whole of the wealth, intelligence and law-making power in its hands, would have freely emancipated its slaves in obedience to a decree from Washington, just as
there are those who would entrust the regulation of the whiskey traffic
to saloon keepers and the bettering of the conditions of child labor to
the employers. It is no attack on the South or on saloon keepers or
on employers to say that such a reform from such a source is unthinkable.
It is simply human nature that men trained to a social system or condition
should be the last to be entirely entrusted with its reformation. It was,
then, not the Emancipation Proclamation but the Fifteenth Amendment
that made slavery impossible in the United States, and those that object
to the Fifteenth Amendment have simply this question to answer: Which
was best, slavery or ignorant Negro voters? The answer is clear as day:
Negro voters never did anything as bad as slavery. If they were guilty
of all the crimes charged to them by the wildest enemies, even then
what they did was less dangerous, less evil and less cruel than the system
of slavery whose death knell they struck. And when in addition to this
we remember that the black voters of the South established the public
schools, gave the poor whites the ballot, modernized the penal code
and put on the statute books of the South page after page of legislation
that still stands today—when we remember this, we have a right to
conclude that the Fifteenth Amendment was a wise and far-sighted piece
of statesmanship.

But today the men who oppose the right of Negroes to vote are no
longer doing so on the ground of ignorance, and with good reason, for
today a majority and an appreciable majority of the black men of the

South twenty-one years of age and over can read and write. In other words, the bottom has been clean knocked out of their ignorance argument and yet the fact has elicited scarcely a loud remark.

Indeed we black men are continually puzzled by the easy, almost unconscious way in which our detractors change their ground. Before emancipation it was stated and reiterated with bitter emphasis and absolute confidence that a free Negro would prove to be a shiftless scamp, a barbarian and a cannibal reverting to savagery and doomed to death. We forget today that from 1830 to 1860 there was not a statement made by the masters of slaves more often reiterated than this, and more dogmatically and absolutely stated. After emancipation, for twenty years and more, so many people looked for the fulfillment of the prophecy that many actually saw it and we heard and kept hearing and now and then still hear that the Negro today is worse off than in slavery days. Then, as this statement grew less and less plausible, its place came to be taken by other assumptions. When a Louisiana senator saw the first Negro school, he stopped and said: "This is the climax of foolishness!" The Negro could not be educated—he could imitate like a parrot but real mental development was impossible.

Then, when Negroes did learn some things, it was said that education spoiled them; they can learn but it does them no practical good; the young educated Negroes become criminals—they neither save nor work, they are shiftless and lazy. Now today are coming uncomfortable facts for this theory. The generation now working and saving is post-bellum and yet no sooner does it come on the stage than accumulated property goes on at an accelerated pace so far as we have measurements. In Georgia the increase of property among Negroes in the last ten years has been 83%. But no sooner do facts like these come to the fore than again the ground of opposition subtly shifts and this last shifting has been so gradual and so insidious that the Negro and his friends are still answering arguments that are no longer being pushed. The most subtle enemies of democracy and the most persistent advocates of the color line admit almost contemptuously most that their forebears strenuously denied: the Negroes have progressed since slavery, they are accumulating some property, some of them work readily and they are susceptible of elementary training; but, they say, all thought of treating black men like white men must be abandoned. They are an inferior stock of men, limited in attainment by nature. You cannot legislate against nature, and philanthropy is powerless against deficient cerebral development.

To realize the full weight of this argument, recall to mind a character like John Brown and contrast his attitude with the attitude of today.

John Brown loved his neighbor as himself. He could not endure, therefore, to see his neighbor poor, unfortunate or oppressed. This natural
sympathy was strengthened by a saturation in Hebrew religion which
stressed the personal responsibility of every man's soul to a just God.
To this religion of equality and sympathy with misfortune, was added
the strong influence of the social doctrines of the French Revolution
with its emphasis on freedom and power in political life. And on all
this was built John Brown's own inchoate but growing belief in a juster
and more equal distribution of property. From all this John Brown
concluded—and acted on that conclusion—that all men were created free
and equal and that the cost of liberty was less than the price of repression.
Up to the time of John Brown's death this doctrine was a growing,
conquering social thing. Since then there has come a change and many
would rightly find reason for that change in the coincidence that the
year John Brown suffered martyrdom was the year that first published
the Origin of Species. Since that day tremendous scientific and economic
advance has been accompanied by distinct signs of moral change in
social philosophy; strong arguments have been made for the fostering
of war, the social utility of human degradation and disease, and the
inevitable and known inferiority of certain classes and races of men.
While such arguments have not stopped the efforts of the advocates
of peace, the workers for social uplift and the believers in human brotherhood, they have, it must be confessed, often made their voices falter
and tinged their arguments with apology.

Why is this? It is because the splendid scientific work of Darwin,
Weissman, Galton and others has been widely and popularly interpreted
as meaning that there is such essential and inevitable inequality among
men and races of men as no philanthropy can or ought to eliminate;
that civilization is a struggle for existence whereby the weaker nations
and individuals will gradually succumb and the strong will inherit the
earth. With this interpretation has gone the silent assumption that the
white European stock represents the strong surviving peoples and that
the swarthy, yellow and black peoples are the ones rightly doomed to
eventual extinction.

One can easily see what influence such a doctrine would have on
the race problem in America. It meant moral revolution in the attitude
of the nation. Those that stepped into the pathway marked by the early
abolitionists faltered and large numbers turned back. They said: They
were good men—even great; but they have no message for us today—John
Brown was a "belated covenanter," William Lloyd Garrison was an
anachronism in the age of Darwin—men who gave their lives to lift
not the unlifted but the unliftable. We have, consequently, the present

reaction—a reaction which says in effect: Keep these black people in their places, and do not attempt to treat a Negro simply as a white man with a black face; to do this would mean moral deterioration of the race and nation—a fate against which a divine racial prejudice is successfully fighting. This is the attitude of the larger portion of the thinking nation today.

It is not, however, an attitude that has brought mental rest or social peace. On the contrary, it is today involving a degree of moral strain and political and social anomaly that gives the wisest pause. The chief difficulty has been that the natural place in which, by scientific law, the black race in America should stay cannot easily be determined. To be sure, the freedmen did not, as the philanthropists of the sixties apparently expected, step in forty years from slavery to nineteenth century civilization. Neither, on the other hand, did they, as the ex-masters confidently predicted, retrograde and die. Contrary to both these views, they chose a third and apparently quite unawaited way: from the great, sluggish, almost imperceptibly moving mass they sent off larger and larger numbers of faithful workmen and artisans, some merchants and professional men, and even men of educational ability and discernment. They developed in a generation no world geniuses, no millionaires, no captains of industry, no artists of first rank; but they did in forty years get rid of the larger part of their illiteracy, accumulate a half billion of property in small homesteads and gained now and then respectful attention in the world's ears and eyes. It has been argued that this progress of the black man in America is due to the exceptional men among them and does not measure the ability of the mass. Such admission is, however, fatal to the whole argument. If the doomed races of men are going to develop exceptions to the rule of inferiority, then no law, scientific or moral, should or can proscribe the race as such.

To meet this difficulty in racial philosophy a step has been taken in America fraught with the gravest social consequences to the world and threatening not simply the political but the moral integrity of the nation: that step is to deny in the case of black men the validity of those evidences of culture, ability and decency which are accepted unquestioningly in the case of other people, and by vague assertion, unprovable assumption, unjust emphasis, and now and then by deliberate untruth, to secure not only the continued proscription of these people, but by caste distinction to shut in the faces of their rising classes many of the paths to further advance.

When a social policy based on a supposed scientific sanction leads to such a moral anomaly, it is time to examine rather carefully the logical foundations of the argument. And so soon as we do this, many things are clear. First, assuming that there are certain stocks of human beings whose elimination the best welfare of the world demands; it is certainly questionable if these stocks include the majority of mankind and it is indefensible and monstrous to pretend that we know today with any reasonable certainty which these stocks are. We can point to degenerate individuals and families here and there among all races, but there is not the slightest warrant for assuming that there do not exist among the Chinese and Hindus, the African Bantus and American Indians as lofty possibilities of human culture as any European race has ever exhibited. It is, to be sure, puzzling to know why the Sudan should linger a thousand years in culture behind the valley of the Seine, but it is no more puzzling than the fact that the valley of the Thames was miserably backward as compared with the banks of the Tiber. Climate, human contact, facilities of communication, and what we call accident have played great part in the rise of culture among nations: to ignore these and to assert dogmatically that the present distribution of culture is a fair index of the distribution of human ability and desert is to make an assertion for which there is not the slightest scientific warrant.

What the age of Darwin has done is to add to the eighteenth-century idea of individual worth the complementary idea of physical immortality of the human race. And this, far from annulling or contracting the idea of human freedom, rather emphasizes its necessity and eternal possibility—the boundlessness and endlessness of possible human achievement. Freedom has come to mean not individual caprice or aberration but social self-realization in an endless chain of selves, and freedom for such development is not the denial but the central assertion of the evolutionary theory. So, too, the doctrine of human equality passes through the fire of scientific inquiry not obliterated but transfigured; not equality of present attainment but equality of opportunity for unbounded future attainment is the rightful demand of mankind.

What now does the present hegemony of the white races threaten? It threatens by the means of brute force a survival of some of the worst stocks of mankind. It attempts to people the best part of the earth and put in absolute authority over the rest not only, and indeed not mainly, the culture of Europe, but its greed and degradation—not only some representatives of the best stocks of the west end of London, upper New York and the Champs Elysées but also, and in as large, if not larger, numbers, the worst stocks of Whitechapel, the East Side and Montmartre; and it attempts to make the slums of white society in all cases and under all circumstances the superior of any colored group, no matter what its ability or culture; it attempts to put the intelligent, property holding, efficient Negroes of the South under the heels and at the absolute mercy of such constituencies as Tillman, Vardaman and Jeff Davis represent.

To be sure, this outrageous programme of wholesale human degeneration is not outspoken yet save in the backward civilizations of the southern United States, South Africa and Australia. But its enunciation is listened to with respect and tolerance in England, Germany and the Northern states and nowhere with more equanimity than right here in New York by those very persons who accuse philanthropy with seeking to degenerate white blood by an infiltration of colored strains. And the average citizen is voting ships and guns to carry out this programme.

This movement gathered force and strength during the latter half of the nineteenth century and reached its culmination when France, Germany and England and Russia began the partition of China and the East. With the sudden self-assertion of Japan, its wildest dreams collapsed, but it is still today a living, virile, potent force and motive, and the most subtle and dangerous enemy of world peace and the dream of human brotherhood. It has a whole vocabulary of its own: the strong races, superior peoples, race preservation, the struggle for survival and a peculiar use of the word "white." And by this it means the right of white men of any kind to club blacks into submission, to make them surrender their wealth and the use of their women, and to submit to the dictation of white men without murmur, for the sake of being swept off the fairest portions of the earth or held there in perpetual serfdom or guardianship. Ignoring the fact that the era of physical struggle for survival has passed away among human beings and that there is plenty of room accessible on earth for all, this theory makes the possession of Krupp guns the main criterion of mental stamina and moral fitness.

Even armed with this morality of the club and every advantage of modern culture, the white races have been unable to possess the earth; many signs of degeneracy have appeared among them; their birthrate is falling, their average ability is not increasing, their physical stamina is impaired, their social condition is not reassuring, and their religion is a growing mass of transparent and self-confessed hypocrisy. Lacking the physical ability to take possession of the world, they are today fencing in America, Australia, and South Africa and declaring that no dark race shall occupy or develop the land which they themselves are unable to use. And all this on the plea that their stock is threatened with deterioration from without, when in fact its most dangerous fate is deterioration from within. We are in fact today repeating in our intercourse between races all the former evils of class injustice, unequal taxation and rigid caste. Individual nations outgrew these fatal things by breaking down the horizontal barriers between classes. We are bringing them back by seeking to erect vertical barriers between races. Men were told that abolition of compulsory class distinction meant leveling down, degradation, disappearance of culture and genius, and the triumph of the mob. As a matter of fact, it has been the salvation of European civilization. Some deterioration and leveling there was, but it was more than balanced by the discovery of new reservoirs of ability and strength. So today we are told that free racial contact—or "social equality" as Southern *patois* has it—means contamination of blood and lowering of ability and culture. It need mean nothing of the sort. Abolition of class distinction does not mean universal intermarriage of stocks, but rather the survival of the fittest by peaceful personal and social selection, a selection all the more effective because free democracy and equality of opportunity allow the best to rise to their rightful place.

The same is true in racial contact. The abolition of the lines of vertical race distinction and their tearing away involves fewer chances of degradation and greater opportunities of human betterment than in the case of class lines. On the other hand, the persistence in racial distinctions spells disaster sooner or later. The earth is growing smaller and more accessible. Race contact will become in the future increasingly inevitable, not only in America, Asia and Africa, but even in Europe. The color line will mean not simply a return to the absurdities of class as exhibited in the sixteenth and seventeenth centuries, but even to the caste of ancient days. This, however, the Japanese, the Chinese, the East Indian and the Negroes are going to resent in just such proportion as they gain the power; and they are gaining the power, and they cannot be kept from gaining more power. The price of repression will then be hypocrisy and slavery and blood.

This is the problem of today, and what is its mighty answer? It is this great word: The cost of liberty is less than the price of repression. The price of repressing the world's darker races is shown in a moral retrogression and economic waste unparalleled since the age of the African slave trade. What would be the cost of liberty? What would be the cost of giving the great stocks of mankind every reasonable help and incentive to self-development—opening the avenues of opportunity freely, spreading knowledge, suppressing war and cheating, and treating men and women as equals the world over whenever and wherever they attain equality? It would cost something. It would cost something in pride and prejudice, for eventually many a white man would be blacking black men's boots; but this cost we may ignore—its greatest cost would be the new problems of racial intercourse and intermarriage which would come to the front. Freedom and equal opportunity in this respect would inevitably bring some intermarriage of whites and yellows and browns and blacks. If such marriages are proven inadvisable, how could they be stopped? Easily. We associate with cats and cows but we do not fear intermarriage with them even though they be given all freedom of development. So, too, intelligent human beings can be trained to breed intelligently without the degradation of such of their fellows as they may not wish to breed with. In the Southern United States, on the contrary, it is assumed that unwise marriage can only be stopped by the degradation of the blacks, the classing of their women with prostitutes, the loading the whole race with every badge of public isolation, degradation and contempt and by burning offenders at the stake.

Is this civilization? No. The civilized method of preventing ill-advised marriage lies in the training of mankind in ethics of sex and childbearing. We cannot ensure the survival of the best blood by the public murder and degradation of unworthy suitors, but we can substitute a civilized human selection of husbands and wives which shall ensure the survival of the fittest. Not the methods of the jungle, not even the careless choices of the drawing room, but the thoughtful selection of the schools and laboratory is the ideal of future marriage. This will cost something in ingenuity, self-control, and toleration, but it will cost less than forcible repression.

Not only is the cost of repression today large—it is a continually increasing cost, because of the fact that furnished the fatal moral anomaly against which physical slavery could not stand—the free Negro—the Negro who in spite of contempt, discouragement, caste and poverty has put himself on a plane where it is simply impossible to deny that he is by every legitimate measurement the equal of his average white neighbor. The former argument was, as I have mentioned, that no such class existed. This assertion was persisted in until it became ludicrous. Today the fashion is come to regard this class as exceptional so far as the logic of the Negro problem is concerned, dangerous so far as social peace is concerned, and its existence more than offset by an abnormal number of criminals, degenerates and defectives.

Right here, then, comes the center of the present problem, namely: What is the *truth* about this? What are the real facts? How far is Negro crime due to inherited and growing viciousness and how far to poverty, degradation and systematic oppression?

How far is Negro labor lazy and how far is it the listless victim of systematic theft?

How far is the Negro woman lewd and how far the helpless victim of social custom?

How far are Negro children being educated today in the public schools of the South and how far is the effort to curtail that training increasingly successful?

How far are Negroes leaving the farms and rushing to the cities to escape work and how far to escape slavery?

How far is this race designated as Negroes the descendants of African slaves and how far is it descended from the most efficient white blood of the nation?

What does actual physical and social measurement prove as to the status of these descendants of black men?

All these are fundamental questions. Not a single valid conclusion as to the future can be absolutely insisted upon without definite skillful scientific answers to these questions and yet not a single systematic effort to answer these questions on an adequate scale has been made in these United States from 1619 to 1909. Not only this, but on all sides opposition ranging from indifference and reluctance to actual force is almost universal when any attempt to study the Negro problem adequately is proposed. Yet in spite of this universal and deliberate ignorance, the demand is made that one line of solution, which a number of good men have assumed is safe and sane, shall be accepted by everybody and particularly by thinking black men. The penalty for not accepting this programme is to be dubbed a radical, a busybody, an impatient dreamer and a dangerous agitator. Yet this programme involves justification of disfranchisement, the personal humiliation of Jim-Crowism, a curtailed and purposely limited system of education and a virtual acknowledgment of the inevitable and universal inferiority of black men. And then in the face of this we are asked to look pleasant and do our very best. I think it is the most cowardly dilemma that a strong people ever thrust upon the weak. And I for one have protested and do protest and shall protest that in my humble opinion the assumption is an outrageous falsehood dictated by selfishness, cowardice and greed and for the righteousness of my cause and the proof of my assertions, I appeal to one arbitrament and one alone and that is: THE TRUTH.

Collateral Reading

Aptheker, Herbert, "Du Bois on Douglass," *Journal of Negro History,* XLIV (October, 1964), 264-266.

Broderick, Francis, *W. E. B. Du Bois, Negro Leader in a Time of Crisis.* Palo Alto, 1959.

Du Bois, W. E. B., *Autobiography.* International Publishers, 1960.

————, *The Souls of Black Folk.* New York, 1903.

Rudwick, Elliott, *W. E. B. Du Bois: A Study in Minority Group Leadership.* Philadelphia, 1966.

————, "The Niagara Movement," *Journal of Negro History,* XLII (July, 1957), 177-200.

————, "W. E. B. Du Bois: In His Role of *Crisis* Editor," *Journal of Negro History,* XLII (July, 1958), 214-241.

Study Questions and Problems

1. W. E. B. Du Bois was well educated and devoted all his intellectual energies to the improvement of the Negro's condition in American society. Do you think that being well informed is sufficient in itself to give a good speech? Debate this important question.

2. What are the ethical implications in the phrase "telling it like it is"?

3. Identify what, if any, pattern of organization emerges from this speech.

4. Compare and contrast Du Bois' views on racial progress with Washington's views. Which position do you favor? Why?

5. In light of the background of the formation of the NAACP in 1910, do you think that the NAACP represented the progressive spirit in race relations?

Marcus Garvey

Marcus Garvey was born in Jamaica in 1887. In 1917 the self-educated Garvey organized the Universal Negro Improvement Association, or "Back-to-Africa" movement, in New York, which had more than a million followers by the middle 1920's. The UNIA collapsed after Garvey was convicted of using the mails to defraud and was deported as an undesirable alien.

Garvey praised all things black and cast suspicion on all things white. He formed such diverse enterprises as the Universal Black Cross Nurses, the Universal African Motor Corps, the Black Flying Eagles, the Black Star (steamship) Line, and the Negro Factory Corporation. The UNIA newspaper, The Negro World, *was read by black discontented masses in New York, Chicago, Cleveland, Detroit, and throughout the country. Garvey was a Messiah who preached a gospel of economic independence and a return to Africa as the solution to the race problem.*

Marcus Garvey's speech, delivered at Liberty Hall in New York City on November 25, 1922, is a clear enunciation of the goals of the UNIA movement together with refutations of misconceptions about the movement. Garvey discredited the notion that his movement was harmful to society and government. He argued that the UNIA respected the rights of all groups and that its main purpose was to unite all black peoples for their own industrial, political, social, and religious emancipation. He argued further that the time had come for blacks to take the lead and formulate a new government of black men in Africa. Garvey refuted the claim that his movement was preaching race hatred. His position was that the races should develop separately, but develop economic interdependence as nations. The UNIA leader cited two impressive examples to illustrate the Negro's humanity. He cited the battle record of Negroes who fought in World War I while many whites shirked their patriotic responsibility, and he cited a biblical reference to Simon the Cyrenian, a black man who bore the cross of Christ to Calvary.

Garvey concluded his address on a climactic note, declaring that the

*black citizens of the world would march out of the nations of the world
to redeem their own country in Africa.*

The UNIA Movement
November 25, 1922

Over five years ago the Universal Negro Improvement Association placed itself before the world as the movement through which the new and rising Negro would give expression of his feelings. This Association adopts an attitude not of hostility to other races and peoples of the world, but an attitude of self-respect, of manhood rights on behalf of 400,000,000 Negroes of the world.

We represent peace, harmony, love, human sympathy, human rights and human justice, and that is why we fight so much. Wheresoever human rights are denied to any group, wheresoever justice is denied to any group, there the UNIA finds a cause. And at this time among all the peoples of the world, the group that suffers most from injustice, the group that is denied most of those rights that belong to all humanity, is the black group of 400,000,000. Because of that injustice, because of that denial of our rights, we go forth under the leadership of the One who is always on the side of right to fight the common cause of humanity; to fight as we fought in the Revolutionary War, as we fought in the Civil War, as we fought in the Spanish-American War, and as we fought in the war between 1914-18 on the battle plains of France and of Flanders. As we fought on the heights of Mesopotamia; even so under the leadership of the UNIA, we are marshaling the 400,000,000 Negroes of the world to fight for the emancipation of the race and of the redemption of the country of our fathers.

We represent a new line of thought among Negroes. Whether you call it advanced thought or reactionary thought, I do not care. If it is reactionary for people to seek independence in government, then we are reactionary. If it is advanced thought for people to seek liberty and freedom, then we represent the advanced school of thought among the Negroes of this country. We of the UNIA believe that what is good for the other folks is good for us. If government is something that is worthwhile; if government is something that is appreciable and helpful and protective to others, then we also want to experiment in government. We do not mean a government that will make us citizens without rights or subjects without consideration. We mean a kind of government that will place our race in control even, as other races are in control of their own governments.

That does not suggest anything that is unreasonable. It was not unreasonable for George Washington, the great hero and father of the country, to have fought for the freedom of America, giving to us this great republic and this great democracy; it was not unreasonable for the Liberals of France to have fought against the Monarchy to give to the world French Democracy and French Republicanism; it was no unrighteous cause that led Tolstoi to sound the call of liberty in Russia, which has ended in giving to the world the social democracy of Russia, an experiment that will probably prove to be a boon and a blessing to mankind. If it was not an unrighteous cause that led Washington to fight for the independence of this country, and led the Liberals of France to establish the Republic, it is therefore not an unrighteous cause for the UNIA to lead 400,000,000 Negroes all over the world to fight for the liberation of our country.

Therefore the UNIA is not advocating the cause of church building, because we have a sufficiently large number of churches among us to minister to the spiritual needs of the people, and we are not going to compete with those who are engaged in so splendid a work; we are not engaged in building any new social institutions, and YMCA or YWCA, because there are enough social workers engaged in those praiseworthy efforts. We are not engaged in politics because we have enough local politicians, Democrats, Socialists, Soviets, etc., and the political situation is well taken care of. We are not engaged in domestic politics, in church building or in social uplift work, but we are engaged in nation building.

Misrepresentations

In advocating the principles of this Association, we find we have been very much misunderstood and very much misrepresented by men from within our own race, as well as others from without. Any reform movement that seeks to bring about changes for the benefit of humanity is bound to be misrepresented by those who have always taken it upon themselves to administer to, and lead the unfortunate, and to direct those who may be placed under temporary disadvantages. It has been so in all other movements whether social or political; hence those of us in the Universal Negro Improvement Association who lead, do not feel in any way embarrassed about this misrepresentation, about this misunderstanding as far as the Aims and Objects of the Universal Negro Improvement Association go. But those who probably would have taken kindly notice of this great movement, have been led to believe that this movement seeks, not to develop the good within the race, but to give expression to that which is most destructive and most harmful to society and to government.

I desire to remove the misunderstanding that has been created in the minds of millions of peoples throughout the world in their relationship to the organization. The Universal Negro Improvement Association stands for the Bigger Brotherhood; the Universal Negro Improvement Association stands for human rights, not only for Negroes, but for all races. The Universal Negro Improvement Association believes in the rights of not only the black race, but the white race, the yellow race and the brown race. The Universal Negro Improvement Association believes that the white man has as much right to be considered, the yellow man has as much right to be considered, the brown man has as much right to be considered, as well as the black man of Africa. In view of the fact that the black man of Africa has contributed as much to the world as the white man of Europe, and the brown man and yellow man of Asia, we of the Universal Negro Improvement Association demand that the white, yellow and brown races give to the black man his place in the civilization of the world. We ask for nothing more than the rights of 400,000,000 Negroes. We are not seeking, as I said before, to destroy or disrupt the society or the government of other races, but we are determined that 400,000,000 of us shall unite ourselves to free our motherland from the grasp of the invader. We of the Universal Negro Improvement Association are determined to unite 400,000,000 Negroes for their own industrial, political, social and religious emancipation.

We of the Universal Negro Improvement Association are determined to unite the 400,000,000 Negroes of the world to give expression to their own feeling; we are determined to unite the 400,000,000 Negroes of the world for the purpose of building a civilization of their own. And in that effort we desire to bring together the 15,000,000 of the United States, the 180,000,000 in Asia, the West Indies and Central and South America, and the 200,000,000 in Africa. We are looking toward political freedom on the continent of Africa, the land of our fathers.

Not Seeking a Government Within a Government

The Universal Negro Improvement Association is not seeking to build up another government within the bounds or borders of the United States of America. The Universal Negro Improvement Association is not seeking to disrupt any organized system of government, but the Association is determined to bring Negroes together for the building up of a nation of their own. And why? Because we have been forced to it. We have been forced to it throughout the world; not only in America, not only in Europe, not only in the British Empire, but wheresoever the black man happens to find himself, he has been forced to do for himself.

To talk about government is a little more than some of our people can appreciate just at this time. The average man does not think that way, just because he finds himself a citizen or a subject of some country. He seems to say, "Why should there be need for any other government? We are French, English, or American." But we of the UNIA have studied seriously this question of nationality among Negroes—this American nationality, this British nationality, this French, Italian, or Spanish nationality, and have discovered that it counts for nought when that nationality comes in conflict with the racial idealism of the group that rules. When our interests clash with those of the ruling faction, then we find that we have absolutely no rights. In times of peace, when everything is all right, Negroes have a hard time, wherever we go, wheresoever we find ourselves, getting those rights that belong to us, in common with others whom we claim as fellow citizens; getting that consideration that should be ours by right of the Constitution, by right of the law; but in the time of trouble they make us all partners in the cause, as happened in the last war, when we were partners, whether British, French, or American Negroes. And we were told that we must forget everything in an effort to save the nation.

We have saved many nations in this manner, and we have lost our lives doing that before. Hundreds of thousands—nay, millions of black men—lie buried under the ground due to that old-time camouflage of saving the nation. We saved the British empire; we saved the French empire; we saved this glorious country more than once; and all that we have received for our sacrifices, all that we have received for what we have done, even in giving up our lives, is just what you are receiving now, just what I am receiving now.

You and I fare no better in America, in the British empire, or in any other part of the white world; we fare no better than any black man wheresoever he shows his head. And why? Because we have been satisfied to allow ourselves to be led, educated, to be directed by the other fellow, who has always sought to lead in the world in that direction that would satisfy him and strengthen his position. We have allowed ourselves for the last 500 years to be a race of followers, following every race that has led in the direction that would make them more secure.

The UNIA is reversing the old-time order of things. We refuse to be followers any more. We are leading ourselves. That means, if any saving is to be done, later on, whether it is saving this one nation or that one government, we are going to seek a method of saving Africa first. Why? And why Africa? Because Africa has become the grand prize of the nations. Africa has become the big game of the nation hunters. Today Africa looms as the greatest commercial, industrial and political prize in the world.

The Difference Between the UNIA and Other Organizations

The difference between the Universal Negro Improvement Association and the other movements of this country, and probably the world, is that the Universal Negro Improvement Association seeks independence of government, while the other organizations seek to make the Negro a secondary part of existing governments. We differ from the organizations in America because they seek to subordinate the Negro as a secondary consideration in a great civilization, knowing that in America the Negro will never reach his highest ambition, knowing that the Negro in America will never get his constitutional rights. All those organizations which are fostering the improvement of Negroes in the British Empire know that the Negro in the British Empire will never reach the height of his constitutional rights. What do I mean by constitutional rights in America? If the black man is to reach the height of his ambition in this country—if the black man is to get all of his constitutional rights in America—then the black man should have the same chance in the nation as any other man to become president of the nation, or a street cleaner in New York. If the black man in the British Empire is to have all his constitutional rights, it means that the Negro in the British Empire should have at least the same right to become premier of Great Britain as he has to become street cleaner in the city of London. Are they prepared to give us such political equality? You and I can live in the United States of America for 100 more years, and our generations may live for 200 years or for 5,000 more years, and so long as there is a black and white population, when the majority is on the side of the white race, you and I will never get political justice or get political equality in this country. Then why should a black man with rising ambition, after preparing himself in every possible way to give expression to that highest ambition, allow himself to be kept down by racial prejudice within a country? If I am as educated as the next man, if I am as prepared as the next man, if I have passed through the best schools and colleges and universities as the other fellow, why should I not have a fair chance to compete with the other fellow for the biggest position in the nation? I have feelings, I have blood, I have senses like the other fellow; I have ambition, I have hope. Why should he, because of some racial prejudice, keep me down and why should I concede to him the right to rise above me, and to establish himself as my permanent master? That is where the UNIA differs from other organizations. I refuse to stultify my ambition, and every true Negro refuses to stultify his ambition to suit anyone, and therefore the UNIA decides if America is not big enough for two presidents, if England is not big enough for two kings, then we are not going to quarrel over the matter; we will leave one president in America, we will leave one king in England, we will leave one president in France and we will have one president in Africa. Hence, the Universal Negro Improvement Association does not seek to interfere with the social and political systems of France, but by the arrangement of things today the UNIA refuses to recognize any political or social system in Africa except that which we are about to establish for ourselves.

Not Preaching Hate

We are not preaching a propaganda of hate against anybody. We love the white man; we love all humanity, because we feel that we cannot live without the other. The white man is as necessary to the existence of the Negro as the Negro is necessary to his existence. There is a common relationship that we cannot escape. Africa has certain things that Europe wants, and Europe has certain things that Africa wants, and if a fair and square deal must bring white and black with each other, it is impossible for us to escape it. Africa has oil, diamonds, copper, gold and rubber and all the minerals that Europe wants, and there must be some kind of relationship between Africa and Europe for a fair exchange, so we cannot afford to hate anybody.

Negroes Ever Ready to Assist Humanity's Cause

The question often asked is, what does it require to redeem a race and free a country? If it takes manpower, if it takes scientific intelligence, if it takes education of any kind, or if it takes blood, then the 400,000,000 Negroes of the world have it.

It took the combined manpower of the Allies to put down the mad determination of the Kaiser to impose German will upon the world and upon humanity. Among those who suppressed his mad ambition were two million Negroes who have not yet forgotten how to drive men across the firing line. Surely those of us who faced German shot and shell at the Marne, at Verdun, have not forgotten the order of our Commander-in-Chief. The cry that caused us to leave America in such mad haste, when white fellow citizens of America refused to fight and said, "We do not believe in war and therefore, even though we are American citizens, and even though the nation is in danger, we will not go to war." When many of them cried out and said, "We are German-Americans and we can not fight," when so many white men refused to answer to the call and dodged behind all kinds of excuses, 400,000 black men were ready without a question. It was because we were told it was a war of democracy; it was a war for the liberation of the weaker peoples of the world. We heard the cry of Woodrow Wilson, not because we liked him so, but because the things he said were of such a nature that they appealed to us as men. Wheresoever the cause of humanity stands in need of assistance, there you will find the Negro ever ready to serve.

He has done it from the time of Christ up to now. When the whole world turned its back upon the Christ, the man who was said to be the Son of God, when the world cried out "Crucify Him," when the world spurned Him and spat upon Him, it was a black man, Simon, the Cyrenian, who took up the cross. Why? Because the cause of humanity appealed to him. When the black man saw the suffering Jew, struggling under the heavy cross, he was willing to go to His assistance, and he bore that cross up to the heights of Calvary. In the spirit of Simon, the Cyrenian, 1,900 years ago, we answered the call of Woodrow Wilson, the call of a larger humanity, and it was for that that we willingly rushed into the war from America, from the West Indies, over 100,000; it was for that that we rushed into the war from Africa, 2,000,000 of us. We met in France, Flanders and in Mesopotamia. We fought unfalteringly. When the white men faltered and fell back on their battle lines, at the Marne and at Verdun, when they ran away from the charge of the German hordes, the black hell fighters stood before the cannonade, stood before the charge, and again they shouted, "There will be a hot time in the old town tonight."

We made it so hot a few months after our appearance in France and on the various battle fronts, we succeeded in driving the German hordes across the Rhine, and driving the Kaiser out of Germany, and out of Potsdam into Holland. We have not forgotten the prowess of war. If we have been liberal minded enough to give our life's blood in France, in Mesopotamia and elsewhere, fighting for the white man, whom we have always assisted, surely we have not forgotten to fight for ourselves, and when the time comes that the world will again give Africa an opportunity for freedom, surely 400,000,000 black men will march out on the battle plains of Africa, under the colors of the red, the black and the green.

We shall march out, yes, as black American citizens, as black British subjects, as black French citizens, as black Italians or as black Spaniards, but we shall march out with a greater loyalty, the loyalty of race. We shall march out in answer to the cry of our fathers, who cry out to us for the redemption of our own country, our motherland, Africa.

We shall march out, not forgetting the blessings of America. We shall march out, not forgetting the blessings of civilization. We shall march out with a history of peace before and behind us, and surely that history shall be our breastplate, for how can man fight better than knowing that the cause for which he fights is righteous? How can man fight more gloriously than by knowing that behind him is a history of slavery, a history of bloody carnage and massacre inflicted upon a race because of its inability to protect itself and fight? Shall we not fight for the glorious opportunity of protecting and forevermore establishing ourselves as a mighty race and nation, nevermore to be disrespected by men. Glorious shall be the battle when the time comes to fight for our people and our race.

We should say to the millions who are in Africa to hold the fort, for we are coming 400,000,000 strong.

Collateral Reading

Aron, Brigit, "The Garvey Movement: Shadow and Substance," *Phylon* (4th Quarter, 1947), 337-343.

Cronon, Edmund D., *Black Moses: The Story of Marcus Garvey and the UNIA*. Madison, Wis., 1955.

Garvey, Amy-Jacques, ed., *The Philosophy and Opinions of Marcus Garvey*. New York, 1969.

Lomas, Ronald, "A Rhetorical Criticism of Selected Speeches of Marcus Garvey." Unpublished Master's thesis, Western Illinois University, 1966.

Starling, Lathan, Sr., and Donald Franklin, "The Life and Work of Marcus Garvey," *The Negro History Bulletin,* XXVI (October, 1962), 36-38.

Study Questions and Problems

1. Did Garvey appeal primarily to reason or to the emotions of his audience? Explain.

2. Read the behavioral experiments on "personality and persuasibility." What types of personalities are most persuasible? Reflect on this phenomenon as it relates to converts to Christianity, Communism, Black Muslimism, and Garvey's Back-to-Africa movement.

3. Read additional speeches by Garvey in Amy-Jacques Garvey, ed., *The Philosophy and Opinions of Marcus Garvey.*

4. Examine the beliefs of the UNIA movement about race relationships. What ideas are similar in the Muslims' cult of Elijah Muhammed?

5. What filled the void created by the collapse of the UNIA movement? What leaders emerged during the Depression?

A. Philip Randolph

Asa Philip Randolph was born in Crescent City, Florida, in 1889, the son of an A.M.E. clergyman. He completed high school at Cookman Institute in Jacksonville, Florida, and then moved to the North, where he studied at the College of the City of New York. In 1917 he helped found The Messenger, considered by many to be a radical Negro magazine.

In 1925 Randolph initiated a campaign to organize the sleeping car porters, and soon became president of the small union that resulted. By 1928 half the porters and maids on railroads were organized, but a contract with the Pullman Company, the most powerful employer of railroad service workers, was not negotiated until 1937. In 1941 Randolph became the leader of the March on Washington Movement together with such other notable black leaders as Walter White of the NAACP and Adam Clayton Powell, Jr. The object of the march was to focus attention on employment discrimination in defense industries and the armed services by bringing fifty thousand black men to the White House. The threatened demonstration led to President Roosevelt's executive order banning discrimination in defense plants, government offices, and the armed services "because of race, creed, color, or national origin."

The "Keynote Address to the Policy Conference of the March On Washington Movement" ("March On Washington Address") set forth to the delegates the ideology behind the movement as well as enumerating an initial practical program.

Randolph argued for a movement that was formulated exclusively for black people.

The essential value of an all-Negro movement such as the March on Washington is that it helps to create faith by Negroes in Negroes. It develops a sense of self-reliance with Negroes depending on Negroes in vital matters. It helps to break down the slave psychology and inferiority complex in Negroes which comes and is nourished with Negroes relying on white people for direction and support.

112

He further urged the Negro masses to organize an aggressive and bold action program which in many respects anticipated the contemporary militant movement for civil rights.

A. Philip Randolph, in the March On Washington speech, called for a practical program including: (1) a national policy conference, (2) a nationwide series of marches, (3) a march on Washington, and (4) picketing of the White House. In addition, Randolph proposed setting up small groups with designated leaders in order to develop a more cohesive organization. He also outlined an educational program to help integrate public facilities and help develop the struggling masses.

Randolph had an athletic appearance and was exceedingly eloquent with voice and language. He was a throwback to the "old school," or oratorical, speaking style. The language and style of the speech conveys something of Randolph's background as a Socialist and labor agitator. He spoke of "economic royalists." He meant Big Business. He constantly referred to the improvement of the "masses." Moreover, he stated that while Communists were prohibited from the movement, they were allowed to participate in the marches. Thus, the speech parallels the style of address common to the labor movement in its early years of industry-wide organization.

March On Washington Address

FELLOW MARCHERS AND DELEGATES TO THE POLICY CONFERENCE OF THE MARCH ON WASHINGTON MOVEMENT AND FRIENDS:

We have met at an hour when the sinister shadows of war are lengthening and becoming more threatening. As one of the sections of the oppressed darker races, and representing a part of the exploited millions of the workers of the world, we are deeply concerned that the totalitarian legions of Hitler, Hirohito, and Mussolini do not batter the last bastions of democracy. We know that our fate is tied up with the fate of the democratic way of life. And so, out of the depth of our hearts, a cry goes up for the triumph of the United Nations. But we would not be honest with ourselves were we to stop with a call for a victory of arms alone. We know this is not enough. We fight that the democratic faiths, values, heritages and ideals may prevail.

Unless this war sounds the death knell to the old Anglo-American empire systems, the hapless story of which is one of exploitation for the profit and power of a monopoly capitalist economy, it will have been fought in vain. Our aim then must not only be to defeat Nazism, fascism, and militarism on the battlefield but to win the peace, for democracy, for freedom and the Brotherhood of Man without regard to his pigmentation, land of his birth or the God of his fathers. . . .

When this war ends, the people want something more than the dispersal of equality and power among individual citizens in a liberal, political democratic system. They demand with striking comparability the dispersal of equality and power among the citizen-workers in an economic democracy that will make certain the assurance of the good life—the more abundant life—in a warless world.

But, withal, this condition of freedom, equality and democracy is not the gift of the gods. It is the task of men, yes, men, brave men, honest men, determined men. . . .

Thus our feet are set in the path toward [the long-range goal of] equality—economic, political and social and racial. Equality is the heart and essence of democracy, freedom and justice. Without equality of opportunity in industry, in labor unions, schools and colleges, government, politics and before the law, without equality in social relations and in all phases of human endeavor, the Negro is certain to be consigned to an inferior status. There must be no dual standards of justice, no dual rights privileges, duties or responsibilities of citizenship. No dual forms of freedom. . . .

But our nearer goals include the abolition of discrimination, segregation, and Jim-Crow in the Government, the Army, Navy, Air Corps, U.S. Marines, Coast Guard, Women's Auxiliary Army Corps and the Waves, and defense industries; the elimination of discriminations in hotels, restaurants, on public transportation conveyances, in educational, recreational, cultural, and amusement and entertainment places such as theatres, beaches, and so forth.

We want the full works of citizenship with no reservations. We will accept nothing less.

But goals must be achieved. They are not secured because it is just and right that they be possessed by Negro or white people. Slavery was not abolished because it was bad and unjust. It was abolished because men fought, bled and died on the battlefield.

Therefore, if Negroes secure their goals, immediate and remote, they must win them and to win them they must fight, sacrifice, suffer, go to jail and, if need be, die for them. These rights will not be given. They must be taken.

Democracy was fought for and taken from political royalists—the kings. Industrial democracy, the rights of the workers to organize and designate the representatives of their own choosing to bargain collectively is being won and taken from the economic royalists—big business.

Now the realization of goals and rights by a nation, race or class requires belief in and loyalty to principles and policies. . . . Policies rest upon principles. Concretely a policy sets forth one's position on vital public questions such as political affiliations, religious alliances. The March on Washington Movement must be opposed to partisan political commitments, religious or denominational alliances. We cannot sup with the Communists, for they rule or ruin any movement. This is their policy. Our policy must be to shun them. This does not mean that Negro Communists may not join the March on Washington Movement.

As to the composition of our movement: Our policy is that it be all-Negro, and pro-Negro, but not anti-white, or anti-semitic, or anti-labor, or anti-Catholic. The reason for this policy is that all oppressed people must assume the responsibility and take the initiative to free themselves. Jews must wage their battle to abolish anti-semitism. Catholics must wage their battle to abolish anti-Catholicism. The workers must wage their battle to advance and protect their interests and rights.

But this does not mean that because Jews must take the responsibility and initiative to solve their own problems that they should not seek the cooperation and support of Gentiles, or that Catholics should not seek the support of Negroes, or that the workers should not attempt to enlist the backing of Jews, Catholics, and Negroes in their fight to win a strike; but the main reliance must be upon the workers themselves. By the same token because Negroes build an all-Negro movement such as the March, it does not follow that our movement should not call for the collaboration of Jews, Catholics, trade unions and white liberals to help restore the President's Fair Employment Practice Committee to its original status of independence, with responsibility to the President. That was done. William Green, President of the AF of L, and Philip Murray, President of CIO, were called upon to send telegrams to the President to restore the Committee to its independence. Both responded. Their cooperation had its effects. Workers have formed citizens committees to back them while on strike, but this does not mean that they take those citizens into their unions as members. No, not at all.

And while the March on Washington Movement may find it advisable to form a citizens committee of friendly white citizens to give moral support to a fight against the poll tax or white primaries, it does not imply that these white citizens or citizens of any racial group should be taken into the March on Washington Movement as members. The essential value of an all-Negro movement such as the March on Washington is that it helps to create faith by Negroes in Negroes. It develops a sense of self-reliance with Negroes depending on Negroes in vital matters. It helps to break down the slave psychology and inferiority complex in Negroes which comes and is nourished with Negroes relying on white people for direction and support. This inevitably happens in mixed organizations that are supposed to be in the interest of the Negro. . . .

Therefore, while the March on Washington Movement is interested in the general problems of every community and will lend its aid to help solve them, it has as its major interest and task the liberation of the Negro people, and this is sound social economy. It is in conformity with the principle of the division of labor. No organization can do everything. Every organization can do something, and each organization is charged with the social responsibility to do that which it can do, it is built to do.

I have given quite some time to the discussion of this question of organizational structure and function and composition, because the March on Washington Movement is a mass movement of Negroes which is being built to achieve a definite objective, and is a departure from the usual pattern of Negro efforts and thinking. As a rule, Negroes do not choose to be to themselves in anything, they are only to themselves as a result of compulsive segregation. Negroes are together voluntarily for the same reason worker[s] join voluntarily into a trade union. But because workers only join trade unions, does not mean that the very same workers may not join organizations composed of some non-workers, such as art museums or churches or fraternal lodges that have varying purposes. This same thing is true of Negroes. Because Negroes only can join the March on Washington Movement, does not indicate that Negroes in the MOWM may not join an interracial golf club or church or Elks Lodge or debating society or trade union.

No one would claim that a society of Filipinos is undemocratic because it does not take in Japanese members, or that Catholics are anti-Jewish because the Jesuits won't accept Jews as members or that trade unions are illiberal because they deny membership to employers. Neither is the March on Washington Movement undemocratic because it confines its members to Negroes. Now this reasoning would not apply to a public school or a Pullman Car because these agencies are public in nature and provide a service which is necessary to all of the people of a community.

Now, the question of policy which I have been discussing involves, for example, the March on Washington Movement's position on the war. We say that the Negro must fight for his democratic rights now, for after the war it may be too late. This is our policy on the Negro and the war. But this policy raises the question of method, programs, strategy, and tactics; namely, how is this to be done. It is not sufficient to say that Negroes must fight for their rights now, during the war. Some methods must be devised, program set up, and strategy outlined.

This Policy Conference is designed to do this very thing. The first requirement to executing the policies of the March on Washington Movement is to have something to execute them with. This brings me to the consideration of organization. Organization supplies the power. The formulation of policies and the planning process furnish direction. Now there is organization and organization. Some people say, for instance, Negroes are already organized and they cite The Sisters of the Mysterious Ten, The Sons and Daughters of I Will Arise, the Holy Rollers, the social clubs, and so forth. But these organizations are concerned about the individual interest of helping the sick and funeralizing the dead or providing amusement and recreation. They deal with no social or racial problem which concerns the entire people. The Negro people as a whole is not interested in whether Miss A. plays Contract Bridge on Friday or not, or whether the deacon of the Methodist Church has a 200 or 500 dollar casket when he dies. These are personal questions. But the Negro race is concerned about Negroes being refused jobs in defense plants, or whether a Negro can purchase a lower in a Pullman Car, or whether the U.S. Treasury segregates Negro girls. Thus, while it is true Negroes are highly organized, the organizations are not built to deal with and manipulate the mechanics of power. Nobody cares how many Whist Clubs or churches or secret lodges Negroes establish because they are not compulsive or coercive. They don't seek to transform the socio-economic racial milieu. They accept and do not challenge conditions with an action program.

Hence, it is apparent that the Negro needs more than organization. He needs mass organization with an action program, aggressive, bold and challenging in spirit. Such a movement is our March on Washington.

Our first job then is actually to organize millions of Negroes, and build them into block systems with captains so that they may be summoned to action overnight and thrown into physical motion. Without this type of organization, Negroes will never develop mass power which is the most effective weapon a minority people can wield. Witness the strategy and maneuver of the people of India with mass civil disobedience and non-cooperation and the marches to the sea to make salt. It may be said that the Indian people have not won their freedom. This is so, but they will win it. The central principle of the struggle of oppressed minorities like the Negro, labor, Jews, and others is not only to develop mass demonstration maneuvers, but to repeat and continue them. The workers don't picket firms today and quit. They don't strike today and fold up. They practice the principle of repetition. . . .

We must develop huge demonstrations because the world is used to big dramatic affairs. . . . Besides, the unusual attracts. We must develop a series of marches of Negroes at a given time in a hundred or more cities throughout the country, or stage a big march of a hundred thousand Negroes on Washington to put our cause into the main stream of public opinion and focus the attention of world interests. This is why India is in the news.

Therefore, our program is in part as follows:

1. A national conference for the integration and expression of the collective mind and will of the Negro masses.

2. The mobilization and proclamation of a nationwide series of mass marches on the City Halls and City Councils to awaken the Negro masses and center public attention upon the grievances and goals of the Negro people and serve as training and discipline of the Negro masses for the more strenuous struggle of a March on Washington, if, as, and when an affirmative decision is made thereon by the Negro masses of the country through our national conference.

3. A march on Washington as an evidence to white America that black America is on the march for its rights and means business.

4. The picketing of the White House following the March on Washington and maintain the said picket line until the country and the world recognize the Negro has come of age and will sacrifice his all to be counted as men, free men.

This program is drastic and exacting. It will test our best mettle and stamina and courage. Let me warn you that in these times of storm and stress, this program will be opposed. Our Movement therefore must be well-knit together. It must have moral and spiritual vision, understanding and wisdom.

How can we achieve this?

Our Movement must be blueprinted. Our forces must be marshalled with block captains to provide immediate and constant contact. Our block captains must hold periodic meetings for their blocks to develop initiative and the capacity to make decisions and move in relation to direction from the central organization of the Division.

Our educational program must be developed around the struggle of the Negro masses.

This can be done by developing mass plans to secure mass registration of the Negro people for the primaries and elections. Through this program the Negro masses can be given a practical and pragmatic view of the mechanics and function of our government and the significance of mass political pressure.

Plans should be mapped by the various divisions to fight for Negro integration in the public utilities as motormen and conductors. During the war women may be placed on these jobs. We must make a drive now to see to it that Negro men and women receive their appropriate consideration in every important field of American industry from which Negroes are now generally barred.

Our day-to-day exercise of our civil rights is a constant challenge. In theatres, hotels, restaurants, amusement places, even in the North now there is discrimination against Negroes. This is true in every large city. Negroes have the moral obligation to demand the right to enjoy and make use of their civil and political privileges. If we don't, we will lose the will to fight for our citizenship rights, and the public will consider that we don't want them and should not have them. This fight to break down these barriers in every city should be carefully and painstakingly organized. By fighting for these civil rights the Negro masses will be disciplined in struggle. Some of us will be put in jail and court battles may ensue, but this will give the Negro masses a sense of their importance and value as citizens and as fighters in the Negro liberation movement and the cause for democracy as a whole. It will make white people in high places and the ordinary white man understand that Negroes have rights that they are bound to respect.

The giant public protest meetings must continue. They are educative and give moral strength to our movement and the Negro masses.

For this task we need men and women who will dedicate and consecrate their life, spirit, mind, and soul to the great adventure of Negro freedom and justice.

Our divisions must serve as Negro mass parliaments where the entire community may debate the day-to-day issues such as police brutality, high rents, and other questions and make judgments and take action in the interest of the community. These divisions should hold meetings at least twice a month. In them every Negro should be made to feel his importance as a factor in the Negro liberation movement. We must have every Negro realize his leadership ability, the educated and uneducated, the poor and wealthy. In the March on Washington Movement the highest is as low as the lowest and the lowest is as high as the highest. Numbers in mass formation is our key, directed, of course, by the collective intelligence of the people.

Let us put our weight behind the fight to abolish the poll tax. This will give the black and white workers of the South new hope. But the Negro people are not the only oppressed section of mankind. India is now waging a world shaking, history making fight for independence. India's fight is the Negro's fight.

Now, let us be unafraid. We are fighting for big stakes. Our stakes are liberty, justice, and democracy. Every Negro should hang his head in shame who fails to do his part now for freedom. This is the hour of the Negro. It is the hour of the common man. May we rise to the challenge to struggle for our rights. Come what will or may, let us never falter.

Collateral Reading

Garfinkel, Herbert, *When Negroes March.* Glencoe, Ill., 1949.

Garland, P., "A. Philip Randolph: Labor's Grand Old Man," *Ebony* XXIV (May, 1969), 31-33.

Marshal, Allan, "A. Philip Randolph: Dean of Negro Leaders," *Ebony,* XXIV (November, 1968).

Velie, L., "Porter Who Carried Hope to His Race," *Readers Digest,* LXX (May, 1957), 121-125.

Villard, Oswald Garrison, "A. Philip Randolph," *Phylon,* VIII (3rd Quarter, 1947), 225-229.

Study Questions and Problems

1. Compare the March on Washington Movement of the early 1940's to the March on Washington of 1963. What similarities and differences do you observe?

2. Do you think that Randolph deserves the label of "Uncle Tom Number Two," which was coined by black power advocates in the 1960's?

3. Read Herbert Garfinkel, *When Negroes March,* for a complete understanding of the background of the March On Washington Movement in 1942.

4. Do you think that the March on Washington Movement is the historical antecedent to the direct action protests of the 1960's? Justify your position.

5. What was the dominant attitude of blacks toward serving in the United States armed forces during World War II? What was the rationale behind this position?

Thurgood Marshall

Thurgood Marshall was born in Baltimore, Maryland, July 2, 1908. He was graduated cum laude from Lincoln University in Pennsylvania in 1929 and received his law degree from Howard University, Washington, D.C., in 1933. In 1936 Marshall joined the legal staff of the NAACP and in 1954 he successfully argued the famous Brown v. Board of Education of Topeka, Kansas *before the Supreme Court. In 1967 Marshall was appointed Justice of the Supreme Court of the United States.*

Speaking at the NAACP Wartime Conference in 1944, Thurgood Marshall made a lucid exposition of the civil rights group's legal approach and the philosophy behind it.

Marshall began his address with a description of the statutes which existed at the time for protecting civil rights because "it is . . . imperative that Negroes be thoroughly familiar with the rights guaranteed them by law in order that they may be in a position to insist that all of their fundamental rights as American citizens be protected." He enumerated the civil rights protections of the Thirteenth, Fourteenth, and Fifteenth Amendments. Marshall then considered the extent to which the civil rights statutes were enforced. He concluded that enforcement was generally a failure primarily due to court decisions, although he did note certain bright spots in the enforcement of the federal statutes. Marshall argued for greater enforcement of civil rights statutes by pointing out the effects of one civil rights statute in the fields of education, voter registration, and job discrimination.

Marshall also discussed the NAACP's legal fight against discrimination as well as their efforts to pass civil rights statutes in the several states.

The speech is a good illustration of a keen legal mind's adapting to a general audience. Marshall's organization and development of ideas is clear. He uses numerous illustrations and examples. At times the speech reads as if Marshall anticipated questions from the lay audience. His language is free of legal technicalities. Thus, he adapted his remarks well to the nature of his audience.

The Legal Attack to Secure Civil Rights
July 13, 1944

On last night we heard a clear statement of some of the problems facing us today. My job tonight is to point out a part of the general program to secure full citizenship rights.

The struggle for full citizenship rights can be speeded by enforcement of existing statutory provisions protecting our civil rights. The attack on discrimination by use of legal machinery has only scratched the surface. An understanding of the existing statutes protecting our civil rights is necessary if we are to work toward enforcement of these statutes.

The titles "civil rights" and "civil liberties" have grown to include large numbers of subjects, some of which are properly included under these titles and others which should not be included. One legal treatise has defined the subject of civil rights as follows: "In its broadest sense, the term *civil rights* includes those rights which are the outgrowth of civilization, the existence and exercise of which necessarily follow from the rights that repose in the subjects of a country exercising self-government."

The Fourteenth and Fifteenth Amendments to the Constitution are prohibitions against action by the states and state officers violating civil rights. In addition to these provisions of the United States Constitution and a few others, there are several statutes of the United States which also attempt to protect the rights of individual citizens against private persons as well as public officers. Whether these provisions are included under the title of "civil rights" or "civil liberties" or any other subject is more or less unimportant as long as we bear in mind the provisions themselves.

All of the statutes, both federal and state, which protect the individual rights of Americans are important to Negroes as well as other citizens. Many of these provisions, however, are of peculiar significance to Negroes because of the fact that in many instances these statutes are the only protection to which Negroes can look for redress. It should also be pointed out that many officials of both state and federal governments are reluctant to protect the rights of Negroes. It is often difficult to enforce our rights when they are perfectly clear. It is practically impossible to secure enforcement of any of our rights if there is any doubt whatsoever as to whether or not a particular statute applies to the particular state of facts.

As to law enforcement itself, the rule as to most American citizens is that if there is any way possible to prosecute individuals who have willfully interfered with the rights of other individuals such prosecution is attempted. However, when the complaining party is a Negro, the rule is usually to look for any possible grounds for *not* prosecuting. It is therefore imperative that Negroes be thoroughly familiar with the rights guaranteed them by law in order that they may be in a position to insist that all of their fundamental rights as American citizens be protected.

The Thirteenth Amendment to the Constitution, abolishing slavery, the Fourteenth Amendment, prohibiting any action of state officials denying due process or the equal protection of its laws, and the Fifteenth Amendment, prohibiting discrimination by the states in voting, are well-known to all of us. In addition to these provisions of the Constitution, there are the so-called Federal "Civil Rights Statutes" which include several Acts of Congress such as the Civil Rights Act and other statutes which have been amended from time to time and are now grouped together in several sections of the United States Code. The Original Civil Rights Act was passed in Congress in 1866, but was vetoed by President Andrew Johnson the same year. It was, however, passed over the veto. It was reintroduced and passed in 1870 because there was some doubt as to its constitutionality, having been passed before the Fourteenth Amendment was ratified. The second bill has been construed several times and has been held constitutional by the United States Supreme Court, which in one case stated that "the plain objects of these statutes, as of the Constitution which authorized them, was to place the colored race, in respect to civil rights, upon a level with the whites. They made the rights and responsibilities, civil and criminal, of the two races exactly the same." (Virginia v. Rives, 100 U.S. 313 [1879])

The Thirteenth and Fourteenth and Fifteenth Amendments, along with the civil rights statutes, protect the following rights:

1. Slavery is abolished and peonage is punishable as a federal crime. (13th amendment)

2. All persons born or naturalized in the U.S. are citizens and no state shall make or enforce any law abridging their privileges or immunities, or deny them equal protection of the law. (14th amendment)

3. The right of citizens to vote cannot be abridged by the United States or by any state on account of race or color. (15th amendment)

4. All persons within the jurisdiction of the United States shall have the same right to enforce contracts, or sue, be parties, give evidence, and to the full and equal benefit of all laws and proceedings as is enjoyed by white citizens.

5. All persons shall be subject to like punishment, pains, penalties, taxes, licenses, and extractions of every kind, and to no other.

6. All citizens shall have the same right in every state and territory, as is enjoyed by white citizens to inherit, purchase, lease, sell, hold and convey property.

7. Every person who, under color of statutes, custom or usage, subjects any citizen of the United States or person within the jurisdiction thereof to the deprivation of any rights, privileges, or immunities secured by the Constitution and laws is liable in an action at law, suit in equity, or other proper proceedings for redress.

8. Citizens possessing all other qualifications may not be disqualified from jury service in federal or state courts on account of race or color; any officer charged with the duty of selection or summoning of jurors who shall exclude citizens for reasons of race or color shall be guilty of a misdemeanor.

9. A conspiracy of two or more persons to deprive any person or class of persons of any rights guaranteed by Constitution and laws is punishable as a crime and the conspirators are also liable in damages.

Most of these provisions only protect the citizen against wrong-doing by public officials, although the peonage statutes and one or two others protect against wrongs by private persons.

Despite the purposes of these Acts which the United States Supreme Court insisted in 1879 "made the rights and responsibilities, civil and criminal, of the two races exactly the same," the experience of all of us points to the fact that this purpose has not as yet been accomplished. There are several reasons for this. In the first place, in certain sections of this country, especially in the deep South, judges, prosecutors and members of grand and petit juries, have simply refused to follow the letter or spirit of these provisions. Very often it happens that although the judge and prosecutor are anxious to enforce the laws, members of the jury are reluctant to protect the rights of Negroes. A third reason is that many Negroes themselves for one reason or another hesitate to avail themselves of the protection afforded by the United States Constitution and statutes.

These statutes protecting our civil rights in several instances provide for both criminal and civil redress. Some are criminal only and others are for civil action only. Criminal prosecution for violation of the federal statutes can be obtained only through the United States Department of Justice.

Up through and including the administration of Attorney General Homer S. Cummings, Negroes were unable to persuade the U.S. Department of Justice to enforce any of the civil rights statutes where Negroes were the complaining parties. The NAACP and its staff made repeated requests and in many instances filed detailed statements and briefs requesting prosecution for lynch mobs, persons guilty of peonage and other apparent violations of the federal statutes. It was not until the administration of Attorney General Frank Murphy that any substantial efforts were made to enforce the civil rights statutes as they apply to Negroes. Attorney General Murphy established a Civil Rights Section in the Department of Justice.

During the present administration of Attorney General Francis Biddle there have been several instances of prosecution of members of lynch mobs for the first time in the history of the United States Department of Justice. There have also been numerous successful prosecutions of persons guilty of peonage and slavery. However, other cases involving the question of the beating and killing of Negro soldiers by local police officers, the case involving the action of Sheriff Tip Hunter, of Browns-ville, Tennessee, who killed at least one Negro citizen and forced several others to leave town, the several cases of refusal to permit qualified Negroes to vote, as well as other cases, have received the attention of the Department of Justice only to the extent of "investigating." Our civil rights as guaranteed by the federal statutes will never become a reality until the U.S. Department of Justice decides that it represents the entire United States and is not required to fear offending any section of the country which believes that it has the God-given right to be above the laws of the United States and the United States Supreme Court.

One interesting example of the apparent failure to enforce the criminal statutes is that although the statute making it a crime to exclude persons from jury service because of race or color was declared unconstitutional by the U.S. Supreme Court in 1879, and is still on the statute books, there have been no prosecutions by the Department of Justice in recent years for the obvious violations of these statutes. The Department of Justice has most certainly on several occasions been put on notice as to these violations by the many cases carried to the Supreme Court by the NAACP and in which cases the Supreme Court has reversed the convictions on the ground that Negroes were systematically excluded from jury service. One wholehearted prosecution of a judge or other official for excluding Negroes from jury service because of their race would do more to make this particular law a reality than dozens of other cases merely reversing the conviction of individual defendants.

There are, however, certain bright spots in the enforcement of the federal statutes. In addition to the lynching and peonage cases handled by the Washington office of the Department of Justice, there have been a few instances of courageous United States Attorneys in such places as Georgia who have vigorously prosecuted police officers who have used the power of their office as a cloak for beating up Negro citizens.

As a result of the recent decision in the Texas Primary Case, it is possible to use an example of criminal prosecution under the civil rights statutes by taking a typical case of the refusal to permit the Negroes to vote in the Democratic Primary elections. Let us see how a prosecution is started: In Waycross, Georgia, for example, we will suppose a Negro elector on July 4, 1944, went to the polls with his tax receipt and demanded to vote in the Democratic Primary. He should, of course, have witnesses with him. Let us also assume that the election officials refused to let him vote solely because of his race or color.

As a matter of law, the election officials violated a federal criminal law and are subject to fine and imprisonment. But how should the voter or the organized Negro citizens, or the local NAACP branch go about trying to get the machinery of criminal justice in motion? Of course, the details of what happens must be put in writing and sworn to by the person who tried to vote and also by his witnesses. Then the matter must be placed before the United States Attorney. This is the *federal* district attorney.

I wonder how many of the delegates here know who is the United States Attorney for their district, or even where his office is. Every branch should know the United States Attorney for that area, even if a delegation goes in just to get acquainted and let him know that we expect him to enforce the civil rights laws with the same vigor as used in enforcing other criminal statutes.

But back to the voting case. The affidavits must be presented to the United States Attorney with a demand that he investigate and place the evidence before the Federal Grand Jury. At the same time copies of the affidavits and statements in the case should be sent to the National Office. We will see that they get to the Attorney General in Washington. I wish that I could guarantee [to] you that the Attorney General would put pressure on local United States Attorneys who seem reluctant to prosecute. At least we can assure you that we will give the Attorney General no rest unless he gets behind these reluctant United States attorneys throughout the South.

There is no reason why a hundred clear cases of this sort should not be placed before the United States Attorneys and the Attorney General every year until the election officials discover that it is both wiser and safer to follow the United States laws than to violate them. It is up to us to see that these officials of the Department of Justice are called upon to act again and again wherever there are violations of the civil rights statutes. Unfortunately, there are plenty of such cases. It is equally unfortunate that there are not enough individuals and groups presenting these cases and demanding action.

The responsibility for enforcement of the civil provisions of the civil rights statutes rests solely with the individual. In the past we have neglected to make full use of these statutes. Although they have been on the books since 1870, there were very few cases under these statutes until recent years. Whereas in the field of general law there are many, many precedents for all other types of action, there are very few precedents for the protection of civil liberties.

The most important of the civil rights provisions is the one which provides that "every person who, under color of any statute, ordinance, regulation, custom or usage of any state or territory subjects or causes to be subjected any citizen of the United States or person within the jurisdiction thereof to the deprivation of any rights, privileges or immunities secured by the Constitution and laws shall be liable to the party injured in an action at law, suit in equity or other proper proceeding for redress." Under this statute any officer of a state, county or municipality who while acting in an official capacity, denies to any citizen or person within the state any of the rights guaranteed by the Constitution or laws is subject to a civil action. This statute has been used to equalize teachers' salaries and to obtain bus transportation for Negro school children. It can be used to attack *every* form of discrimination against Negroes by public school systems.

The statute has also been used to enjoin municipalities from refusing to permit Negroes to take certain civil service examinations and to attack segregation ordinances of municipalities. It can likewise be used to attack all types of discrimination against Negroes by municipalities as well as by states themselves.

This statute, along with other of the civil rights statutes, can be used to enforce the right to register and vote throughout the country. The threats of many of the bigots in the South to disregard the ruling of the Supreme Court of the United States in the recent Texas Primary decision has not intimidated a single person. The United States Supreme Court remains the highest court in this land. Election officials in states affected by this decision will either let Negroes vote in the Democratic Primaries, or they will be subjected to both criminal and civil prosecution under the civil rights statutes. In every state in the deep South Negroes have this year attempted to vote in the primary elections. Affidavits concerning the refusal to permit them to vote in Alabama, Florida and Georgia have already been sent to the United States Department of Justice. We will insist that these election officials be prosecuted and will also file civil suits against the guilty officials.

It can be seen from these examples that we have just begun to scratch the surface in the fight for full enforcement of these statutes. The NAACP can move no faster than the individuals who have been discriminated against. We only take up cases where we are requested to do so by persons who have been discriminated against.

Another crucial problem is the ever-present problem of segregation. Whereas the principle has been established by cases handled by the NAACP that neither states nor municipalities can pass ordinances segregating residences by race, the growing problem today is the problem of segregation by means of restrictive covenants, whereby private owners band together to prevent Negro occupancy of particular neighborhoods. Although this problem is particularly acute in Chicago, it is at the same time growing in intensity throughout the country. It has the full support of the real estate boards in the several cities, as well as most of the banks and other leading agencies. The legal attack on this problem has met with spotty success. In several instances restrictive covenants have been declared invalid because the neighborhood has changed, or for other reasons. Other cases have been lost. However, the NAACP is in the process of preparing a detailed memorandum and will establish procedure which will lead to an all-out legal attack on restrictive covenants. Whether or not this attack will be successful cannot be determined at this time.

The National Housing Agency and the Federal Public Housing Authority have established a policy of segregation in federal public housing projects. A test case has been filed in Detroit, Michigan, and is still pending in the local federal courts. The Detroit situation is the same as in other sections of the country. Despite the fact that the Housing Authority and other agencies insist that they will maintain separate but equal facilities, it never develops that the separate facilities are equal in all respects. In Detroit separate projects were built and it developed that by the first of this year every single white family in the area eligible for public housing had been accommodated and there were still some 800 "white" units vacant with "no takers." At the same time there were some 45,000 Negroes inadequately housed and with no units open to them. This is the inevitable result of "separate but equal" treatment.

I understand that in Chicago a public housing project to be principally occupied by Negroes is being opposed by other Negroes on the ground that it will depreciate their property. It is almost unbelievable that Negroes would oppose public housing for the same reason used by real estate boards and other interests who are determined to keep Negroes in slum areas so that they may be further exploited. The NAACP is in favor of public housing and works toward that end every day. It will continue to do so despite real estate boards and other selfish interests opposing public housing whether they be white or Negro. The NAACP is, of course, opposed to segregation in public housing and will continue to fight segregation in public housing.

We should also be mindful of the several so-called civil rights statutes in the several states. There are civil rights acts in at least 18 states, all of which are in the North and Middle West. These statutes are in California, Colorado, Connecticut, Illinois, Indiana, Iowa, Kansas, Massachusetts, Michigan, Minnesota, Nebraska, New Jersey, New York, Ohio, Pennsylvania, Rhode Island, and Washington. California provides only for civil action. Illinois, Kansas, Minnesota, New York, and Ohio have both civil and criminal provisions. In New Jersey the only action is a criminal action, or an action for penalty in the name of the state, the amount of the penalty going to the state.

In those states not having civil rights statutes it is necessary that every effort be made to secure passage of one. In states having weak civil rights statutes efforts should be made to have them strengthened. In states with reasonably strong civil rights statutes, like Illinois and New York, it is necessary that every effort be made to enforce them.

The Chicago branch has the record of more successful prosecutions for violation of the local civil rights statute than any other branch of the NAACP. In New York City resort to the enforcement of the criminal provisions has greatly lessened the number of cases. Outside of New York City there are very few successful cases against the civil rights statutes because of the fact that members of the jury are usually reluctant to enforce the statutes. I understand the same is true for Illinois. The only method of counteracting this vicious practice is by means of educating the general public, from which juries are chosen, to the plight of the Negro.

It should also be pointed out that many of our friends of other races are not as loud and vociferous as the enemies of our race. In Northern and Mid-Western cities it repeatedly happens that a prejudiced Southerner on entering a hotel or restaurant, seeing Negroes present makes an immediate and loud protest to the manager. It is very seldom that any of our friends go to the managers of places where Negroes are excluded and complain to them of this fact. Quite a job can be done if our friends of other races will only realize the importance of this problem and get up from their comfortable chairs and actually go to work on the problem.

Thus it seems clear that although it is necessary and vital to all of us that we continue our program for additional legislation to guarantee and enforce certain of our rights, at the same time we must continue with ever-increasing vigor to enforce those few statutes, both federal and state, which are now on the statute books. We must not be delayed by people who say "the time is not ripe," nor should we proceed with caution for fear of destroying the "status quo." Persons who deny to us our civil rights should be brought to justice now. Many people believe the time is always "ripe" to discriminate against Negroes. All right then—the time is always "ripe" to bring them to justice. The responsibility for the enforcement of these statutes rests with every American citizen regardless of race or color. However, the real job has to be done by the Negro population with whatever friends of the other races are willing to join in.

Collateral Reading

Blaustein, Albert P., ed., *Civil Rights and the American Negro: A Documentary History.* New York, 1969.

Hughes, Langston, *Fight for Freedom: The Story of the NAACP.* New York, 1962.

Marshall, Thurgood and Roy Wilkins, "Interpretations of the Supreme Court Decisions and the NAACP Program," *Crisis* (July, 1955), 329-337.

————, "Gradualism," *Newsweek* (September 17, 1956), 36-37.

St. James, Warren D., *The NAACP: A Case Study in Pressure Groups.* New York, 1958.

Study Questions and Problems

1. Why was the NAACP legal program so effective in the postwar years and only marginally successful prior to that time? How do you account for the change?

2. How do you explain the fact that at the height of its success, the NAACP civil rights program became passé for many black protestors?

3. Analyze the language that Marshall uses in his speech. He was a skilled lawyer, yet he spoke quite simply to his audience. Was his word choice good or bad rhetorical language?

4. Is Marshall's purpose to inform or to persuade? Perhaps you might argue that there are elements of both information and persuasion in this speech and that his goal was multi-purposed.

5. Compare Marshall's speech to Roy Wilkins' speech. Has the NAACP changed its program in your opinion?

6. Segregation has been described as the problem of the white man. What is meant by this observation?

TWO

The Contemporary Scene

Introduction

According to the history of post-World War II race relations presented in the *Report of the National Advisory Commission on Civil Disorder,* the end of World War II marked the beginning of an era of accelerated agitation by blacks and sympathetic whites for an end to racial discrimination in the United States. Decades of legal opposition to racial barriers by the NAACP's legal department finally bore fruit. In 1946 the *Sweatt* v. *Painter* Case provided for the admission of a Negro to an all-white educational institution. The armed services were integrated by President Truman's 1948 executive order which declared, "There shall be equality of treatment and opportunity for all persons in the Armed Services without regard to race, color, religion, or national origin." The "separate but equal" doctrine of long standing was at last ruled unconstitutional by the Supreme Court when it decided that separation of the races was psychologically harmful to Negroes and thus inherently unequal. In the 1954 case of *Brown* v. *Board of Education of Topeka, Kansas* and other similar cases, the court decisions served as catalysts in stimulating greater demands for civil rights reform. The contemporary rhetoric of black Americans was initially stimulated by development of direct action protest techniques. Then, the rise of the black power movement further stimulated agitational oratory among black rhetors.

A first indication of direct action as a means of seeking reform came in 1956 when Negroes effectively boycotted the Montgomery Bus Company for its policy of segregated seating. The Montgomery bus boycott ended discrimination on Montgomery's buses and catapulted a twenty-seven-year-old minister, Dr. Martin Luther King, Jr., to a position of national prominence in the civil rights movement. Shortly after the Montgomery bus boycott had ended, Dr. King organized the Southern Christian Leadership Conference (SCLC), a civil rights group dedicated to securing full citizenship rights by using direct action, nonviolent techniques of protest.

The first two speeches presented in this section are addresses by the charismatic leader of nonviolence, Dr. Martin Luther King, Jr. Through his effective rhetoric, Dr. King was able to involve thousands of white and black people in the civil rights struggle. Dr. King's "I Have a Dream" was selected because it is perhaps the most eloquent articulation of the hopes of many black Americans for the realization of social equality in America. In addition, Dr. King's views on nonviolence are presented in the speech "Nonviolence and Social Change." According to rhetorical critic Haig Bosmajian:

> After 1957, a sustained series of verbal confrontations by Negroes and their white allies was brought to bear to persuade Negroes and whites that it was now time for both to act to bring about equality and justice in a segregated and unjust society . . . The civil rights movement brought with it not only these acts of "creative dissent," these "controlled creative disorders," but also a great increase in speech-making and pamphleteering by Negro civil rights leaders and organizations. Speeches, pamphlets, protest songs, like the physical confrontations, had a rhetorical or suasory function.[1]

Direct action protest accelerated during the early 1960's. In 1960 young Negro college students in the South protested segregated lunch counters by staging a series of "sit-ins." The sit-ins were the direct cause of the creation of the Student Nonviolent Coordinating Committee, a group composed of students engaged in civil rights protest. In 1961 CORE, the Congress of Racial Equality, dramatically protested segregated transportation facilities in the South by organizing Freedom Rides through Southern cities on Greyhound buses. The rides achieved their goal when interstate carriers and terminals were ordered to desegregate by the Interstate Commerce Commission. Finally, the 1963 March on Washington brought 250,000 citizens to Washington, D.C., to urge passage of the Civil Rights Bill which was then being deliberated. The march was the turning point in the protest movement, since it was clear to many that it dissipated its energies in a gathering of no final significance.

During the decade between 1954 and 1964, such nonverbal forms of protest as marches, mass meetings, and sit-ins were used in an attempt to achieve significant change in the black man's social, economic, and political condition in America. Failure of direct action techniques to meet the expectations of the black masses was a major influence in the development of the Black Power movement.

Since 1964, the black protest movement has tended to stress ideals of economic improvement, political solidarity, and race pride above the ideal of integration and assimilation. It appears that the traditional approach of nonviolent demonstration and appeal to the courts for redress

[1]Haig A. Bosmajian and Hamida Bosmajian, *The Rhetoric of the Civil-Rights Movement* (New York, 1969), pp. 4-5.

of wrongs has been eclipsed by the notion of a more militant show of force with greater antagonism directed toward the so-called "white power structure." Marxist ideology appears in the rhetoric of some militant leaders, as we shall observe.

A series of speeches were selected by the editor to represent the spectrum of opinion from conservative to radical views by spokesmen for black America. Speeches by James Farmer, Martin Luther King, Jr., Roy Wilkins, Carl Rowan, and Whitney M. Young, Jr., were chosen to represent expressions of a more-or-less integrationist approach to race relations. Expressions of black power are voiced in this collection by Adam Clayton Powell, Jr., and Floyd McKissick. Finally, sentiments of alienation are voiced in the views of Malcolm X and Eldridge Cleaver. The latter speakers question the long-held assumption by many whites that the goal of the black protest movement is assimilation by the white majority.

Contemporary black American speakers have tended to express one of three views regarding the black man's position in American society. During the early post-World War II era, black spokesmen emphasized the notion of integration as an objective of the black race. King's notion of nonviolent confrontation was so appealing to blacks and whites alike because both racial groups could accept the techniques of nonviolence and the goal of social assimilation. The eloquent "I Have a Dream" speech is indeed the typification of the goal of assimilation of the black man into the dominant white society.

A less attractive notion to blacks and whites alike is the notion of separation. While Malcolm X was the most articulate spokesman for this point of view in contemporary times, the concept of separation has a long history. Separation of blacks from whites was the cornerstone of the colonization movement of nineteenth-century America. The Garvey movement appealed to dispirited, disenfranchised black masses during the 1920's with the movement's notion of withdrawing from the United States to form a black expatriot state in Africa. In more recent times, the Muslim religious sect, led by Elijah Mohammad, advocates the separation of white and black. The idea has never been a popular one among most blacks. However, its persistence throughout the nineteenth and twentieth century is symptomatic of American society's failure to include blacks in the mainstream of economic, political, and social life.

A third notion, currently popular, is the notion of self-improvement within the society. Again the notion is not new. Booker T. Washington dominated a generation with his notion of separate self-improvement of the black race. In contemporary times, the failure of the integrationist objective to meet the expectations of the black masses has revitalized interest in this notion under the rubric "black power."

An interesting phenomenon of the post-World War II civil rights movement was the receptiveness of many white Americans to the black speaker. Then, as never before, the black civil rights leader was a much sought-after speaker by liberal organizations and university lecture series. Black leaders like King, Marshall, Wilkins, Farmer, and Whitney Young were moderate in their views, and embraced the notion of nonviolent integration. Liberal white audiences could easily identify with these aims. As the protest movement became more militant and less concerned with evoking cooperation from sympathetic whites, as the protest movement became more concerned with developing black awareness, black speakers have not been able to keep the continued enthusiasm of many white auditors.

Thus, the voices of black Americans speak a complex message. Some speak for accommodation between the races. Some speak for racial improvement by following a program of separate racial development. Others agitate for revolt and revolution. Interestingly, all these tendencies were expressed by earlier black American speakers throughout our long history of racial strife.

From the Report of the National Advisory Commission on Civil Disorders[2]

The Postwar Period

White opinion in some quarters of America had begun to shift to a more sympathetic regard for Negroes during the New Deal, and the war had accelerated that movement. Thoughtful whites had been painfully aware of the contradiction in opposing Nazi racial philosophy with racially segregated military units. In the postwar years, American racial attitudes became more liberal as new nonwhite nations emerged in Asia and Africa and took increasing responsibilities in international councils.

Against this background, the growing size of the Northern Negro vote made civil rights a major issue in national elections and, ultimately, in 1957, led to the establishment of the Federal Civil Rights Commission, which had the power to investigate dis-

[2]Reprinted from *Report of The National Advisory Commission on Civil Disorders,* March 1, 1968, pp. 105-114.

criminatory conditions throughout the country and to recommend corrective measures to the President. Northern and Western states outlawed discrimination in employment, housing and public accommodations, while the NAACP, in successive court victories, won judgments against racially restrictive covenants in housing, segregation in interstate transportation and discrimination in publicly-owned recreational facilities. The NAACP helped register voters, and in 1954, *Brown* v. *Board of Education* became the triumphant climax of the NAACP's campaign against educational segregation in the public schools of the South.

CORE, which had been conducting demonstrations in the Border states, its major focus on public accommodations, began experimenting with direct-action techniques to open employment opportunities. In 1947, in conjunction with the Fellowship of Reconciliation, CORE conducted a "Journey of Reconciliation"—what would later be called a "Freedom Ride"—in the states of the upper South to test compliance with the Supreme Court decision outlawing segregation on interstate buses. The resistance met by riders in some areas and the sentencing of two of them to 30 days on a North Carolina road gang dramatized the gap between American democratic theory and practice.

The Montgomery, Ala., bus boycott of 1955-56 captured the imagination of the nation and of the Negro community in particular, and led to the growing use of direct-action techniques. It catapulted into national prominence the Reverend Martin Luther King, Jr., who, like the founders of CORE, held to a Gandhian belief in the principles of pacifism.

Even before a court decision obtained by NAACP attorneys in November, 1956, desegregated the Montgomery buses, a similar movement had started in Tallahassee, Fla. Afterward, another one developed in Birmingham, Ala. In 1957, the Tuskegee Negroes undertook a 3-year boycott of local merchants after the state legislature gerrymandered nearly all of the Negro voters outside of the town's boundaries. In response to a lawsuit filed by the NAACP, the Supreme Court ruled the Tuskegee gerrymander illegal.

These events were widely heralded. The "new Negro" had now emerged in the South—militant, no longer fearful of white hoodlums or mobs and ready to use his collective strength to achieve his ends. In this mood, King established the Southern Christian Leadership Conference in 1957 to coordinate direct-action activities in Southern cities. Nonviolent direct action attained popularity not only because of the effectiveness of King's leadership, but because the older techniques of legal and legislative action had had limited success. Impressive as the advances in the 15 years after World War II were, in spite of state laws and Supreme Court decisions, something was still clearly wrong. Negroes remained disfranchised in most of the South, though in the 12 years following the outlawing of the white primary in 1944, the number of Negroes registered in Southern states had risen from about 250,000 to nearly a million and a quarter. Supreme Court decisions desegregating transportation facilities were still being largely ignored in the South. Discrimination in employment and housing continued, not only in the South but also in Northern states with model civil rights laws. The Negro unemployment rate steadily moved upward after 1954. The South reacted to the Supreme Court decision on school desegregation by attempting to outlaw the NAACP, intimidating civil rights leaders, calling for "massive resistance" to the Court's decision, curtailing Negro voter registration and forming White Citizens' Councils.

Revolution of Rising Expectations

At the same time, Negro attitudes were changing. In what has been described as a "revolution in expectations," Negroes were gaining a new sense of self-respect and a new self-image as a result of the civil rights movement and their own advancement. King and others were demonstrating that nonviolent direct action could succeed in the South. New laws and court decisions and the increasing support of white public opinion gave American Negroes a new confidence in the future.

Negroes no longer felt they had to accept the humiliations of second-class citizenship. Ironically it was the very successes in the legislatures and the courts that, more perhaps than any other single factor, led to intensified Negro expectations and resulting dissatisfaction with the limitations of legal and legislative programs. Increasing Negro impatience accounted for the rising tempo of nonviolent direct action in the late 1950's, culminating in the student sit-ins of 1960 and the inauguration of what is popularly known as the "Civil Rights Revolution" or the "Negro Revolt."

Many believe that the Montgomery boycott ushered in this Negro Revolt, and there is no doubt that, in its importance, by projecting the image of King and his techniques, it had great importance. But the decisive break with traditional techniques came with the college student sit-ins that swept the South in the winter and spring of 1960. In dozens of communities in the upper South, the Atlantic coastal states and Texas, student demonstrations secured the deseg- regation of lunch counters in drug and variety stores. Arrests were numbered in the thousands, and brutality was evident in scores of communities. In the Deep South, the campaign ended in failure, even instances where hundreds had been arrested, as in Mont- gomery, Orangeburg, South Carolina, and Baton Rouge. But the youth had captured the imagination of the Negro community and to a remarkable extent of the whole Nation.

Student Involvement

The Negro protest movement would never be the same again. The Southern college students shook the power structure of the Negro community, made direct action temporarily preeminent as a civil rights tactic, speeded up the process of social change in race relations, and ultimately turned the Negro protest organi- zations toward a deep concern with the economic and social prob- lems of the masses.

Involved in this was a gradual shift in both tactics and goals: from legal to direct action, from middle and upper class to mass action, from attempts to guarantee the Negro's constitutional rights to efforts to secure economic policies giving him equality of oppor- tunity, from appeals to the sense of fair play of white Americans to demands based upon power in the black ghetto.

The successes of the student movement threatened existing Negro leadership and precipitated a spirited rivalry among civil rights organizations. The NAACP and SCLC associated themselves with the student movement. The organizing meeting of the Student Nonviolent Coordinating Committee (SNCC) at Raleigh, North Carolina, in April 1960, was called by Martin Luther King, but within a year the youth considered King too cautious and broke with him.

The NAACP now decided to make direct action a major part of its strategy and organized and reactivated college and youth chapters in the Southern and Border states.

CORE, still unknown to the general public, installed James Farmer as national director in January, 1961, and that spring joined the front rank of civil rights organizations with the famous Freedom Ride to Alabama and Mississippi that dramatized the persistence of segregated public transportation. A bus-burning resulted in Alabama. Hundreds of demonstrators spent a month or more in

Mississippi prisons. Finally, a new order from the Interstate Commerce Commission desegregating all interstate transportation facilities received partial compliance.

Organizational Differences

Disagreement over strategy and tactics inevitably became intertwined with personal and organizational rivalries. Each civil rights group felt the need for proper credit in order to obtain the prestige and financial contributions necessary to maintain and expand its own programs. The local and national, individual and organizational clashes stimulated competition and activity that further accelerated the pace of social change.

Yet there were differences in style. CORE was the most interracial. SCLC appeared to be the most deliberate. SNCC staff workers lived on subsistence allowances and seemed to regard going to jail as a way of life. The NAACP continued the most varied programs, retaining a strong emphasis on court litigation, maintaining a highly effective lobby at the national capital and engaging in direct-action campaigns. The National Urban League under the leadership of Whitney M. Young, Jr., appointed executive director in 1961, became more outspoken and talked more firmly to businessmen who had previously been treated with utmost tact and caution.

The role of whites in the protest movement gradually changed. Instead of occupying positions of leadership, they found themselves relegated to the role of followers. Whites were likely to be suspect in the activist organizations. Negroes had come to feel less dependent on whites, more confident of their own power, and they demanded that their leaders be black. The NAACP had long since acquired Negro leadership but continued to welcome white liberal support. SCLC and SNCC were from the start Negro-led and Negro-dominated. CORE became predominantly Negro as it expanded in 1962 and 1963; today all executives are Negro, and a constitutional amendment adopted in 1965 officially limited white leadership in the chapters.

A major factor intensifying the civil rights movement was widespread Negro unemployment and poverty; an important force in awakening Negro protest was the meteoric rise to national prominence of the Black Muslims, established around 1930. The organization reached the peak of its influence when more progress toward equal rights was being made than ever before in American history, while at the same time the poorest groups in the urban ghettos were stagnating.

The Black Muslims preached a vision of the doom of the white "devils" and the coming dominance of the black man, promised a utopian paradise of a separate territory within the United States for a Negro state, and offered a practical program of building Negro business through hard work, thrift and racial unity. To those willing to submit to the rigid discipline of the movement, the Black Muslims organization gave a sense of purpose and dignity.

"Freedom Now!" And Civil Rights Laws

As the direct-action tactics took more dramatic form, as the civil rights groups began to articulate the needs of the masses and draw some of them to their demonstrations, the protest movement in 1963 assumed a new note of urgency, a demand for complete "Freedom Now!" Direct action returned to the Northern cities, taking the form of massive protests against economic, housing and educational inequities, and a fresh wave of demonstrations swept the South from Cambridge, Maryland, to Birmingham, Alabama. Northern Negroes launched street demonstrations against discriminations in the building trade unions, and the following winter, school boycotts against de facto segregation.

In the North, 1963 and 1964 brought the beginning of the waves of civil disorders in Northern urban centers. In the South, incidents occurred of brutal white resistance to the civil rights movement, beginning with the murders of Mississippi Negro leader Medgar Evers, and of four Negro schoolgirls in a church in Birmingham. These disorders and the events in the South are detailed in the introduction to Chapter 1, the *Profiles of Disorder.*

The massive anti-Negro resistance in Birmingham and numerous other Southern cities during the spring of 1963 compelled the nation to face the problem of race prejudice in the South. President Kennedy affirmed that racial discrimination was a moral issue and asked Congress for a major civil rights bill. But a major impetus for what was to be the Civil Rights Act of 1964 was the March on Washington in August, 1963.

Early in the year, A. Philip Randolph issued a call for a March on Washington to dramatize the need for jobs and to press for a Federal commitment to job action. At about the same time, Protestant, Jewish and Catholic churches sought and obtained representation on the March committee. Although the AFL-CIO national council refused to endorse the March, a number of labor leaders and international unions participated.

Reversing an earlier stand, President Kennedy approved the March. A quarter of a million people, about 20 percent of them white, participated. It was more than a summation of the past years of struggle and aspiration. It symbolized certain new directions: a deeper concern for the economic problems of the masses, more involvement of white moderates and new demands from the most militant, who implied that only a revolutionary change in American institutions would permit Negroes to achieve the dignity of citizens.

President Kennedy had set the stage for the Civil Rights Act of 1964. After his death, President Johnson took forceful and effective action to secure its enactment. The law settled the public accommodations issue in the South's major cities. Its voting section, however, promised more than it could accomplish. Martin Luther King and SCLC dramatized the issue locally with demonstrations at Selma, Alabama, in the spring of 1965. Again the national government was forced to intervene, and a new and more effective voting law was passed.

Failures of Direct Action

Birmingham had made direct action respectable; Selma, which drew thousands of white moderates from the North, made direct action fashionable. Yet as early as 1964, it was becoming evident that, like legal action, direct action was of limited usefulness.

In Deep South states like Mississippi and Alabama, direct action had failed to desegregate public accommodations in the sit-ins of 1960-1961. A major reason was that Negroes lacked the leverage of the vote. The demonstrations of the early 1960's had been successful principally in places like Atlanta, Nashville, Durham, Winston-Salem, Louisville, Savannah, New Orleans, Charleston, and Dallas—where Negroes voted and could swing elections. Beginning in 1961, Robert Moses, of SNCC, with the cooperation of CORE and NAACP established voter registration projects in the cities and county seats of Mississippi. He succeeded in registering only a handful of Negroes, but by 1964, he had generated enough support throughout the country to enable the Mississippi Freedom Democratic Party, which he had created, to challenge dramatically the seating of the official white delegates from the state at the Democratic National Convention.

In the black ghettos of the North, direct action also largely failed. Street demonstrations did compel employers, from supermarkets to banks, to add Negroes to their work force in Northern and Western cities, and even in some Southern cities where the Negroes had considerable buying power. However, separate and inferior schools, slum housing, and police hostility proved invulnerable to direct attack.

New Directions

Although Negroes were being hired in increasing numbers, mass unemployment and underemployment remained. As economist Vivian Henderson pointed out in his testimony before the Commission:

> No one can deny that all Negroes have benefitted from civil rights laws and desegregation in public life in one way or another. The fact is, however, that the masses of Negroes have not experienced tangible benefits in a significant way. This is so in education and housing. It is critically so in the area of jobs and economic security. Expectations of Negro masses for equal job opportunity programs have fallen far short of fulfillment.
> Negroes have made gains. . . . There have been important gains. But . . . the masses of Negroes have been virtually untouched by those gains.

Faced with the intransigence of the Deep South and the inadequacy of direct action to solve the problems of the slumdwellers, Negro protest organizations began to diverge. The momentum toward unity, apparent in 1963, was lost. At the very time that white support for the movement was rising markedly, militant Negroes felt increasingly isolated from the American scene. On two things, however, all segments of the protest movement agreed: (1) Future civil rights activity would have to focus on economic and social discrimination in the urban ghettos; and (2) while demonstrations would still have a place, the major weapon would have to be the political potential of the black masses.

By the middle of the decade, many militant Negro members of SNCC and CORE began to turn away from American society and the "middle-class way of life." Cynical about the liberals and the leaders of organized labor, they regarded compromise, even as a temporary tactical device, as anathema. They talked more of "revolutionary" changes in the social structure and of retaliatory violence, and increasingly rejected white assistance. They insisted that Negro power alone could compel the white "ruling class" to make concessions. Yet they also spoke of an alliance of Negroes

and unorganized lower class whites to overthrow the "power structure" of capitalists, politicians, and bureaucratic labor leaders who
exploited the poor of both races by dividing them through an appeal
to race prejudice.

At the same time that their activities declined, other issues,
particularly Vietnam, diverted the attention of the country, and
of some Negro leaders, from the issue of equality. In civil rights
organizations, reduced financing made it increasingly difficult to
support staff personnel. Most important was the increasing frustration of expectations that affected the direct-action advocates of
the early 1960's—the sense of futility growing out of the feeling
that progress had turned out to be "tokenism," that the compromises
of the white community were sedatives rather than solutions and
that the currect methods of Negro protest were doing little for
the masses of the race.

As frustration grew, the ideology and rhetoric of a number of
civil rights activists became angrier. One man more than any
other—a black man who grew up believing whites had murdered
his father—became a spokesman for this anger: Malcolm X, who
perhaps best embodied the belief that racism was so deeply in-
grained in white America that appeals to conscience would bring
no fundamental change.

"Black Power"

In this setting, the rhetoric of black power developed. The pre-
cipitating occasion was the Meredith March from Memphis to
Jackson in June, 1966, but the slogan expressed tendencies that
had been present for a long time and had been gaining strength
in the Negro community.

"Black power" first articulated a mood rather than a program:
disillusionment and alienation from white America and independence, race pride, and self-respect, or "black consciousness."
Having become a household phrase, the term generated intense
discussion of its real meaning, and a broad spectrum of ideologies
and programmatic proposals emerged.

In politics, "black power" meant independent action—Negro
control of the political power of the black ghettos and its use to
improve economic and social conditions. It could take the form
of organizing a black political party or controlling the political
machinery within the ghetto without the guidance or support of
white politicans. Where predominantly Negro areas lacked Negroes

in elective office, whether in the rural Black Belt of the South or in the urban centers, black power advocates sought the election of Negroes by voter registration campaigns, by getting out the vote, and by working for redrawing electoral districts. The basic belief was that only a well-organized and cohesive bloc of Negro voters could provide for the needs of the black masses. Even some Negro politicians allied to the major political parties adopted the term "black power" to describe their interest in the Negro vote.

In economic terms, "black power" meant creating independent, self-sufficient Negro business enterprise not only by encouraging Negro entrepreneurs but also by forming Negro cooperatives in the ghettos and in the predominantly black rural counties of the South. In the area of education, black power called for local community control of the public schools in the black ghettos.

Throughout, the emphasis was on self-help, racial unity, and, among the most militant, retaliatory violence, the latter ranging from the legal right of self-defense to attempts to justify looting and arson in ghetto riots, guerilla warfare, and armed rebellion.

Phrases like "black power," "black consciousness," and "black is beautiful," enjoyed an extensive currency in the Negro community, even within the NAACP and among relatively conservative politicians, and particularly among young intellectuals and Afro-American student groups on predominantly white college campuses. Expressed in its most extreme form by small, often local, fringe groups, the black power ideology became associated with SNCC and CORE.

Generally regarded today as the most militant among the important Negro protest organizations, they have developed different interpretations of the black power doctrine. SNCC calls for totally independent political action outside the established political parties, as with the Black Panther Party in Lowndes County, Ala.; rejects the political alliances with other groups until Negroes have themselves built a substantial base of independent political power; applauds the idea of guerilla warfare; and regards riots as rebellions.

CORE has been more flexible. Approving the SNCC strategy, it also advocates working within the Democratic Party, forming alliances with other groups and, while seeking to justify riots as the natural explosion of an oppressed people against intolerable conditions, advocates violence only in self-defense. Both groups favor cooperatives, but CORE has seemed more inclined toward job-training programs and developing a Negro entrepreneurial class, based upon the market within the black ghettos.

Old Wine in New Bottles

What is new about black power is phraseology rather than substance. Black consciousness had roots in the organization of Negro churches and mutual benefit societies in the early days of the Republic, the antebellum Negro convention movement, the Negro colonization schemes of the 19th century, Du Bois' concept of Pan-Africanism, Booker T. Washington's advocacy of race pride, self-help, and racial solidarity, the Harlem Renaissance, and the Garvey Movement. The decade after World War I—which saw the militant, race-proud "new Negro," the relatively widespread theory of retaliatory violence and the high tide of the Negro-support-of-Negro-business ideology—exhibits striking parallels with the 1960's.

The theme of retaliatory violence is hardly new for American Negroes. Most racial disorders in American history until recent years were characterized by white attacks on Negroes. But Negroes have retaliated violently in the past.

Black Panther rhetoric and ideology actually express a lack of power. The slogan emerged when the Negro protest movement was slowing down, when it was finding increasing resistance to its changing goals, when it discovered that nonviolent direct action was no more a panacea than legal action, when CORE and SNCC were declining in terms of activity, membership, and financial support. This combination of circumstances provoked anger deepened by impotence. Powerless to make any fundamental changes in the life of the masses—powerless, that is, to compel white America to make those changes, many advocates of black power have retreated into an unreal world, where they see an outnumbered and poverty-stricken minority organizing itself entirely separately from whites and creating sufficient power to force white America to grant its demands. To date, the evidence suggests that the situation is much like that of the 1840's, when a small group of intellectuals advocated slave insurrections, but stopped short of organizing them.

The black power advocates of today consciously feel that they are the most militant group in the Negro protest movement. Yet they have retreated from a direct confrontation with American society on the issue of integration and, by preaching separatism, unconsciously function as an accommodation to white racism. Much of their economic program, as well as their interest in Negro history, self-help, racial solidarity and separation, is reminiscent of Booker T. Washington. The rhetoric is different, but the ideas are remarkably similar.

The Meaning

By 1967, whites could point to the demise of slavery, the decline of illiteracy among Negroes, the legal protection provided by the constitutional amendments and civil rights legislation, and the growing size of the Negro middle class. Whites would call it Negro progress, from slavery to freedom and toward equality.

Negroes could point to the doctrine of white supremacy, its persistence after emancipation and its influence on the definition of the place of Negroes in American life. They could point to their long fight for full citizenship when they had active opposition from most of the white population and little or no support from the Government. They could see progress toward equality accompanied by bitter resistance. Perhaps most of all, they could feel the persistent, pervasive racism that kept them in inferior segregated schools, restricted them to ghettos, barred them from fair employment, provided double standards in courts of justice, inflicted bodily harm on their children and blighted their lives with a sense of hopelessness and despair.

In all of this and in the context of professed ideals, Negroes would find more retrogression than progress, more rejection than acceptance.

Until the middle of the 20th century, the course of Negro protest movements in the United States, except for slave revolts, was based in the cities of the North, where Negroes enjoyed sufficient freedom to mount sustained protest. It was in the cities, North and South, that Negroes had their greatest independence and mobility. It was natural, therefore, for black protest movements to be urban-based—and, until the last seven years or so, limited to the North. As Negroes emigrated from the South, the mounting strength of their votes in Northern cities became a vital element in drawing the Federal Government into the defense of the civil rights of Southern Negroes. While rural Negroes today face great racial problems, the major unsolved questions that touch the core of Negro life stem from discrimination embedded in urban housing, employment, and education.

Over the years the character of Negro protest has changed. Originally, it was a white liberal and Negro upper class movement aimed at securing the constitutional rights of Negroes through propaganda, lawsuits, and legislation. In recent years, the emphasis in tactics shifted first to direct action and then—among the most militant—to the rhetoric of "black power." The role of white liberals declined as Negroes came to direct the struggle. At the same time, the Negro protest movement became more of a mass movement, with increasing participation from the working classes. As these changes were occurring, and while substantial progress was being made to secure constitutional rights for the Negroes, the goals of the movement were broadened. Protest groups now demand special efforts to overcome the Negro's poverty and cultural deprivation—conditions that cannot be erased simply by ensuring constitutional rights.

The central thrust of Negro protest in the current period has aimed at the inclusion of Negroes in American society on a basis of full equality, rather than at a fundamental transformation of American institutions. There have been elements calling for a revolutionary overthrow of the American social system or for a complete withdrawal of Negroes from American society. But these solutions have had little popular support. Negro protest, for the most part, has been firmly rooted in the basic values of American society, seeking not their destruction but their fulfillment.

Martin Luther King, Jr.

Martin Luther King, Jr., was born in Atlanta, Georgia, in 1929, the son of a Baptist preacher. He received a B.A. from Morehouse College in Atlanta in 1948, a B.D. from Crozer Theological Seminary, Chester, Pennsylvania, in 1951, and a Ph.D. from Boston University in 1955. While studying at Boston University, King spent three summers preaching at his father's church. He was still working on his dissertation when he accepted a position at the Dexter Avenue Baptist Church in Montgomery, Alabama. One year later, King was asked to direct the Montgomery Improvement Association's bus boycott. He accepted the position, making a speech militant enough to keep people aroused and yet moderate enough to keep them under control.

During the ensuing years, King articulated a philosophy of nonviolent protest to racial discrimination. As a civil rights leader, he traveled 780,000 miles and made 208 speeches during 1957 and made a comparable number of major speeches each year thereafter, as he became the most prominent leader of direct action civil rights demonstrations.

As a speaker, King had an indescribable capacity for empathizing with his audience. According to one observer, the cadence of his voice and the earnestness of his tone tended to obscure occasional mixed metaphors. He stood five feet seven inches with broad shoulders and a muscular neck. He added to these physical attributes a rich baritone voice.

His speeches reflect appeals to the highest ethical and moral values, and they helped establish the enormous credibility which he enjoyed. He sincerely believed that unwarranted suffering by righteous people was re-demptive.

Dr. King received numerous awards and degrees, including the Nobel Peace Prize in 1964. In accepting the award, he stated that "nonviolence is the answer to the crucial political and moral question of our time—the need for man to overcome oppression and violence without resorting to violence and oppression."

The "I Have a Dream" speech was delivered at the Lincoln Memorial,

Washington, D.C., August 28, 1963, before a crowd of 250,000 people who had marched to Washington in support of civil rights legislation. The speech was intended to evoke strong feelings in the hearts of civil rights supporters throughout the nation, and it was an outstanding rhetorical success. It was a speech full of patriotic and religious metaphors coupled with effective use of repetition. The speech contained a chronological pattern of arrangement. It began with a reference to the emancipation of the Negro slave. A brief series of repeated phrases emphasized the notion that "now is the time" for social action. It concluded with the "dream" that one day the American dream would be realized.

The heart of the speech is a series of effective images related to the notion "I have a dream." Within this passage, King appealed to motives of justice and decency and reverence for life in the best sense of the Judeo-Christian heritage. The speech should be read again and again by those who wish an example of how to evoke strong emotion in an audience.

Another speech by King, "Nonviolence and Social Change," is included in this book because it articulates King's philosophy of nonviolence with clarity and force at a time when many black leaders were questioning nonviolent civil disobedience as an effective strategy for social change. King briefly reviewed the civil rights successes of the technique and then discussed whether nonviolence would continue to be effective psychologically after the urban riots of 1967. He maintained in his speech that Negroes showed restraint during the riots by attacking property rather than people. He contended that experience had demonstrated to him that the most militant black leader could demonstrate constructively by channeling his energies into nonviolent protest.

Dr. King further proposed to organize a massive nonviolent army of the poor to move on Washington to improve the conditions of the poor. He suggested that a nonviolent direct action movement might be developed on the international scene to improve conditions for all the people of the world. He eloquently concluded that "nonviolence is no longer an option for intellectual analysis, it is an imperative for action."

I Have a Dream

August 28, 1963

I am happy to join with you today in what will go down in history as the greatest demonstration for freedom in the history of our nation.

Five score years ago, a great American, in whose symbolic shadow we stand today, signed the Emancipation Proclamation. This momentous decree came as a great beacon light of hope to millions of Negro slaves, who had been seared in the flames of withering injustice. It came as a joyous daybreak to end the long night of their captivity.

But one hundred years later, the Negro is still not free. One hundred years later, the life of the Negro is still sadly crippled by the manacles of segregation and the chains of discrimination. One hundred years later, the Negro lives on a lonely island of poverty in the midst of a vast ocean of material prosperity. One hundred years later, the Negro is still languished in the corners of American society and finds himself an exile in his own land. So we have come here today to dramatize a shameful condition.

Martin Luther King, Jr.   *Frederic Lewis Photo*

In a sense we've come to our nation's Capitol to cash a check. When the architects of our republic wrote the magnificent words of the Constitution and the Declaration of Independence, they were signing a promissory note to which every American was to fall heir. This note was a promise that all men—yes, black men as well as white men—would be guaranteed the unalienable rights of life, liberty, and the pursuit of happiness.

It is obvious today that America has defaulted on this promissory note insofar as her citizens of color are concerned. Instead of honoring this sacred obligation, America has given the Negro people a bad check; a check which has come back marked "insufficient funds." But we refuse to believe that the bank of justice is bankrupt. We refuse to believe that there are insufficient funds in the great vaults of opportunity of this nation. So we've come to cash this check—a check that will give us upon demand the riches of freedom and the security of justice. We have also come to this hallowed spot to remind America of the fierce urgency of *now*. This is no time to engage in the luxury of cooling off or to take the tranquilizing drug of gradualism. *Now is the time* to make real the promises of Democracy. *Now is the time* to rise from the dark and desolate valley of segregation to the sunlight of racial justice. *Now is the time* to lift our nation from the quicksands of racial injustice to the solid rock of brotherhood. *Now is the time* to make justice a reality for all of God's children.

It would be fatal for the nation to overlook the urgency of the moment. This sweltering summer of the Negro's legitimate discontent will not pass until there is an invigorating autumn of freedom and equality. Nineteen sixty-three is not an end, but a beginning. Those who hope that the Negro needed to blow off steam and will now be content will have a rude awakening if the nation returns to business as usual. There will be neither rest nor tranquility in America until the Negro is granted his citizenship rights. The whirlwinds of revolt will continue to shake the foundations of our nation until the bright day of justice emerges.

But that is something that I must say to my people who stand on the warm threshold which leads into the palace of justice. In the process of gaining our rightful place we must not be guilty of wrongful deeds. Let us not seek to satisfy our thirst for freedom by drinking from the cup of bitterness and hatred.

We must forever conduct our struggle on the high plane of dignity and discipline. We must not allow our creative protest to degenerate into physical violence. Again and again we must rise to the majestic heights of meeting physical force with soul force. The marvelous new militancy which has engulfed the Negro community must not lead us to a distrust of all white people, for many of our white brothers, as evidenced by their presence here today, have come to realize that their destiny is tied up with our destiny. And they have come to realize that their freedom is inextricably bound to our freedom. We cannot walk alone.

And as we walk we must make the pledge that we shall always march ahead. We cannot turn back. There are those who ask the devotees of civil rights, "When will you be satisfied?" We can never be satisfied as long as the Negro is the victim of the unspeakable horrors of police brutality. We can never be satisfied as long as our bodies, heavy with the fatigue of travel, cannot gain lodging in the motels of the highways and the hotels of the cities. We cannot be satisfied as long as the Negro's basic mobility is from a smaller ghetto to a larger one. We can never be satisfied as long as our children are stripped of their selfhood and robbed of their dignity by signs stating "For Whites Only." We cannot be satisfied as long as a Negro in Mississippi cannot vote and a Negro in New York believes he has nothing for which to vote. No, no, we are not satisfied, and we will not be satisfied until justice rolls down like waters and righteousness like a mighty stream.

I am not unmindful that some of you have come here out of great trials and tribulations. Some of you have come fresh from narrow jail cells. Some of you have come from areas where your quest for freedom left you battered by the storms of persecution and staggered by the winds of police brutality. You have been the veterans of creative suffering. Continue to work with the faith that unearned suffering is redemptive.

Go back to Mississippi, go back to Alabama, go back to South Carolina, go back to Georgia, go back to Louisiana, go back to the slums and ghettos of our Northern cities knowing that somehow this situation can and will be changed. Let us not wallow in the valley of despair.

I say to you today, my friends, so even though we face the difficulties of today and tomorrow, I still have a dream. It is a dream deeply rooted in the American dream.

I have a dream that one day this nation will rise up and live out the true meaning of its creed: "We hold these truths to be self-evident; that all men are created equal."

I have a dream that one day on the red hills of Georgia the sons of former slaves and the sons of former slaveowners will be able to sit down together at the table of brotherhood; I have a dream—

That one day even the state of Mississippi, a state sweltering with the heat of injustice, sweltering with the heat of oppression, will be transformed into an oasis of freedom and justice; I have a dream—

That my four little children will one day live in a nation where they will not be judged by the color of their skin but by the content of their character; I have a dream today.

I have a dream that one day down in Alabama, with its vicious racists, with its governor having his lips dripping with the words of interposition and nullification, one day right there in Alabama little black boys and black girls will be able to join hands with little white boys and white girls as sisters and brothers; I have a dream today.

I have a dream that one day every valley shall be exalted, every hill and mountain shall be made low, and rough places will be made plane and crooked places will be made straight, and the glory of the Lord shall be revealed, and all flesh shall see it together.

This is our hope. This is the faith that I go back to the South with. With this faith we will be able to hew out of the mountain of despair a stone of hope. With this faith we will be able to transform the jangling discords of our nation into a beautiful symphony of brotherhood. With this faith we will be able to work together, to pray together, to struggle together, to go to jail together, to stand up for freedom together, knowing that we will be free one day.

This will be the day. . . . This will be the day when all of God's children will be able to sing with new meaning "My country 'tis of thee, sweet land of liberty, of thee I sing. Land where my fathers died, land of the pilgrim's pride, from every mountainside, let freedom ring," and if America is to be a great nation—this must become true.

So let freedom ring—from the prodigious hilltops of New Hampshire, let freedom ring; from the mighty mountains of New York, let freedom ring—from the heightening Alleghenies of Pennsylvania!

Let freedom ring from the snowcapped Rockies of Colorado!

Let freedom ring from the curvaceous slopes of California!

But not only that; let freedom ring from Stone Mountain of Georgia!

Let freedom ring from Lookout Mountain of Tennessee!

Let freedom ring from every hill and molehill of Mississippi. From every mountainside, let freedom ring, and when this happens. . . .

When we allow freedom to ring, when we let it ring from every village and every hamlet, from every state and every city, we will be able to speed up that day when all of God's children, black men and white men, Jews and Gentiles, Protestants and Catholics, will be able to join hands and sing in the words of the old Negro spiritual, "Free at last! free at last! thank God almighty, we are free at last!"

Nonviolence and Social Change

November, 1967

There is nothing wrong with a traffic law which says you have to stop for a red light. But when a fire is raging, the fire truck goes right through that red light, and normal traffic had better get out of its way. Or, when a man is bleeding to death, the ambulance goes through those red lights at top speed.

There is a fire raging now for the Negroes and the poor of this society. They are living in tragic conditions because of the terrible economic injustices that keep them locked in as an "underclass," as the sociologists are now calling it. Disinherited people all over the world are bleeding to death from deep social and economic wounds. They need brigades of ambulance drivers who will have to ignore the red lights of the present system until the emergency is solved.

Massive civil disobedience is a strategy for social change which is at least as forceful as an ambulance with its siren on full. In the past ten years, nonviolent civil disobedience has made a great deal of history, especially in the Southern United States. When we and the Southern Christian Leadership Conference went to Birmingham, Alabama, in 1963, we had decided to take action on the matter of integrated public accommodations. We went knowing that the Civil Rights Commission had written powerful documents calling for change, calling for the very rights we were demanding. But nobody did anything about the Commission's report. Nothing was done until we acted on these very issues, and demonstrated before the court of world opinion the urgent need for change. It was the same story with voting rights. The Civil Rights Commission, three years before we went to Selma, had recommended the changes we started marching for, but nothing was done until, in 1965, we created a crisis the nation couldn't ignore. Without violence, we totally disrupted the system, the life style of Birmingham, and then of Selma, with their unjust and unconstitutional laws. Our Birmingham struggle came to its dramatic climax when some 3,500 demonstrators virtually filled every jail in that city and surrounding communities, and some 4,000 more continued to march and demonstrate nonviolently. The city knew then in terms that were crystal-clear that Birmingham could no longer continue to function until the demands of the Negro community were met. The same kind of dramatic crisis was created in Selma two years later. The result on the national scene was the Civil Rights Bill and the Voting Rights Act, as President and Congress responded to the drama and the creative tension generated by the carefully planned demonstrations.

Of course, by now it is obvious that new laws are not enough. The emergency we now face is economic, and it is a desperate and worsening situation. For the 35 million poor people in America—not even to mention, just yet, the poor in the other nations—there is a kind of strangulation in the air. In our society it is murder, psychologically, to deprive a man of a job or an income. You are in substance saying to that man that he has no right to exist. You are in a real way depriving him of life, liberty, and the pursuit of happiness, denying in his case the very creed of his society. Now, millions of people are being strangled that way. The problem is international in scope. And it is getting worse, as the gap between the poor and the "affluent society" increases.

The question that now divides the people who want radically to change that situation is: can a program of nonviolence—even if it envisions massive civil disobedience—realistically expect to deal with such an enormous, entrenched evil?

First of all, will nonviolence work, psychologically, after the summer of 1967? Many people feel that nonviolence as a strategy for social change was cremated in the flames of the urban riots of the last two years. They tell us that Negroes have only now begun to find their true manhood in violence; that the riots prove not only that Negroes hate whites, but that, compulsively, they must destroy them.

This blood-lust interpretation ignores one of the most striking features of the city riots. Violent they certainly were. But the violence, to a startling degree, was focused against property rather than against people. There were very few cases of injury to persons, and the vast majority of the rioters were not involved at all in attacking people. The much publicized "death toll" that marked the riots, and the many injuries, were overwhelmingly inflicted on the rioters by the military. It is clear that the riots were exacerbated by police action that was designed to injure or even to kill people. As for the snipers, no account of the riots claims that more than one or two dozen people were involved in sniping. From the facts, an unmistakable pattern emerges: a handful of Negroes used gunfire substantially to intimidate, not to kill; and all of the other participants had a different target—property.

I am aware that there are many who wince at a distinction between property and persons—who hold both sacrosanct. My views are not so rigid. A life is sacred. Property is intended to serve life, and no matter how much we surround it with rights and respect, it has no personal being. It is part of the earth man walks on; it is not man.

The focus on property in the 1967 riots is not accidental. It has a message; it is saying something.

If hostility to whites were ever going to dominate a Negro's attitude and reach murderous proportions, surely it would be during a riot. But this rare opportunity for bloodletting was sublimated into arson, or turned into a kind of stormy carnival of free-merchandise distribution. Why did the rioters avoid personal attacks? The explanation cannot be fear of retribution, because the physical risks incurred in the attacks on property were no less than for personal assaults. The military forces were treating acts of petty larceny as equal to murder. Far more rioters took chances with their own lives, in their attacks on property, than threatened the life of anyone else. Why were they so violent with property then? Because property represents the white power structure, which they were attacking and trying to destroy. A curious proof of the symbolic aspect of the looting for some who took part in it is the fact that, after the riots, police received hundreds of calls from Negroes trying to return merchandise they had taken. Those people wanted the experience of taking, of redressing the power imbalance that property represents. Possession, afterward, was secondary.

A deeper level of hostility came out in arson, which was far more dangerous than the looting. But it, too, was a demonstration and a warning. It was directed against symbols of exploitation, and it was designed to express the depth of anger in the community.

What does this restraint in the summer riots mean for our future strategy?

If one can find a core of nonviolence toward persons, even during the riots when emotions were exploding, it means that nonviolence should not be written off for the future as a force in Negro life. Many people believe that the urban Negro is too angry and too sophisticated to be nonviolent. Those same people dismiss the nonviolent marches in the South and try to describe them as processions of pious, elderly ladies. The fact is that in all the marches we have organized some men of very violent tendencies have been involved. It was routine for us to collect hundreds of knives from our own ranks before the demonstrations, in case of momentary weakness. And in Chicago last year we saw some of the most violent individuals accepting nonviolent discipline. Day after day during those Chicago marches I walked in our lines and I never saw anyone retaliate with violence. There were lots of provocations, not only the screaming white hoodlums lining the sidewalks, but also groups of Negro militants talking about guerrilla warfare. We had some gang leaders and members marching with us. I remember walking with the Blackstone Rangers while bottles were flying from the sidelines, and I saw their noses being broken and blood flowing from their wounds; and I saw them continue and not retaliate, not one of them, with violence. I am convinced that even very violent temperaments can be channeled through nonviolent discipline, if the movement is moving, if they can act constructively and express through an effective channel their very legitimate anger.

But even if nonviolence can be valid, psychologically, for the protesters who want change, is it going to be effective, strategically, against a government and a status quo that have so far resisted this summer's demands on the grounds that "we must not reward the rioters"? Far from rewarding the rioters, far from even giving a hearing to their just and urgent demands, the Administration has ignored its responsibility for the causes of the riots, and instead has used the negative aspects of them to justify continued inaction on the underlying issues. The Administration's only concrete response was to initiate a study and call for a day of prayer. As a minister, I take prayer too seriously to use it as an excuse for avoiding work and responsibility. When a government commands more wealth and power than has ever been known in the history of the world, and offers no more than this, it is worse than blind, it is provocative. It is paradoxical but fair to say that Negro terrorism is incited less on ghetto street corners than in the halls of Congress.

I intended to show that nonviolence will be effective, but not until it has achieved the massive dimensions, the disciplined planning, and the intense commitment of a sustained, direct-action movement of civil disobedience on the national scale.

The dispossessed of this nation—the poor, both white and Negro—live in a cruelly unjust society. They must organize a revolution against that injustice, not against the lives of the persons who are their fellow citizens, but against the structures through which the society is refusing to take means which have been called for, and which are at hand, to lift the load of poverty.

The only real revolutionary, people say, is a man who has nothing to lose. There are millions of poor people in this country who have very little, or even nothing, to lose. If they can be helped to take action together, they will do so with a freedom and a power that will be a new and unsettling force in our complacent national life. Beginning in the New Year, we will be recruiting three thousand of the poorest citizens from ten different urban and rural areas to initiate and lead a sustained, massive, direct-action movement in Washington. Those who choose to join this initial three thousand, this nonviolent army, this "freedom church" of the poor, will work with us for three months to develop nonviolent action skills. Then we will move on Washington, determined to stay there until the legislative and executive branches of the government take serious and adequate action on jobs and income. A delegation of poor people can walk into a high official's office with a carefully, collectively prepared list of demands. (If you're poor, if you're unemployed anyway, you can choose to stay in Washington as long as the struggle needs you.) And if that official says, "But Congress would have to approve this," or, "But the President would have to be consulted on that," you can say, "All right, we'll wait." And you can settle down in his office for as long a stay as necessary. If you are, let's say, from rural Mississippi, and have never had medical attention, and your children are undernourished and unhealthy, you can take those little children into the Washington hospitals and stay with them there until the medical workers cope with their needs, and in showing it your children you will have shown this country a sight that will make it stop in its busy tracks and think hard about what it has done. The many people who will come and join this three thousand, from all groups in the country's life, will play a supportive role, deciding to be poor for a time along with the dispossessed who are asking for their right to jobs or income—jobs, income, the demolition of slums and the rebuilding by the people who live there of new communities in their place; in fact, a new economic deal for the poor.

Why camp in Washington to demand these things? Because only the federal Congress and Administration can decide to use the billions of dollars we need for a real war on poverty. We need, not a new law, but a massive, new national program. This Congress has done nothing to help such measures, and plenty to hinder them. Why should Congress care about our dying cities? It is still dominated by senior representatives of the rural South, who still unite in an obstructive coalition with unprogressive Northerners to prevent public funds from going where they are socially needed. We broke that coalition in 1963 and 1964, when the Civil Rights and Voting Rights laws were passed. We need to break it again by the size and force of our movement, and the best place to do that is before the eyes and inside the buildings of these same congressmen. The people of this country, if not the congressmen, are ready for a serious economic attack on slums and unemployment, as two recent polls by Lou Harris have revealed. So we have to make Congress ready to act on the plight of the poor. We will prod and sensitize the legislators, the administrators, and all the wielders of power until they have faced this utterly imperative need.

I have said that the problem, the crisis we face, is international in scope. In fact, it is inseparable from an international emergency which involves the poor, the dispossessed, and the exploited of the whole world.

Can a nonviolent, direct-action movement find application on the international level, to confront economic and political problems? I believe it can. It is clear to me that the next stage of the movement is to become international. National movements within the developed countries—forces that focus on London, or Paris, or Washington, or Ottawa—must help to make it politically feasible for their governments to undertake the kind of massive aid that the developing countries need if they are to break the chains of poverty. We in the West must bear in mind that the poor countries are poor primarily because we have exploited them through political or economic colonialism. Americans in particular must help their nation repent of her modern economic imperialsim.

But movements in our countries alone will not be enough. In Latin America, for example, national reform movements have almost despaired of nonviolent methods; many young men, even many priests, have joined guerrilla movements in the hills. So many of Latin America's problems have roots in the United States of America that we need to form a solid, united movement, nonviolently conceived and carried through, so that pressure can be brought to bear on the capital and government power structures concerned, from both sides of the problem at once. I think that may be the only hope for a nonviolent solution in Latin America today; and one of the most powerful expressions of nonviolence may come out of that international coalition of socially aware forces, operating outside governmental frameworks.

Even entrenched problems like the South African Government and its racial policies could be tackled on this level. If just two countries, Britain and the United States, could be persuaded to end all economic interaction with the South African regime, they could bring that government to its knees in a relatively short time. Theoretically, the British and American governments could make that kind of decision; almost every corporation in both countries has economic ties with its government which it could not afford to do without. In practice, such a decision would represent such a major reordering of priorities that we should not expect that any movement could bring it about in one year or two. Indeed, although it is obvious that nonviolent movements for social change must internationalize, because of the interlocking nature of the problems they all face, and because otherwise those problems will breed war, we have hardly begun to build the skills and the strategy, or even the commitment, to planetize our movement for social justice.

In a world facing the revolt of ragged and hungry masses of God's children; in a world torn between the tensions of East and West, white and colored, individualists and collectivists; in a world whose cultural and spiritual power lags so far behind her technological capabilities that we live each day on the verge of nuclear co-annihilation; in this world, nonviolence is no longer an option for intellectual analysis, it is an imperative for action.

Collateral Reading

Bosmajian, H. A., "Rhetoric of Martin Luther King's Letter from Birmingham Jail," *Midwest Quarterly,* VIII (January, 1967), 127-143.

Cook, S. D., "Martin Luther King," *Journal of Negro History,* LIII (October, 1968), 348-354.

King, Martin Luther, Jr., *Stride Toward Freedom.* New York, 1958.
————, *Where Do We Go From Here? Community or Chaos?* Boston, 1968.

————, *Why We Can't Wait.* New York, 1963.

Melhuish, Lucy Anne, "Rhetoric of Racial Revolt." Unpublished Master's thesis, University of Oregon, 1964.

Sharma, M. L., "Martin Luther King: Modern America's Greatest Theologian of Social Action," *Journal of Negro History,* LIII (July, 1968), 257-263.

Warren, Mervyn A., "A Rhetorical Study of the Preaching of Dr. Martin Luther King, Jr., Pastor and Pulpit Orator." Unpublished Ph.D. dissertation, Michigan State University, 1966.

Study Questions and Problems

1. Describe the tone of the "Nonviolence and Social Change" speech. Does King sound defensive and apologetic?

2. Argue the merit of nonviolence as a technique for social protest. What arguments can be made for and against its use?

3. Read the *Report of the National Advisory Commission on Civil Disorders.* Is Dr. King's analysis of the violence of 1967 validated by this report?

4. How would you describe the language of "I Have a Dream"? Do you think that the language was suitable to the occasion?

5. Discuss the importance of repetition as an interest device using King's "I Have a Dream" as an illustration of the effective use of repetition.

6. Read some of King's published speeches found in Martin Luther King, Jr., *Trumpet of Conscience,* and formulate a judgment about Dr. King's effectiveness as a speaker.

7. What were some of the factors beyond Martin Luther King's speeches which created high credibility for him among white and black citizens alike?

8. What factors within King's speeches created high credibility?

Roy Wilkins

Roy Wilkins was born in St. Louis, Missouri, in 1901. He grew up in St. Paul, Minnesota, and received his A.B. from the University of Minnesota in 1923. One account of Wilkins' life tells of a speech which he gave while a university student. Prompted by a mass lynching that occurred in Duluth, Minnesota, Wilkins entered the university oratorical contest and won first prize with his antilynching speech.

During his forty years of service with the NAACP, Wilkins was associated with numerous activities of the civil rights organization. In 1934 he succeeded W. E. B. Du Bois as editor of the NAACP journal, Crisis. In 1949 he was appointed Acting Executive Secretary of the NAACP, and in 1955 he was unanimously elected as the Executive Secretary of the organization.

Over the years, Wilkins has emerged as a spokesman for a moderate approach to the contemporary racial crisis, thus exposing himself to the charge by more militant blacks that he is an "Uncle Tom."

As a speaker Wilkins has expressed a philosophy of social change within the bounds of law, believing in the effectiveness of court decisions, corrective legislation, and direct action protest in contrast to the notions of violent confrontation and black separatism.

Roy Wilkins' "Keynote Address" to the 57th Annual Convention of the NAACP in Los Angeles, California, July 5, 1966, is an excellent example of adapting a speech to the times and to the convictions of the audience.

Wilkins began his speech by observing that the convention was meeting at a critical moment in the history of the civil rights movement. He noted that divergent forces were arising within the civil rights movement. He argued that historically the NAACP had defended the right of blacks to retaliate in self-defense, but he indicted the separatist concept of Black Power as morally reprehensible.

He then stated the immediate program of the NAACP in strong and forceful terms, calling for continuation of (1) voter registration, (2) efforts *to improve employment opportunities for Negro workers, (3) agitation to end discrimination in housing, (4) improvement of unsegregated, high quality education, and (5) the struggle with the complex social problems of millions of urban black citizens.*

Finally, Wilkins praised the work of the numerous local chapters for the contributions which they had made in the past year. He cited a number of examples of unusually praiseworthy local NAACP groups.

Of special rhetorical importance is the forceful and aggressive tone of the address. Rather than presenting an apologia, Wilkins took the offensive by attacking "black power" and outlining a positive-action program. The speech illustrates the principle that the best defense is a good offense. It is rhetorically interesting because of the speaker's excellent use of illustration and anecdotes and because of his effective adaptation to the audience and occasion.

Sail Our NAACP Ship—Keynote Address
July 5, 1966

In the transition period of the civil rights movement, 1966 is developing into a critical year.

The 57th annual convention of our NAACP is thus a gathering of more than ordinary significance.

All about us are alarums and confusions as well as great and challenging developments. Differences of opinion are sharper. For the first time since several organizations began to function where only two had functioned before, there emerges what seems to be a difference in goals.

Heretofore there were some differences in methods and in emphases, but none in ultimate goals. The end was always to be the inclusion of the Negro American, without racial discrimination, as a full-fledged equal in all phases of American citizenship. The targets were whatever barriers, crude or subtle, which blocked the attainment of that goal.

There has now emerged, first, a strident and threatening challenge to a strategy widely employed by civil rights groups, namely, nonviolence. One organization, which has been meeting in Baltimore, has passed a resolution declaring for defense of themselves by Negro citizens if they are attacked.

This position is not new as far as the NAACP is concerned. Historically our Association has defended in court those persons who have defended themselves and their homes with firearms. Extradition cases are not as frequent or as fashionable as they once were, but in past years we have fought the extradition of men who had used firearms to defend themselves when attacked.

We freed seventy-nine Arkansas sharecroppers in a four-year court battle beginning in 1919. They had returned gunfire directed at a meeting they were holding in a church.

We employed the late Clarence Darrow in 1926 to defend a man and his family when a member of a mob threatening his newly-purchased Detroit home was shot and killed. The NAACP has subscribed to nonviolence as a humane as well as a practical necessity in the realities of the American scene, but we have never required this as a deep personal commitment of our members. We never signed a pact either on paper or in our hearts to turn the other cheek forever and ever when we were assaulted.

But neither have we couched a policy of manly resistance in such a way that our members and supporters felt compelled to maintain themselves in an armed state, ready to retaliate instantly and in kind whenever attacked. We venture the observation that such a publicized posture could serve to stir counter-planning, counter-action and possible conflict. If carried out literally as instant retaliation, in cases adjudged by aggrieved persons to have been grossly unjust, this policy could produce—in extreme situations—lynchings, or, in better-sounding phraseology, private, vigilante vengeance.

Moreover, in attempting to substitute for derelict law enforcement machinery, the policy entails the risk of a broader, more indiscriminate crackdown by law officers under the ready-made excuse of restoring law and order.

It seems reasonable to assume that proclaimed protective violence is as likely to encourage counter-violence as it is to discourage violent persecution.

But the more serious division in the civil rights movement is the one posed by a word formulation that implies clearly a difference in goals.

No matter how endlessly they try to explain it, the term "black power" means anti-white power. In a racially pluralistic society, the concept, the formation and the exercise of an ethnically-tagged power, means opposition to other ethnic powers, just as the term "white supremacy" means subjection of all non-white people. In the black-white relationship, it has to mean that every other ethnic power is the rival and the antagonist of "black power." It has to mean "going-it-alone." It has to mean separatism.

Now, separatism, whether on the rarefied debate level of "black power" or on the wishful level of a secessionist Freedom City in Watts, offers a disadvantaged minority little except the chance to shrivel and die.

The only possible dividend of "black power" is embodied in its offer to millions of frustrated and deprived and persecuted black people of a solace, a tremendous psychological lift, quite apart from its political and economic implications.

Ideologically it dictates "up with black and down with white" in precisely the same fashion that South Africa reverses that slogan.

It is a reverse Mississippi, a reverse Hitler, a reverse Ku Klux Klan.

If these were evil in our judgment, what virtue can be claimed for black over white? If, as some proponents claim, this concept instills pride of race, cannot this pride be taught without preaching hatred or supremacy based upon race?

Though it be clarified and clarified again, "black power" in the quick, uncritical and highly emotional adoption it has received from some segments of a beleaguered people can mean in the end only black death. Even if, through some miracle, it should be enthroned briefly in an isolated area, the human spirit, which knows no color or geography or time, would die a little, leaving for wiser and stronger and more compassionate men the painful beating back to the upward trail.

We of the NAACP will have none of this. We have fought it too long. It is the ranging of race against race on the irrelevant basis of skin color. It is the father of hatred and the mother of violence.

It is the wicked fanaticism which has swelled our tears, broken our bodies, squeezed our hearts and taken the blood of our black and white loved ones. It shall not now poison our forward march.

We seek, therefore, as we have sought these many years, the inclusion of Negro Americans in the nation's life, not their exclusion. This is our land, as much so as it is any American's—every square foot of every city and town and village. The task of winning our share is not the easy one of disengagement and flight, but the hard one of work, of short as well as long jumps, of disappointments, and of sweet successes.

In our Fight for Freedom we choose:

1. The power and the majesty of the ballot, the participation of free men in their government, both as voters and as honorable and competent elected and appointed public servants. Year in and year out, the NAACP voter registration work has proceeded. No one except the Federal Government has registered more Negro voters in Mississippi than the NAACP. In six weeks last summer more than twenty thousand new names were added by our workers alone, with additional thousands during an intensive renewal last winter. That work is continuing under the leadership of our Mississippi state president, Dr. Aaron Henry, and

of our state director, Charles Evers. Later this month a summer task force will be at work in Louisiana. Already our South Carolina NAACP is busy on registration, as is our Alabama organization.

We are aware that a Louisiana young man, born along the Mississippi border, has been named and confirmed as one of the seven governors of the Federal Reserve Bank. We know that his extraordinary ability finally tipped the scales, but we know also, that, without ballot power, he would not even have been on the scales ready to be tipped.

2. We choose employment for our people—jobs not hidden by racial labels or euphemisms, not limited by racial restrictions in access and promotion, whether by employers or organized labor. We commend a growing number of corporations for expanding their employment of Negro applicants in technical and professional posts, but we insist that only the surface has been scratched.

We commend the "good guys" among the trade unions for the improvement in opportunities and advancement for the Negro worker, but we condemn the policies of some unions which have either barred or heavily handicapped the Negro worker. Negro employment is in a crisis stage. The rate of unemployment ranges from twice that of whites to four and five times the white rate in some areas. The answer to the complaint of employers that workers are not trained is to institute in-plant training, just as they have in other shortages. The apprentice training stranglehold must be broken, the racially separate seniority lines, the still-persisting segregated local and the remaining crude segregation in plant facilities must be abolished. The demonstrations before the U.S. Steel Corporation offices and plants under the cooperative leadership of Dr. John Nixon, our Alabama president, and Henry Smith, our Pennsylvania president, had wide and beneficial impact.

The Negro migrant worker, the forgotten man in the employment picture, must have attention.

In the Watts district of Los Angeles last year the unemployment rate was more than 30 per cent, a rate higher than that during the great, nationwide Depression of the Nineteen Thirties. The Negro teenage rate is nearly 25 per cent as against 13 per cent for white teenagers.

Negro employment is a disaster area demanding the strict enforcement of Title VII of the 1964 Civil Rights Act. The NAACP has filed more than one thousand complaints with the Equal Employment Opportunity Commission and will file more until the law accomplishes what it was enacted to do. As evidence of his continuing concern, Congressman Augustus Hawkins of Los Angeles succeeded in having his bill relating to federal employment passed by the House as an amendment to Title VII of the 1964 Civil Rights Act.

3. We choose to combat the color line in housing. In one breath our opinion-makers decry the existence of the poverty and filth and crime and degradation of the slums, but in the next they decry low-cost housing and fair housing laws. Here in California the hysteria over whether Negro Americans should live in gullies or be pushed into the sea reached the Proposition 14 stage which the state's highest court has declared unconstitutional. But who cares about the Constitution when a Negro might be enabled to move into the neighborhood? One could think black Americans were men from Mars. Instead, we have been here, side by side with the white folks (some of whom just got here), for 345 years.

They tell us to work hard and save our money, to go to school and prepare ourselves, to be "responsible," to rear and educate our children in a wholesome and directed family atmosphere, to achieve, to "get up in the world."

After we do all this, they look us in the eye and bar us from renting or buying a home that matches our achievements and one in keeping with our aspirations for further advancement.

Some public officials, including mayors of cities, and many candidates for election to public office are not above public double talk and private single talk on this issue. Any candidate who orates about basic Americanism or "the American way," but who hems and haws over fair housing legislation is no friend of the Negro citizen.

The Administration's civil rights bill of 1966 with its vital section barring discrimination in the rental or sale of housing must be enacted with the amendment, already inserted by the committee, providing for administrative redress as well as court action.

Your congressmen and senators are at home until July 11 celebrating Independence Day—Freedom Day for the United States. See them or have your branch officers back home see them in person. Urge them to rub some freedom off on twenty million loyal Americans by voting for a strong civil rights bill. Of course the section on punishing in the federal courts those who attack civil rights workers must pass. And we must have indemnification for victims.

4. Most of all, we choose to secure unsegregated, high quality public education for ourselves and our children. A new report, made public only last week, is a jolt for anyone who thought the 1954 Supreme Court decision or subsequent legislation solved the problem.

The report says officially and professionally what we have contended all along: that predominantly Negro schools are inferior to those attended largely by whites. Also that the achievement gap widens between the first grade and the twelfth. In other words, the longer our children attend racially segregated schools, the farther they fall behind white children.

And, lest the non-Southerners feel smug, the report found that segregation for both whites and Negroes is more complete in the South, but "is extensive in other regions where the Negro population is concentrated: the urban North, Midwest and West."

The Federal Government, whose Office of Education has made some strong statements, must follow up with a strong enforcement of Title VI of the 1964 law. The empty promises of school officials and the defiance of the whole State of Alabama must not be accepted meekly by federal officials. The furor over the guidelines issued by HEW is another version of the Dixie bluff on race which has worked so well for so many decades. The guidelines are mild. They are legal and not illegal as Governor Wallace proclaimed to his state's educators. They ask the Southerners to do what is for them a strange thing: obey the school desegregation law. On this point the Federal Government must not yield. The Attorney General and the Department of Justice must back up resolutely the legality of federal action. There can be no temporizing.

Outside the South the call is for unrelenting activity to wipe out de facto school segregation. Boston, Massachusetts, has proved to be the Mississippi of the North. In fact, in fairness to Mississippi and in consideration of the starting points and traditions of the two places, Boston is *below* Mississippi on this issue. The details, the traps, the methods and the progress will be covered in workshop discussions, but here it must be said that before we can get jobs to earn increased income to buy and rent better homes, before we can contribute to the enrichment of our nation, we must have free access to quality education.

The man who shoots and burns and drowns us is surely our enemy, but so is he who cripples our children for life with inferior public education.

5. We also choose to wrestle with the complex problems of urban life, all of which include an attitude toward and a treatment of millions of Negro citizens. The solution of urban problems will become the solution of living in the last third of our century since more than 70 per cent of Americans now live in urban communities.

If it has been asked once, it has been asked a hundred times: Are we going to have a long, hot summer? The answer has many facets, some extremely complex and difficult. But one quick answer is that the police everywhere can make or break urban racial tensions by their conduct toward minority group citizens.

Last summer you had here an upheaval that shook the world. To many of us who looked from afar, it appeared to be a wild, senseless rampage of hate and destruction. But that was far from the whole truth.

There was powder in Watts, piled up and packed down through the years: wide-scale unemployment, both adult and teenage, slum housing, crowded schools, non-existent health facilities, inadequate transportation and—the Parker police attitude. Everyone was suspect and everyone was subject to harassment in one form or another. The community smoldered under the peculiar brand that police place upon a whole section with their constant sirens, their contemptuous searches, their rough talk, their ready guns and their general "Godalmightiness."

The lesson they and city officials have learned from last year is to seek not correction and improvement, but still more repression. Mayor Yorty and whoever writes his scripts testified in Sacramento in support of a so-called riot-control bill.

The only thing one has to remember about this bill is that it would allow a policeman to judge whether an utterance or an act is an incitement to riot! On his own judgment he could arrest or club or otherwise deter—or shoot—a person whom he (not the law or the courts) deemed to be an inciter of riot. Down the drain goes freedom of speech and down, too, possibly, goes a life.

The McCone Report on the 1965 riot called for "costly and extreme" remedies for Watts, undertaken with a "revolutionary attitude." The answer of the City of Los Angeles was to vote down a hospital bond issue. The answer of Mayor Yorty and of his man, Chief Parker, is a trampling-tough riot-control bill which, if enacted, would loose the police, almost without restraint, upon a populace sick to death—literally—of race control. To blot out any remaining fitful light, one of the gubernatorial candidates, full of disavowals, is the darling of those ultraconservatives who believe in iron control of what they call "violence in the streets"—their code name for Negroes.

If this is the best that a great city can bring to a hard urban problem, one largely of its own making, then God pity both the whites and the Negroes!

We have no panacea for all these problems. We do not proclaim that what we declare here this week is going to change the course of the whole civil rights movement. We do not know all the answers to the George Wallace problem in Alabama, the James Eastland problem in Mississippi, or to the Boston, Massachusetts, school committee and its Louise Day Hicks problem. We certainly don't know the answers to foreign policy and to tax and interest rate puzzlers.

But in this unsettled time when shifts are the order of the day and when change is in the air, we can sail our NAACP ship "steady as she goes," with more drive to the turbines, more skill at the wheel, but no fancy capers for the sake of capers.

We can follow down into each community the really advanced blueprint of the White House Conference "To Fulfill These Rights," which covered four principal areas: economic security and welfare, education, housing, and the administration of justice.

We can expand and point up the community services of our NAACP branches, each of which is, in reality, a citizenship clinic. Just as medical clinics need specialists to cure physical ills, so our branch clinics should recruit volunteer specialists to diagnose and minister to social ills.

We must involve people in the communities in the solution of our problem—not limiting ourselves to our church or lodge or club group.

We must keep the pressure on our local and state education systems through the employment of every legitimate technique: protests, surveys, discussions, demonstrations, picketing and negotiation. Nothing should be overlooked in fighting for better education. Be persistent and ornery; this will be good for the lethargic educational establishment and will aid the whole cause of public education.

Our branches are at work in their territories. In Baltimore, the NAACP won a case against the police commissioner which the Fourth Circuit Court of Appeals declared revealed the most flagrant police practices ever to come before the court. The Blair County, Pennsylvania, NAACP is busy rooting out the remaining discrimination in public accommodations in Clearfield, Pennsylvania.

The Wilmington, Ohio, NAACP has a program for tutoring adults and drop-outs and has recruited college professors and students and textbooks to make the project effective. The Bay City, Michigan, NAACP also has a tutorial program under way as well as continuous work on industrial employment practices and housing. The Stillwater, Oklahoma, NAACP is active on a child care center project and on high school desegregation.

And the Montgomery County, West Virginia, NAACP, bless its heart, is 112 per cent above last year in membership and 500 per cent above last year in funds raised.

Thirty-one branches found time and funds to be present at the Meredith march rally in Jackson, Mississippi, even though the Association, at the last minute, was insulted by the barring of Charles Evers as an NAACP spokesman.

This is only part of the chronicle of "steady as she goes." In a world where the Mayor of Los Angeles is yelling "riot control," where Rhodesia says "never!" to black representation while in America SNCC raises the chant of black power, where the Federal Government at long last is committed, but both the far right and the far left offer vocal and vicious objection, someone has to drive the long haul toward the group goal of Negro Americans and the larger ideal of our young nation.

Our objective is basically as it was laid down in 1909 by the interracial founders of our NAACP. Back there William Lloyd Garrison [speaker means Oswald Garrison Villard] expressed the strong feeling that the first NAACP conference "will utter no uncertain sound on any point affecting the vital subject. No part of it is too delicate for plain speech. The republican experiment is at stake, every tolerated wrong to the Negro reacting with double force upon white citizens guilty of faithlessness to their brothers."

As it was then, so it is today. The republican experiment *is* at stake in 1966. More than that, the dream of a brotherhood in equality and justice is imperiled.

Our fraternity tonight, as it was then, is the fraternity of man, not the white, or brown, or yellow, or black man, but man.

Collateral Reading

Ferris, Maxine S., "The Speaking of Roy Wilkins," *Central States Speech Journal,* XVI (1965), 91-98.

Hughes, Langston, *Fight for Freedom: The Story of the NAACP.* New York, 1962.

Marshall, Thurgood and Roy Wilkins, "Interpretations of the Supreme Court Decisions and the NAACP Program," *Crisis,* LXII (July, 1955), 329-334.

St. James, Warren D., *The NAACP: A Case Study in Pressure Groups.* New York, 1958.

Wilkins, Roy, "Whither 'Black Power'?" *Crisis,* LXXIII (September, 1966), 353-354.

Study Questions and Problems

1. Evaluate Wilkins' position on "black power." In your opinion, does the NAACP leader thoroughly understand the concept?

2. The NAACP social-action program has been criticized as catering to white liberals and middle-class blacks. Do you think such criticism is accurate?

3. What figure of speech is used in Wilkins' address to denote a continuation of the NAACP's traditional program?

4. Argue for or against Wilkins' view that separation of the races is not in the best interest of American society.

5. Discuss whether or not legal redress is a viable means for eliminating racial discrimination.

Whitney M. Young, Jr.

Whitney M. Young, Jr., was born in 1921 at Lincoln Ridge, Kentucky. He received a B.S. from Kentucky State College and an M.A. from the University of Minnesota. In 1954 Young was appointed Dean of the School of Social Work at Atlanta University in Georgia. He became Executive Director of the National Urban League in 1961.

Young's speech "Can the City Survive?" was delivered on October 28, 1968, before a luncheon at the 54th Annual Fall Conference of the National Association of Bank Loan and Credit Officers. The speech was delivered before predominantly white bank officials who represented perhaps the most powerful economic group in the nation. Young's main purpose was to talk about expanding employment opportunities for black people. He also sought to inform his audience about the economic and social condition of blacks in contemporary America and to present an entertaining and interesting speech at the same time.

The speech develops the concept that the country is in a deep crisis created by the anger of the disadvantaged and the sensitivity of the younger generation to the inequities in American society. Young revised the question "Can the city survive?" by including the qualifying phrase "with honor and justice?" According to Young, the inequities between the haves and the have-nots can be eliminated if intelligent people, working for their own self-interest, would take immediate and effective action to improve economic and educational opportunities for black people. The Urban League Executive Secretary refuted the idea that blacks can be assimilated into the American economic and social system in the same way as earlier ethnic groups. To the speaker, segregation was an ever-increasing reality for black people. He lauded the black power movement and local control of education as healthy indications of black people's attempting to solve their problems.

Young urged the bank officials to hire more blacks at all levels of employment. He further suggested that they do something about attitudes regarding housing and education in the community where they live.

Can the City Survive?

October 28, 1968

I'm sure all of us experienced a variety of reactions to the recent successful space flight. For my own part, as I thought of the manned flight, loping around the globe, I was quite aware that the shrill beeps which came back to us told us of temperature and radiation and all of the secrets of the ionosphere. But I'm sure that they should have told us something vastly more important; namely, that this tiny planet which we are all privileged to inhabit has now become so shriveled and so diminished that every man is, in fact, every other man's next door neighbor. In this kind of enforced intimacy, friendship with other human beings, to the intelligent person, must become our most prized possession. We must make friends and be friends with all mankind. As Dr. Martin Luther King used to put it, "We will either live together in this world as brothers, or we will surely die together as fools."

Only the most hopeless optimist would fail to acknowledge that our country is in deep crisis. The issues before us are several. We face a depolarization, a division between the young and the unyoung, between black and white, and between urban and rural populations. This is not a crisis that one can easily dismiss. It is one, I assure you, that is not a fad or a phenomena of a few months. The real situation is that the disinherited, the poor, the disadvantaged (many of whom are black in our society) are today a different breed than in the past.

They are determined, they are impatient, they are angry, and unlike the past, they are fully aware of the gap between themselves and other Americans. They are no longer concentrated in rural areas—share croppers on some isolated Southern farm where they have not the benefit of modern communication media. Today, for the most part, the disadvantaged are located in urban areas, side by side with affluence where they witness how the other half lives through their television sets or their newspapers.

They're not only aware of the difference in their status and that of other human beings, but they are also aware that that status was not God-made and God-decreed but man-made. They're not at all of a mood to assume that they are congenitally inferior but rather that they are victims of a historically selfish, callous, and sometimes brutal society. Furthermore, the disinherited today are quite aware of how other groups who felt themselves previously suppressed went about righting the wrongs and securing for themselves the advantages and the privileges and the elimination of injustice. They are aware how America rid itself of the domination of England. They are aware of how the labor movement brought about its economic freedom. They are aware of the struggles of women to get suffrage. They are aware of all of the fights of other ethnic groups and all of the techniques that they have used. And so today, they feel it is in the best American tradition to engage in similar kinds of activities that so many of us are so quick to forget.

Another very important addition and new dimension to this struggle is that the disadvantaged today are joined by a very strong and powerful new ally—namely, young people. And I do not refer to the "hippies" and the "yippies." I'm talking about all young people—your daughters

Whitney M. Young, Jr.   *Los Angeles Times Photo*

and sons as well as mine. The young people of our country today are, themselves, of a different breed—though some of you may wish to console yourselves by saying, "Well, this is normal. Young people have, historically, in their teens been radical only to become liberals in their twenties and conservatives in their thirties and finally, reactionaries in their forties." This won't happen with this young generation for a very good and valid reason. For the most part, they have never known great poverty.

Over 80% of the young people in our society today were born to inherit a certain amount of economic security. They have had things, they have taken them for granted and so their preoccupation with material things, understandably, is not the same as our generation's might have been because we knew poverty. It will not be as easy to seduce them and to co-opt them into a system which at best they are cynical about and at worst they are contemptuous of. I say this as one who speaks to young people in, literally, dozens (maybe a hundred) of universities, colleges, and high schools around the country. And I'm deeply impressed by their awareness of the gross inequities, by their accurate documentation of the inconsistencies and the hypocrisy in our society, and by their attitudes toward the adult behavior. I think we ignore this new dimension at our peril both as individual parents and as collective leaders of the society with a great stake in it.

Unfortunately, the response to this new challenge to our society has not been a good one. We have, for the most part, responded with ideas of suppression rather than massive programs of prevention. We have responded with making George Wallace a serious candidate for President—a man who is the very epitome of racism and bigotry; a man who created a climate in his own state which gave license to the bombing of little children in churches and the bombing of many other churches and to the suppression and persecution of people; a man who has defied the highest court of the land and the highest laws of the land; a man who conducted his own civil disobedience campaign and who has preached race against race. And when he becomes a serious candidate for President, we, as a country, are in deep trouble. It comes as no surprise to black people. It comes as no surprise to the Kerner Commission (composed of conservatives and for the most part an all white group) who, after intensive exploration announced that we were, in fact, guilty of racism in the country.

The question is often asked, "Can the City Survive?" I think we can qualify that and say, "Can the City Survive with Order?", and say yes, I suppose. Russia would claim that it has brought about order in Prague and has continued the survival of Prague, I suppose the leaders of South Africa would say they had brought about the survival of Johannesburg

and there exists order. I'm sure Hitler felt that after the conscious exter-
mination of some six million people in ovens and concentration camps
in Germany and a few million others throughout Europe that he had
brought about order in those communities and in Berlin; that with his
massive secret police, his Gestapo, that he had brought about perfect
order. And there are those in our society who would contend that we
too can bring about order through similar kinds of methods. The issue
to me, though, isn't whether we can survive with order because I don't
think we can. The issue is can we survive with honor, with justice, with
some semblance of values that better bespeak the American credo and
our Judeo-Christian ethic. I think we as a nation can, but it won't be
easy.

I know of no group of people in this society who are better equipped,
in fact who must inevitably provide the leadership in the business community, than the bankers in the business community. For better or for
worse (I'm not always sure which) you occupy a status, a leadership
role. You occupy a position of influence. You are the role model. Historically, in American society the banker has been the person that people
looked up to. You can't have it both ways, gentlemen. You cannot,
as you so often do, accept the plaudits for all of the great things that
have happened in America for our unprecedented technological and
industrial advances, for our great gross national product. You can't accept
credit for all of the television sets and automobiles in mass production
and then silently slip off to the side and defer any blame for the things
that have happened in America that are not too good. And I know
of no other group that has a greater stake in the bringing about of
stability in our society. But I can assure you that stability and order
are but pious hopes and dreams if we do not, in fact, eliminate the
inequities between the haves and the have-nots in our society.

This will not be an easy task. It will require guts, it will require the
same kind of coming together collectively of the intelligent people in
our society—people who may not even be compassionate and humane,
but who at least are intelligent and who are concerned about their own
self-interest—it will require their coming together in the type of response
this country showed when it faced other crises. I can remember when
Sputnick first shot out of Russia. Overnight we had a massive program
and a timetable and an allocation of funds to assure that in a short
time we, too, would have our space program under way. I can remember
in the early 1930's when there was about to be a major, a true revolution
in this country when white people were all out of work. Overnight this
country passed massive measures to put people to work—NYA, FERA,
WPA, CCC, Social Security, and all kinds of welfare programs. I know

how we of the country have responded to war. Overnight, when asked to build 10,000 planes, we build 100,000. I know how we responded after the war with over $17 billion in the massive Marshall Plan to rebuild Western Europe, even West Germany.

And so today, in the land of our former enemies, there are no slums, there is little unemployment. There is none of the kind of talk that you heard in the business council meeting recently where in order to get rid of inflation we might have to up the unemployment rate from 3½ to 4 to 5 and 5½. This is said by people who themselves I'm sure are not willing to become unemployed. But to black people this means 11½ to 12%. For a country with a gross national product of one trillion dollars, for a country with a kind of creativity and imagination, for a country whose cities are, literally, havens of despair, whose cities are growing blacker and older and deteriorating the very foundation, cities where we have problems of air pollution and water pollution and transportation, our answer to the problem of inflation is "let's increase the number of people who are unemployed."

Our response has also been to echo that familiar phrase, "We made it, why can't they." And there's no statement I know that's more hypocritical. The reason white people and earlier immigrants made it and black people have not made it is so simple and so clear that I find it difficult that people would even utter the phrase, "We made it, why can't they." The reason black people haven't made it is because we were the first and only involuntary immigrants to the country. For 250 years we were required to give free labor to the country as slaves during a period of time when it was illegal for us to marry and to produce families that were stable, and when it was unlawful for us to get an education. And then we have another 100 years of cheap labor because the economy then needed cheap labor.

In addition we had the added handicap of being black. We couldn't lose our identity by changing our last names like the two vice-presidential candidates, Mr. Agnew and Mr. Muskie. We couldn't have a little operation and sort of change some identifying feature. We did try a salve called "Black No More" and it didn't work so we decided to make black beautiful. And that's why so many people are going to the Caribbean and getting suntan these days. We've got a major campaign on—since we can't become white, we're going to make white people black.

The others made it because there was a period when immigrants were given land. Because they came to this country during a time when all you needed was a strong back and a willing mind—before it became a highly technological and industrial age. They made it because they were not only given land but were given very good loans at low interest

rates and then given farm agents by the Federal Government to teach
them how to farm and now they are being given money not to farm.
Others have made it because once they pursued a course of education
and acquired some of the culture and some of the sophistication they
could escape. They had freedom of choice. They could move where they
want to. But a man, if he was black, regardless of his education, was
caught in the ghetto. And so an Al Capone could move to Cicero, but
a Ralph Bunch could not and cannot now move to Cicero. Nor can
he move to Bronxville, New York—and there are many Bronxvilles and
Ciceros and Grosse Points that are much worse than some places in
the South. They don't have a sign like some of the Southern cities used
to have about "Nigger, don't let the sun set on you."

They do it much more subtly in the North—through real estate opera-
tors cooperating with people like you. You have helped to create this
mess in America. It has been the genius, imagination, and creativity
of your predecessors which led to the white noose around the central
cities. It has been you with the cooperation of the Federal Government
which had clearly written into its FHA rulings that such loans will be
guaranteed only if these communities were homogeneous and compatible.
All of us knew what that meant. The Federal Government built the
suburbs with your help. The Federal Government put public housing
all in the central city which led to the kind of immigration, containment,
and segregation that has increased in our society. And this situation
is not going to change unless, hopefully, we have developed a new
generation of people who have as much creativity, imagination, and
commitment to inclusion and to decency as your forefathers had to
exclusion and to cruelty, and to segregation in this society.

But it's got to take your leadership. We have responded in this society
by the familiar phrase that I heard after a speech to the home builders
not so long ago. A fellow got up and he said, "Mr. Young, I must
confess that I've lost sympathy with your people. I have been a great
friend and have loved your people very much and I've been very sympathetic, but because of the riots and the shouts of 'black power' I've
now lost sympathy." I told him I didn't want to debate with him the
logic in a decision to indict twenty million people, a whole ethnic group,
because of the excesses of a handful which, in itself, was unprecedented
in history. But I would like to find out precisely the extent of our loss
now that he'd lost sympathy. So I took out a pencil and a piece of
paper and I said, "Now, sir, would you mind telling me, before you
lost sympathy, how many subdivisions did you build? How many black
people did you employ and at what level? How many black people
did you help to get into your neighborhood, into your school, into your

country club, into your church?" I said, "Now, say it slowly so that I can write it down and document it for posterity—our great loss now that we have lost your sympathy." And he said, "Well, well, I didn't do any of those things." I pointed out that nothing from nothing leaves nothing and that did it ever occur to him that if he had been doing all these things when he loved my people so much and was so sympathetic then we wouldn't have had the riots and the shouts of "black power". And so I say to you that you forfeit your right to be indignant and to be angry and to lose sympathy if you have not been in the forefront doing these concrete tangible things—giving black people a piece of the action and a chance to share in the rewards of America and not just its responsibilities; the chance to live in America, not to just die for America in Vietnam in disproportionate numbers like we are doing at this present time.

Well, I've said what we shouldn't do; what should we do? I think that we need to understand the mood. But more than the mood, we need to understand some of the language—what are people talking about when they shout "black power"? What is the significance behind decentralization which is something that all of you are going to have to face up to? We have had to face up to it in the Urban League. I suppose there was nobody who was more anxious for the slogan of "black power" to disappear the day after it was uttered than Whitney Young and all of us in the Urban League because we knew its overtones and the implications, the interpretations that would be given to it, of violence and of separatism. But it didn't go away—thanks to a sensation-seeking press and because it was born in an atmosphere of violence. So it seemed to us that we should take a hard look at it and try to sanitize it and try to give it a more constructive interpretation. There is really nothing new about the concept of a group seeking power. There is nothing new—every other group in American society has done it. To the Urban League, "black power" means first—"Look at me, I exist. I am somebody. I have pride. I have roots. I have an identity. I've made a contribution. I'm tired of being an invisible man, an asterisk in American life, a footnote." It says also that "I want the opportunity to participate in the decisions that affect my community—that if you want me to be responsible then give me responsibility and quit treating me like I am a colonial in American society." It says also that "We should organize our economic and political strength as all other groups have done to reward our friends and punish our enemies." The Irish did it, the Italians did it, the Catholics have done it, the Jews have done it, all other groups have done this. They just didn't make the mistake of shouting "Jewish power," "Italian power," or "Irish power"—the Irish just kept their mouths shut and took over the police departments of most cities in the country. And they made mistakes. They elected Curly, at first, not Jack Kennedy. Curly would make Adam Powell look like the epitome of political morality. All groups have made their mistakes and learned through trial and error and the black man should have the same opportunity to learn from trial and error. He will learn no other way. He has as much right to fail as anybody else. And incidentally, he has as much right to his crackpots as anybody else. There is no reason why white people should have a monopoly on crackpots. At least our crackpots don't go around bombing little children in churches and they don't go around denying to other human beings certain elementary rights. This is what decentralization is really all about.

The issue of separatism versus integration is an academic issue. For, the black poor of this country are, in fact, segregated. Almost without exception in the major cities of this country, black people are contained. The index of segregation has gone higher and higher and, today, we are a far more segregated society than we were twenty years ago. We do have in this country more of a condition of apartheid than one would want to admit. We aren't likely, overnight, to change this situation in spite of all of the good wishes and the laws. And in this segregated situation that we find ourselves, it is now clear that we will not be able to move into the mainstream and to compete with other Americans unless the institutions to which we are forced to accept services become not just equal but superior institutions. And those institutions cannot be run forever by outside absentee landlords and owners of business and policy makers in our schools. The Oceanhill-Brownsville controversy is much more than a labor dispute. It is first a recognition of the failure of the old and nobody today disputes the fact that the old system failed in Ocean[hill]-Brownsville. The union, Mr. Shanker, and everybody admits that when a black child in Ocean[hill]-Brownsville gets to the twelfth grade they are four to five years behind in their achievement scores and when a youngster is in the fifth grade, they are one to three years behind already in reading comprehension and word comprehension. The parents have not been participating in the PTA meetings. There has been little or no involvement. The principals, the superintendent, the district superintendent had been from outside of the community and felt that he was not particularly responsible to the community. Oceanhill-Brownsville is not just a few blocks. It's a school system larger than the whole city of Buffalo. It's larger than most any other city except about 12 in the United States. It's of enormous size and the people in that district want and need the opportunity to participate. And so they've begun the experiment. And you've heard most of the negative things but you haven't heard some of the positive things. I have been there. I spent most of last week there. I've talked to the teachers. First of all, this board employed 500 teachers and of that 500, 70% were white and 50% were Jewish. But they are different—they are different. They are teachers who have as much feeling, as much heart, as they have head. They are people who care and there is nobody in a better situation to know when somebody cares about them than a suppressed minority. He does have a built-in radar. He has to have it to survive. He has to learn early the little nuances that indicate that people like him or they don't like him. And today, the climate of that school, that whole district, is entirely different. Parent-teachers meetings are packed and jammed. The eagerness to learn in the classroom is unprecedented. The whole climate of discipline is so much more improved over what it was a year ago when I was in the same district, the kind of respect, pupil for teacher and parent for teacher, is unprecedented.

The real issue around the fight in Ocean[hill]-Brownsville is an issue that is going to face us in business. It is going to face us in relation to health and welfare services. The issue is, does white America have the capability, the moral responsibility to give up power and privilege. It's easy to say I will support a civil rights bill. It's easy to applaud a Supreme Court decision. It's easy to write out a directive. The real test of the moral sensibility or the moral bankruptcy is now the issue before us. The real test is, can we, in fact, give up some power, give up to Americans who are colored what we have given up to other Americans who are white.

What happens in this determines, I think, the future of our cities. If the responsible leadership in this country, black leadership, is denied this opportunity to show what we can do, then the country is in trouble. Because it immediately will fall into the clutches of the white and black revolutionists who have now formed a nice little alliance—the Black Panthers and the SDS people are working hand-in-hand today. And these are the people who say to the Whitney Youngs, "You know, you're a fool if you think that this problem can be worked out within the framework of this system. The system must be destroyed and its institutions must be destroyed." And they go farther and say, "We have no responsibility to provide alternatives, but this, we know, we must destroy."

Now, you will determine who are the prophets in history. Can the system be compassionate, intelligent enough, flexible enough to permit black people this kind of a piece of the action? I was down in Miami, Florida, not too long ago to the AFL-CIO executive council meeting. I walked into the lobby of this very luxurious hotel and some of the labor leaders' wives were down there with their mink stoles and their

Pekingese dogs. They were getting into their chauffeured limousines and they had just left their well-stocked suites upstairs. Their husbands were not up there debating on how to destroy the system, I can assure you. Forty years ago they were. But what had happened was, they had gotten a piece of the action, they had gotten a stake in the system. And you don't destroy that that you have a stake in. And that's the answer. When the black man in this country and the responsible leadership are given victories, then we can walk in the ghetto and say, "Cool it." And when asked "Why?" we don't have to respond in terms of little token programs, or little "cool it" summer programs, or little pacifiers to keep the natives quiet; when we can talk about a massive program based upon a national commitment that's willing to appropriate the money like it did for the rebuilding of Western Europe and that sets a timetable on it that people can count on and not have their hopes raised only to be dashed by the passage of model cities legislation and rent supplements and poverty programs immediately to be sabotaged by the appropriation committee. And so no money goes out to amount to anything for model cities or rent supplements. The poverty program is supposed to be up around $8 billion now and it's barely creaking along at about a billion and a half while in every other area we are escalating. We spend much more money for the national guard and then, we kill a program of rat control.

The reason for this is that the leadership, the Congress today, hears from the lower middle class white person who is a victim of great fear. This guy who just made it on WPA and NYA, one generation removed from welfare, who is now saying, "We are against all these government programs." Rank and file union members who invented demonstrations and picketing and boycotting and violence in order to achieve their end are saying, "We're sick and tired of demonstrations. We're going to vote for Wallace." They write to their congressmen. They proudly wear their Wallace buttons. But the nice decent people, you, the bankers, have up to very recent months distinguished yourselves by your thunderous silence and this has got to change. Not for my benefit, and the benefit of black people, but for the benefit of your country in which you have a greater stake than anybody else.

Now this means doing a lot of things. It means first of all making sure your own house is in order in terms of employment. As I look around this room, I would say that you've got an awful lot to do. I feel very much like Mr. Stanley looking for Dr. Livingston in Africa in reverse. I keep hoping I'll run across a credit official or bank loan official who is black. I finally met one, I think, this morning and I started to rush up to him and say, "Dr. Livingston, I presume." You can find

them. Everybody else is finding them in industry generally. Some banks
are in New York City. I know that there are some in Philadelphia.
But obviously, if you are finding them you are not upgrading them
or you are not taking those who you already have and upgrading them
fast enough. Unless you do this, unless you get those road models, unless
you get people in visible top spots then there will be no incentive and
motivation. Don't come to the Urban League and say, "How do we
motivate these people?" This is what an automobile manufacturer said
to me not so long ago. "I hired, Whitney, 2,000 of those hard-core people
you told me to but after the first pay day 500 quit. And they are late
on Monday mornings, too." I told him we looked into this and we found
that there was one institution where this didn't happen and that's in
organized sports. Ever since Bill Russell became the head of the Boston
Celtics (and that's like being president of AT & T in the commercial
business), ever since Wilt Chamberlin began to make a couple hundred
thousand dollars a year, ever since Willy Mays began to make a hundred
and twenty-five thousand, we haven't had a single Negro basketball
or baseball player to quit after the first pay day. We haven't had a
single one late to work—there's no example of where they have been
late to work on Monday mornings. So I said to him, "Who is your
Willy Mays, who is the Bill Russell in your company." That's the answer.
Black people are motivated like anyone else. They are motivated by
the knowledge that through perseverance, extra study, and hard work
they, too, can move upstairs.

   And in our banks today like in a lot of other industries, you can
still tell what floor you are on by the color—sort of checkerboard on
the first floor, the basement is mainly black, but as you go up it gets
whiter and whiter. So, I don't need to know what floor I'm on. I know
I'm getting near the top just by the color of the employees for the most
part. Except maybe for one instant black man who is out front to lead
the way. Now this has to change. You can do it. You have the creative
skills. I don't have to tell you how to do it. I did it in the Urban League
in reverse. We had 1% white employees when I came in and now we've
got 30%. And we did it through extra special recruiting techniques. We
did it through lowering some of our standards that the white people
couldn't meet. (I'm really not being completely facetious.) We wanted
people who knew what it meant to be rejected. We wanted people who
understood the language of the ghetto. We wanted people who understood the psychology of the poor. In our work this is a valid kind of
qualification. Most white people couldn't meet it. And so we took in
people like young Rusk, Secretary Rusk's son, who was a Phi Beta Kappa
from Cornell. We took in Adrian Zucker whose father was then head

of the Air Force. We took in some law review graduates. Adrian was a Phi Beta Kappa from Radcliffe. We took Yale Law Review editors. We took bright people from public relations and from industrial relations. And we put them in a special provisional training course and gave them remedial teaching to help bring them up to our standards. I'm delighted to report that it works and that they are doing as well, if not better, than many of our black employees. But we were willing to change our screening process. We were willing to change some of our scores. We know you can't ask white people what to do when a rat comes in the room? How do you kill a bed bug? What's a syringe? What's chitlins? I mean, white people don't know anything about this. We have this intelligence test in Harlem that I sent to Scottie Reston (New York Times) the other day and he turned out to be an idiot, he said. He'd been taking the same kind of intelligence test based upon white middle class norms, about whether caviar smells like fish or fruit or whether you use red or white wine with chicken or steak and the slum kids don't know this. The tests aren't valid as a test of potential, as a test of intelligence.

Don't stop at just your jobs. Please do something about the attitudes, do something about housing, do something about education. You see, in the same breath that you tell me that you can't find any qualified people, you are also telling me how dumb you are because you are taxed twice. You pay the big taxes to maintain a public school system. And then you have to train people again for your companies. Why don't you get involved and see to it that these schools turn out people who can go to work for you right away. You need to disperse the housing and you play a crucial role in dispersal. You've got in New Haven and Newark now some banks who have set up a consortium in which they have set aside money for not just the development of black businesses but also for providing technical assistance and also for housing developments. And not all in the black community. I know it's better to get together collectively so one or two of you can't sneak out and appeal to the bigots. All of you feel a little scared. So what you do is get together so then they can't boycott any of you. All of you are in it together. That's what we had to do in Detroit and some other places. And this is what you've got to do to be credible to the black community. You are the one that suffers if this community becomes blacker and poorer. If people become tax eaters rather than tax producers, if people produce crime and welfare costs instead of producing goods and services, you pay the costs. And those are the sheer alternatives.

One final alternative is that you will either support responsible black leadership in this country or irresponsible leadership will take over. An organization like the Urban League that has been in business 58 years deserves better than what banks are doing for them now. Overnight, banks have given $100,000 to the Urban Coalition and then given the Urban League $5,000. Any kind of new idea that comes along they take off and say let's invest in that. You don't do that when it comes to building airplanes in time of war. You invest in Boeing and North America who've been producing airplanes. You don't go out and say let's start a new airplane manufacturing company. And yet when it comes to this problem the Urban League which tries to provide sane, intelligent, militantly responsible leadership does not get the resources to work with. The Urban League budgets ought to be quadrupled in these cities.

It isn't easy today to be a responsible leader. If you think you have to go home and apologize to somebody for associating with me, I want you to know that many times I have to apologize for associating with you. And I don't mind defending you to the black angry people in the ghetto (and that's not easy) if you don't mind defending me. Because we may have all come over here on different ships but at this moment we are in the same boat and we must never forget it. We'll sink or swim together. The stakes are high not just in terms of our cities and your banks. The stakes are high in terms of what kind of human being you want to be. What kind of husband, what kind of father.

I started talking about the children, let me close by talking about them. Mel Batton, who is chairman of the board of J. C. Penney, told me recently about his having breakfast one Sunday morning with his 21-year-old girl and his 23-year-old son. In just making conversation the girl said, "Where are you going this week, Dad?" And he said, "I'm going out with Whitney Young to three or four cities where I'm hosting some luncheons to talk about expanding employment opportunities for black people." And the boy almost fell off the stool and said, "You're going to do what?" And he explained it to him again. The boy said, "You mean you aren't going out this week and try to maximize the profits of J. C. Penney? You're not going out to find some product you can get a greater margin of profit on?" He said, "No." There was silence for a moment. And then his daughter with tears in her eyes jumped over and hugged and kissed him. And he said to me, "You know, Whitney, I've given my kids everything—cars, clothes, great allowances, tuitions, they've traveled all over the world." He said "but I never got more genuine respect and affection and love from my children than I got in that one moment." He said, "I want to thank you and the Urban League for giving me this opportunity to, for the first time, begin real communication with my child."

And that's what's at stake. These kids are serious today. They're not moved by money you give them. They know that you are getting ahead in your business and making money because of your own ambition, not because you want to give them more things. You say that but it is your own ambition, it's your own challenge. And they take it for granted just like my kids do. But the one thing they don't take for granted is when you tell them to stand up for what they believe in and not to conform to all the other kids but do what they know is right and then they turn around and they say, "But Mom and Daddy never do. They never stand up for what they believe in. They never lift their finger to get a black man a much better job or get a black man in the neighborhood or in the school. They are afraid."

Gentlemen, you teach by example and not by exhortation. You teach by precept and not by concept. And that's what's at stake. What kind of human being, what kind of man, what kind of American—this problem more than any other separates the real from the phony. An ancient Greek scholar was once asked to name when they would have justice in Athens. And he said, "We will have justice in Athens when those who are not injured are as indignant as those who are." And so shall it be in this society. We will have true justice in America when people like you who are not injured are as indignant as those who are.

―――――――

Collateral Reading

"Fifty Years of the Urban League," *Negro History Bulletin,* XXIV (October, 1960), 13-14.

Wood, L. Hollingsworth, "The Urban League Movement," *Journal of Negro History,* IX (April, 1924).

Young, Whitney M., Jr., "The Urban League and Its Strategy," *The Annals of the American Academy of Political and Social Science,* CCCLVII (January, 1965), 102-107.

―――――――, *Beyond Racism.* New York, 1969.

―――――――

Study Questions and Problems

1. How does Whitney M. Young, Jr., adapt his message to his specific audience?

2. Identify Young's forms of supporting material, i.e., illustrations, specific instances, statistics, etc. How well informed is Young?

3. Compare Young's position on "black power" to Wilkins'. Which speaker do you think understands the concept better?

4. Reread the conclusion of Young's address and comment on its effectiveness.

5. How do you account for Young's popularity among blacks and whites who represent views varying from moderate to militant?

6. What signs, if any, do you observe of elimination of job discrimination in the 1970's?

Adam Clayton Powell, Jr.

Adam Clayton Powell, Jr., was born in New Haven, Connecticut, on November 29, 1908. He received his B.A. from Colgate University, Hamilton, New York, his M.A. from Columbia University in New York City, and his D.D. from Shaw University, Raleigh, North Carolina. Powell was elected to the City Council of New York in 1941 and to Congress in 1945. He was Chairman of the House Education Committee until barred from sitting in the House of Representatives in 1967. He was legally permitted to resume his position in Congress in 1969. Powell lost the Democratic congressional primary election in 1970.

Powell delivered the commencement address at Howard University, Washington, D.C., May 29, 1966. The speech is an evocative appeal for black leadership to emerge from the graduating class of 1966. "In this commencement of your life, the world will ask: Can there any good thing come out of Howard?" In a series of striking contrasts, Powell described the problems of racial discrimination in contemporary American. He argued for race consciousness and counseled against conciliation with white liberals and black integrationists. He called for "audacious power—more black power" as the means to improve the economic, educational, and social condition of black citizens.

In this speech, Powell employed a number of rhetorical strategies which he had learned from his years as a pulpit preacher. For example, the speech contains some important religious symbolism. The text is from the Book of John, referring to the fact that Jesus, representing great good, came from Nazareth. So might great good come from the graduates of Howard. Powell counseled for more militant black leaders, quoting the Book of Hebrews to support his claim. He drew a biblical parallel between Nicodemus and Howard University. "Like Nicodemus, Howard must be born again—born again in the image of black greatness gone before." Finally, he called for a sustaining faith in God.

Powell also called for his youthful audience to emulate great black men and women of the past. He recited the names of black scholars who had graduated from Howard University generations before, and whom he hoped would inspire emulation.

Finally, he raised the question of what contribution black people might make to America. He answered that blacks were the last purifying agent of the democratic ideal.

"Can There Any Good Thing Come Out of Nazareth?"
May 25, 1966

Almost 2,000 years ago, that question was a contemptuous inquiry in the book of John.

"And Nathanael said unto Philip, 'Can there any good thing come out of Nazareth?' Philip saith, 'Come and see.' "

Nazareth was the Mississippi of Galilee. There were no great artists or philosopher-kings or musicians. There was no center of learning such as Howard University.

In this commencement of your life, the world will ask: Can there any good thing come out of Howard?

As black students educated at America's finest black institution of higher learning, you are still second-class citizens.

A mere 100 years in the spectrum of time separates us from the history of slavery and a lifetime of indignities.

Next year, on March 2, 1967, Howard will celebrate the centennial of its founding. Next year, on March 21, 1967, the Committee on Education and Labor of which I am the Chairman will also celebrate its 100th anniversary.

How ironic that the Committee on Education and Labor which was formed immediately after the Civil War to help black slaves make the transition into freedom should have a black man 100 years later as its Chairman.

One of the purposes of the Committee's founding was to take care of Howard University. It is too late for you who are graduating to know this unless you plan to pursue graduate work here, but it is not too late for the faculty to know it: the Education and Labor Committee is in charge of Howard University. Howard, along with other Federal institutions such as St. Elizabeth's and Gallaudet College, is under the jurisdiction of my Committee.

While both Howard and I as Chairman of this Committee will celebrate our 100 years together, joy of our success is tempered by the sobering fact that our status as black people has been denied first-class acceptance.

Keith E. Baird, writing in the spring edition of "Freedomways," gives eloquent voice to these thoughts in his poem, "Nemesis":

> You snatched me from my land,
> Branded my body with your irons
> And my soul with the slave-name, "Negro"
> (How devilish clever to spell it upper case
> And keep me always lower!)

To possess a black skin today in America means that if you are in Los Angeles driving your pregnant wife to a hospital, you'll be shot to death by a white policeman.

A black skin means that if your family lives in Webster County, Mississippi, your average family income will be $846 a year—$16.30 a week for an entire family.

A black skin today is an unemployment rate twice that of whites, despite a skyrocketing gross national product of $714 billion dollars and an unprecedented level of employment.

A black skin means you are still a child, that all the white liberals who have helped you to take your first steps toward freedom and manhood now believe they own your soul, can manage your lives and control your civil rights organizations. Only SNCC has been able to resist the seductive blandishments of white liberals.

So beware not only of Greeks bearing gifts, but colored men seeking loans and Northern white liberals!

At this graduation today, this is the reality of self you must face. Your graduation comes at a particularly critical period of the black man's searching re-assessment of who he is, what he should become, and how he should become *it*.

The history of the last 25 years of the freedom struggle has been capsuled in only two concepts: integration and civil rights.

During those years, our leaders—and black people are the only people who have "leaders"—other groups have politicians, statesmen, educators, financiers and businessmen—but during those years, our leaders drugged us with the LSD of integration. Instead of telling us to seek audacious power—more black power—instead of leading us in the pursuit of excellence, our leaders led us in the sterile chase of integration as an end in itself in the debasing notion that a few white skins sprinkled amongst us would somehow elevate the genetics of our development.

As a result, ours was an integration of intellectual mediocrity, economic inferiority and political subservience.

Like frightened children, we were afraid to eat the strong meat of human rights and instead sucked the milk of civil rights from the breasts of white liberals, black Uncle Toms and Aunt Jemimas.

From the book of Hebrews, a diet of courage is offered to black people:

For every one that useth milk is unskillful in the word of righteousness: for he is a babe. But strong meat belongeth to them that are of full age, even those who by reason of use have their senses exercised to discern both good and evil.

Historically, strong meat was too risky for most black people for it would have enabled them to discern both good and evil, the difference between civil rights and human rights.

I

Human rights are God-given. Civil rights are man-made.

Civil rights has been that grand deception practiced by those who have not placed God first, who have not believed that God-given rights can empower the black man with superiority as well as equality.

II

Our life must be purposed to implement human rights:

*the right to be secure in one's person from the excessive abuses of the state and its law-enforcing officials.

*the right to freedom of choice of a job to feed one's family.

*the right to freedom of mobility of residence.

*the right to the finest education man's social order can provide.

*and most importantly, the right to share fully in the governing councils of the state as equal members of the body politic.

III

To demand these God-given human rights is to seek black power, what I call audacious power—the power to build black institutions of splendid achievement.

Howard University was once well on its way toward becoming a lasting black institution of splendid achievement when it struggled to contain the intellectual excitement and dynamic creativity of such black scholars as Alain Locke, Sterling Brown, E. Franklin Frazier, Sam Dorsey, Eugene Holmes, James Nabrit, and Rayford Logan—all on the campus at the same time. What glorious symbols they were of black creativity!

But where are the black symbols of creativity of 1966? Where is the greatness of our yesteryears? Where are the sonnets black poets once sang of the black man's agony of life? Can any good thing come out of Howard today?

IV

There can and there must. I call today for a black renaissance at Howard University. Resurrect black creativity, not only in literature, history, law, poetry and English, but more so in mathematics, engineering, aerodynamics and nuclear physics.

Like Nicodemus, Howard must be born again—born again in the image of black greatness gone before.

Will one black woman here today dare to come forth as a pilgrim of God, a Sojourner Truth—as a black Moses, Harriet Tubman—or a Nannie Burroughs?

Will one black man here today dare to be a Denmark Vesey, a Nat Turner, a Frederick Douglass, a Marcus Garvey, a W. E. B. Du Bois, or a Malcolm X?

One with God is a majority.

This divine oneness can restore Howard to the Glory of Charlie Houston whose classrooms were the womb of the civil rights movement—a womb that birthed a Thurgood Marshall.

But the womb has aborted and the good thing which must come out of Howard must also come out of black people.

V

Ask yourselves that higher question: Can any good thing come of black people?

We are the last revolutionaries in America—the last transfusion of freedom into the blood stream of democracy.

Because we are, we must mobilize our wintry discontent to transform the cold heart and white face of this nation.

Indeed, we must "drop our buckets" where we are. We must stop blaming "Whitey" for all our sins and oppressions and deal from situations with strength. Why sit down at the bargaining table with the white man when you have nothing with which to bargain? Why permit social workers and various Leagues and Associations to represent us when they are representing the decadent white power structure which pays their salaries, their rent and tells them what to say? Such men cannot possess the noble arrogance of power that inspires men, moves nations and decides the fate of mankind.

VI

I call for more arrogance of power among black people, but an arrogance of power that is God-inspired, God-led and God-daring.

As Cassius said: "The fault, dear Brutus, is not in our stars, but in ourselves, that we are underlings."

So, every bondman in his own hand bears the power to cancel his captivity.

We can cancel the captivity of our souls and destroy the enslavement of our minds by refusing to compromise any of our human rights.

The era of compromise for the black man is gone!

Birmingham, Harlem and Watts have proved this. You cannot compromise man's right to be free, nor can you sit down and "reason together" whether man should have some rights today and full rights tomorrow.

Let somebody reason with Mrs. Barbara Deadwyler in Los Angeles that a white policeman really did not intend to kill her black husband.

Let somebody tell her that the passion of her love for her husband should bow to the reason of diaphanous official alibis.

Only God can reason with her and soothe her grief. And there is a "God who rules above with a hand of power and a heart of love, and if I'm right He'll fight my battle and I shall be free this day."

This same God calls us first to the conference table, and His Son, when the word of reason was no longer heeded, went into the temple and "began to cast out those that sold."

Those that sell black people down the river must be cast out. Those conference tables which defile the human spirit must be overturned.

Conferences are for people who have time to contemplate the number of angels dancing on a civil rights pin. Conferences are for people who seek a postponement until tomorrow of a decision which screams for a solution today.

Conferences are an extravagant orgy of therapy for the guilt-ridden and a purposeless exercise in dialectics for the lazy.

America has been holding too many conferences, conducting too many seminars; writing too many books and articles about the black man and his right to freedom for over a century.

This week, 3,000 black and white people will gather once again in our nation's capital to whisper words of futility into the hurricane of massive indifference.

Certainly the Federal Government should cease to be a partner in this cruel, historic charade with the black man's rights.

To fulfill these rights? Let us begin with first things first.

The largest single employer in the United States is the Federal Government—2,574,000 employees.

Yet, racial discrimination within the Government—more subtle, more sophisticated, more elegantly structured—continues almost as rampant as yesterday. The times have changed, but the system hasn't.

Though racial persecution presses its crown of thorns on our brows, our faith in God must never falter.

We must sustain that faith which helps us to cast off the leprosy of self-shame in our black skins and lift us up to the glorious healing power of belief in the excellence of black power.

We must have the faith to build mighty black universities, black businesses and elect black men as governors, mayors and senators.

Our faith must be sustained by our passion for dignity and our trust in God, not man's faithless reason in himself.

What is easier—"to say to the sick of the palsy Thy sins be forgiven thee; or to say, Arise and take up thy bed and walk?"

Black children of Howard, take up thy beds and walk into the new era of excellence.

Arise, and walk into a new spirit of black pride.

"Can there any good thing come out of Nazareth?" "Come and see," said Philip.

Nathanael came and saw Jesus and the world felt, as he did, the power of his love and the beauty of his words.

Can there any good thing come out of Howard University here today?

"Come and see," you Howard graduates must say.

"Come and see" us erect skyscrapers of economic accomplishment, scale mountains of educational excellence and live among the stars of audacious political power.

"Come and see" us labor for the black masses—not the black leaders—but the black masses who have yearned for audacious leadership.

Collateral Reading

Hickey, Neil, and Edwin, eds., *Adam Clayton Powell.* New York, 1965.

Powell, Adam Clayton, Jr., *Keep the Faith, Baby.* New York, 1967.

————, *Marching Blacks.* New York, 1946.

Warren, Robert Penn, *Who Speaks for the Negro?* New York, 1965.

Study Questions and Problems

1. What effect do you think being barred from sitting in the United States House of Representatives had on Powell's *ethos* with (1) the white majority, (2) his constituents, (3) young black militants?

2. Locate portions of Powell's speech which are indicative of the style of a Negro preacher.

3. As an exercise in organization, outline Powell's speech. Did Powell usually argue from general to specific or from specific to general?

4. Do you think Powell's address is well adapted to his audience? Explain your position.

5. What legislative proposals did Powell sponsor in the field of race relations? Make an assessment of Rep. Powell's effectiveness as a political leader.

Carl T. Rowan

Carl T. Rowan was born in Ravenscroft, Tennessee, August 11, 1925. He graduated from high school in 1942 as class president and valedictorian. Rowan became one of the first black men to earn a commission in the Navy. After serving as a communications officer on two ships in the Atlantic, he returned to enroll at Oberlin College, Ohio, where he earned a B.A. in mathematics. He later received an M.A. in journalism from the University of Minnesota while working for two Negro weeklies.

During his professional career, Carl Rowan won numerous awards for his journalistic expertise. In 1956 he became the only newspaperman to win three successive annual awards from Sigma Delta Chi, the journalism fraternity. He has written South of Freedom *(Knopf, 1952)*, The Pitiful and the Proud *(Random, 1956), and* Go South to Sorrow *(Random, 1957)*. Rowan's reporting ranges the spectrum of social issues in our time from race relations to social unrest in Asia, to the plight of the American Indian. In 1964 President Johnson appointed Rowan head of the United States Information Agency, a post which he held from 1964-1965. Mr. Rowan now writes a syndicated column and lectures extensively throughout the United States.

Carl Rowan's speech, "New Frontiers in Racial Relations," was delivered at Youngstown State University as part of the university's Artist Lecture series. The speech calls for a multiplicity of techniques to solve race conflict in America. While he understands the psychology behind the black man's call for separation of the races, Rowan's personal credo rejects that particular alternative: "There is not a white man alive who is mean enough, powerful enough, or clever enough to make me flee this land made great in part by so much of the labor, the sweat, the tears of black men. I said to him, believe me, I'm here for the duration." Through the use of statistical evidence, Rowan's speech punctures the illusion of many white Americans that blacks are closing the economic gap. He uses common observation to refute the belief by many whites that Negroes are now given preferential treatment in job recruitment.

In tone, the speech is anecdotal, containing a simple topical pattern of organization. Rowan gains and maintains the attention of his audience through his ability to illustrate an idea with vivid examples. Statistics are made vivid by Rowan's interpreting their significance to his audience. Moreover, he calls on a lifetime of professional experiences to enrich the content of his lecture.

———————

New Frontiers in Racial Relations

October 24, 1968

Thank you very much, ladies and gentlemen, and thank you, Dr. Kiriazis, for making that introduction as short as it was. I got here just in time to tell him that I used to like the longer, more syrupy kind but my wife has put me in the position where I can't say that any more. I say that because not long before leaving the directorship of USIA, I went home one evening and in what I thought was total innocence, I turned to my wife and said, "Darling, I'll bet you don't know how many famous ex-newspapermen are holding top government jobs?" She thought about it awhile and said, "Well, Carl, I don't know the exact number, but I'll bet it's one fewer than you think!" Now having given you just a little glimpse into the kind of wife I've got, I think you'll know that I speak with honesty when I say I'm delighted to be here today. Although that is sort of a half-truth because I tell you that I'm always a little bit nervous when I have to go out on one of these lecture trips and I was particularly nervous about coming into Youngstown until I looked at my television screen and knew it would be absolutely safe because you ran out of rocks and toilet paper yesterday.

But I must say, any time a newspaperman books a speech in this season, he trembles nervously because he never knows whether he can make it or not. Just yesterday morning I was in Boston, my secretary called and said, "Mr. Rowan, don't you think we'd better put into effect some kind of contingency plan for Youngstown?" I said, "Contingency plan—you sound like a bureaucrat—you weren't in government with me." She said, "No sir, but I did have lunch with a girl who was your secretary for four and one-half years, and she tells me that you always had a contingency plan in case you were supposed to speak here but Lyndon Johnson said 'No, don't go there,' you always had someone designated to take your place." And I said, "Yes, that part's true, but she didn't tell you the whole story. Did she tell you my favorite story about President

Wilson?" And she said, "No sir." So I told her about the time when they awakened President Wilson in the wee hours and said, "Mr. President, I'm terribly sorry to disturb you, but there's a man on the phone who has called at least a half dozen times and he says it's a matter of life and death that he talk to you." Rather grouchily, President Wilson picked up the phone and said "YES." The voice on the other end said, "Mr. President, I'm one of your loyal customs workers here in New York and I called to let you know your chief customs collector just dropped dead." "Oh, that's too bad," said President Wilson, "but my good citizen, couldn't you have waited until breakfast to give me that sad news?" "Heavens no!" said the voice on the other end, "I'm next in line of seniority and I had to find out if I can take his place." Without a pause, President Wilson said, "Well, if it's all right with the undertaker, it's sure as hell all right with me!"

I think my secretary fairly well got the message that I was determined to be in Youngstown today, because quite seriously I relish the opportunity to visit the campuses of America where part of that great struggle goes on to try to prove that reason is more powerful than emotions—that we can construct a society in which men can live by brain power rather than their glands. And I must say that if there ever were a time when Americans needed to try to prove their stability, it is now. Because I have come before you during a period of grim contradictions. This is an era in which men yearn for peace as they've never yearned for anything else, but when they still fight with a savagery unexceeded in human history. I speak to you at a time when black men fight and die in disproportionate numbers in distant paddies and jungles all in the name of freedom; but a time when a black man can also die in a street in South Carolina because some stupid man wants to keep his bowling alley white. I stand before you at a time when we can plant a rocket on the moon with robot ditch digger, and when we on earth give the signal "Dig," the robot digs—a marvel of communications; but an era when fathers can't communicate with their sons, their mothers with their daughters, or black Americans with white. I stand here at a time when we Americans have a gross national product of some 889 billion dollars a year, when we're enjoying an abundance never before known by any society, when booze, baubles, and banquets are within easy reach of all who can hear my voice, but a time also when people cry that the dollar is sick and the treasury is bad and that we can afford various foreign follies, but that we can't meet the deepest human needs of 26 million Americans who live in hunger, squalor, and abject poverty.

Oh, I could go on to cite enough grim contradictions to cause someone to cry out, "Is there a psychiatrist in the house?" But I didn't come here to exercise anybody's schizophrenia today, although I confess there may be some of that before I'm through. You asked me to talk a bit about some new frontiers of race relations. I'm happy to do so, although I want to tell you at the outset, it will not be the kind of race relations talk I would have given ten years ago if you'd invited me to this university. Had I come here then, I expect, I'd have had to stand here as a black man and plead with the white members of this audience to go out and do a little bit of justice to the black man in this country. I'd have talked to you about what it is you owe the black people, but that's not the case today. Because when I stand here and talk about what we need to restore some measure of sanity, some measure of justice, some measure of dignity to a society that shows some signs of going a little bit out of its mind, I'm talking about not just the future of black children, but of every white child who walks this country's dirt and of every parent who hopes that its child is going to live in some measure of freedom and dignity.

Indeed, as I sat down in Pittsburgh today, waiting for that late plane, I thought about this speech and what it is that I really want to put across here, and how I could best indicate to you that it's for each of you that the bell tolls today, and I couldn't help but recall a recent visit to Africa to the little country Zambia. And in Usaka I agreed to go out and give a speech to the university there, and I even reached the audacious point of agreeing to answer questions after. And things went along swimmingly until a young African got up and he said, "Mr. Rowan, when you answer this question, now I want you to tell the people the truth." I said, "Yes." He said, "Now isn't it a fact that your foreign aid program is nothing but dirty dollar diplomacy. That you're taking your ill gotten wealth that you dredged out of your raw resources and the sweat and the labor of the peoples of the underdeveloped world, and you're dribbling a little bit of it back here in the hope that you can buy the hearts and minds of our people?" Well, needless to say, that audience fell silent. And I looked at that young man and said to him that his mind seemed so completely made up, I'd hate to confuse him with any facts. That, indeed, I wasn't sure there were facts that would go to the heart of his question and the only way I could explain to him why I thought the American people had shelled out 130 billion dollars in foreign aid since World War II was to tell him my favorite story about Abraham Lincoln. And I think this same story will illustrate why it is that you ought to be interested in what's happening in race relations in this country.

It seems that Lincoln and his law partner Herndon were riding down a muddy road in a rainstorm arguing a point of philosophy as they often did. This time they argued about whether or not there's such a thing as a completely unselfish act. Herndon was sure there was. Lincoln was just as sure there was not. Well the argument raged furiously until they came upon a point where a pig had his head stuck in a rail fence and was squealing to beat the dickens. "Whoa," Lincoln said. He pulled the old wagon to a halt, jumped down, sloshed through the mud and rain, walked over, put a knee against one rail, pulled the other, the pig jerked his head out and ran squealing across the pasture. Lincoln sloshed back, clambered into the wagon, "Git up," he said, and the old horse trotted on down the road, as Herndon leaned back, laughing for all he was worth. Finally, Lincoln couldn't ignore him any longer. He turned and said, "All right, my silly friend, what the devil do you find so funny?" "You," said Herndon. "Well what's so funny about me?" He said, "You silly man. You just got out of the wagon and proved my side of the argument. You went over to free that stupid pig when anybody can tell that as wet as it is today, the pig would have freed himself sooner or later. Now that was an unselfish act if I ever saw one." Lincoln gave a wry smile and said, "No, Herndon. If I proved anything, I proved my side of the argument. You see Herndon, that pig might very well have freed itself, but I wouldn't have known it, and it would have been squealing in my dreams for many a night to come. Herndon, that was a terribly selfish thing I did."

Well, I told that young man in Zambia that a great many Americans had given to a foreign aid program out of various kinds of selfishness. That some were told that if you don't give to country X, they'll go communist, and that scared them to death and, oh, they shelled out with both hands for awhile. And others were simply told that a world in which half the people go to bed a little bit hungry every night will never be a very safe world, and they gave out of that kind of enlightened self-interest. And there were others who got very close to unselfishness who just didn't like the notion of hungry children crying in their dreams for many a night to come.

Well, I don't know how many of you read my column, I hope all of you do, but if you did, you saw a couple of columns I wrote in the past week or ten days about the possibilities of fascism coming to this country. About how there are people like George Wallace who are trying to exploit the rioting in the streets to make it what the Reichstag fire of 1933 was to Adolph Hitler; and I answered a young man who said in so many words, fascism can't come here because our constitution is a great bulwark against fascism, and I said in so many words to that young man, nonsense! What's on parchment hasn't ever been much of a bulwark against fascism, or any other kind of dictatorial regime. No constitution, however beautifully written, is any stronger than the judicial and other safeguards built around that constitution, and most certainly, no stronger than the people's determination to protect those safeguards from the tamperings of men filled with fear and emotion. So the great danger in this society, as I pointed out, is not George Wallace himself. Some people say to me, "Hey did you hear about George Wallace's military record, he's got some kind of mental disability." And I say, I'm not so much concerned about the state of George Wallace's mind. What I'm concerned about is the state of the mind of the people who are going into the polls on November 5, because it is obvious to me that just as I predicted months ago, the war in Vietnam, for all the frustration it has aroused, is not the dominant issue in this campaign.

The dominant issue is precisely my subject today—Race Relations in These United States. It is the white backlash that is the central force in the American people's decision as to who is going to be the next president of this country. A man who is going to have far more power than Alexei Kosygin. A man who is going to have far more power than Breshnev. We are going to give one man the power to call out the National Guard, send troups into Youngstown in an emergency, conduct foreign policy, indeed dominate it as is the case in Vietnam. And there is every likelihood that this is going to be done on the basis of the fears and frustrations of a great many white blue-collar workers, and a great many suburbanites who want to embrace the silly notion that if they elect the right man, he'll go out and buy enough stone or rifles and enough tanks and beef up the police force to the point where he can quiet the black man's revolution, put the niggers back in their places and everybody will live in sweet tranquility ever after. Well, I think before I get through, you'll know that it just isn't going to happen that way. I don't care how you vote when you go into the polls on November 5. But let me talk first about why this mood exists.

I can understand part of the reason why there would be many, many thousands of frustrated and perhaps even frightened white people in this country today. The Negro in his rebellion has created a great many reasons why a great many whites think they ought to be frightened, because the truth is that the Negro has frustrated himself with good reason. The black man in America is angry with justification. The colored American is confused, understandably. No American ought doubt that the black man is in revolt. He's groping, he's feeling, he's thrashing for a place of dignity under the American sun. He's rebelling against centuries of unfulfilled promises, decades of broken dreams, ages of bitter discrimination and suppression. But, one of the reasons for the confusion which exists in America today, I tell you quite frankly, is that black

Americans as a whole have no sense of direction. One man preaches nonviolence. He wants me to love my enemy. Another man speaks of guerrilla warfare. He believes, as does Mao Tse Tung, justice comes only from the barrel of a gun. One man tells me, "Rowan, we've got to stay here and struggle under the rule of law," and another man says, "Forget it, buddy, only the law of the jungle prevails in American race relations, so let's get the hell out of here." Now some of them want to free the struggle only part way. There is, for example, a group that preaches separatism within these shores. A. Milton Henry of Detroit would be a spokesman for this group. He's the man who recently proposed that Florida, Louisiana, South Carolina, Mississippi, and I believe one other state, be turned over to America's two million black people, and we're all supposed to pick up and move down there and set up a separate country, and in exchange for this real estate, we will promise the white man trouble-free summers. Now, why does this group of separatists arise? Well, they say, and they believe it with a passion, they say that racial integration is an unattainable goal. They say that this is a dream that the black man now rejects because he knows the white man never really believed in it. So he wants the Negro to become a nation within a nation, a Detroit within a Detroit, a Youngstown within a Youngstown, a Washington within a Washington. And out of this separatism, we're told, will emerge a black community that's self-governing, and self-sustaining. There will be Negro credit unions, Negro banks, Negro supermarkets, black distilleries, black king makers. In short, the white man's hand will be forever out of the black man's pocket. The white man's voice barred forever from black man's decision making, and everybody will live happily ever after. Well, you know, I can almost buy this nonsense, were it not for the fact that I've had a rather lot of intimate looks at an American minority that tried to remain a nation within a nation. I've roamed for weeks among the Chippawas of Minnesota and the Sioux of the Dakotas, but I didn't see all those credit unions and banks, and the political power, the abundance that supposedly accrued from getting yourself outside the mainstream of American life. What I saw was poverty, misery, squallor, hopelessness, aimlessness, despair, and no likelihood of change for as far ahead as man can see or hope.

But this notion of a self-governing Negro nation within the white nation at large is also being rejected by some of the people at the extremes of black consciousness. There are those who think the only solution is a Negro nation outside the United States. It was only a few days ago that I got a beautifully written letter from a young man in Los Angeles. Let me share a paragraph or two. He said, "Dear Mr. Rowan, For some time now I have been talking almost endlessly with a number of black people who would like to establish a black nation outside of the United States. The conviction to do so comes from a close and realistic look at American history as well as a very strong desire to really build something meaningful and lasting. We see the anger, the poverty, the frustration, the aimlessness, the wasted time and energy, and we see no early resolution here. Black people must formulate and execute their own destiny, and this has not happened in America, nor is there any significant evidence that it's about to happen. The lives of too many black people are hopelessly linked with perpetual domestic conflict." And that young man wanted to know whether I would in my column endorse his proposal and his group's proposal that black Americans pick up and go find themselves some idyllic island and set up a black republic where they can build something without wasting their time fighting white men. Well, my answer to that young man was simple. I wrote him that there is not a white man alive who is mean enough, powerful enough, or clever enough to make me flee this land made great in part by so much of the labor, the sweat, the tears of black men. I said to him, believe me, I'm here for the duration. And for those white Americans who are confused today, let me say that I make no pretense of speaking for anybody who says, Rowan doesn't speak for me; but if you want my guess, my guess is that there aren't more than a handful of black Americans who are going to cop out. I don't think there are any of them going to give up by default what they consider to be the birthright of their children and their children's children. Oh, don't get me wrong. I'm perfectly willing to lay claim to a little bit of Harlem, but I'm reaching out for a piece of Wall Street and Madison Avenue, too. But, as I've said, this has helped to create a tremendous amount of confusion in the white community.

Now, let me tell you. I think I can understand why some black people feel this way, why they've concluded that integration is an unattainable goal. It is because the white American businessman, politician, educator, preacher—they've all given abundant ammunition to the people who argue that integration is unattainable. In the fields of housing, employment, government, religion, social life, the white man's actions have shouted loudly to the Negro, "Our consciences for political expediency, or a variety of other pressures, force us to accept token desegregation, but real integration on a mass basis is simply not acceptable." Now, I run into hundreds of intelligent white Americans who express what they claim is a total inability to understand why the American Negro is so aroused in 1968 when he is "so much better off than he was in 1948." I am amazed and dismayed that those white Americans are not more aware of the extent to which they are reading tokenism as a sign of genuine across-the-board advance by the black man in this country. Oh, they look at Carl Rowan, who admittedly has moved a fair distance from that little red clay town in McMinnville, Tennessee, where he lived across the street from the junkyard. So they see me eating a little high off the hog and riding down the street in a big, fine car, and all of a sudden, their consciences are clear, and they say, "Boy, everything's all right, the black man has sure come a long way in this country." And if you want to show on a census bureau report that says the medium income of the Negro family in this country is today 59% of the medium income of the white family, they want to turn and say, "Statistics always did confuse me, let's not talk about that." But, this is not the dryness of statistics. The simple fact of life is—that if I have $5,900 a year and you have $10,000 a year and your family, you're going to be able to buy better food, better clothing, provide better education, bring more magazines and records into the family, all sorts of little cultural attributes; and the point is that from the very day your child is born, that child is a few jumps ahead of mine in that race we Americans call the pursuit of happiness. And you don't have to do any great figuring out as to why there's more divorce in the black community, why there's more crime out in that ghetto, why more people are dropping out of high school, why fewer of them get to college, why there is just a greater general weakness in the black family in this country. You don't have to go any further than that very first statistic about who can get his hand on that dollar that controls darn near everything in this society. Yet, they want to give you another cliché and say, well, yes, education is the answer. There is no doubt that Negroes have been caught in this vicious circle where there is an educational gap or that it's a gap in attainment as between the average black American and the average white American, but that's not the whole story. The Bureau of Labor Statistics recently reported that a black American with a college degree will, in his lifetime, earn exactly the same amount of money as a white American with three years of high school. So it shows you that even after you equalize the education or make it superior, there is still an awful lot of hanky-panky going on.

Now, let me give you a little example of tokenism at work. I tell you I want to leave a little time for you to get back at me with a question or two, so I'll not talk as long as I normally do at colleges. I normally talk long enough to prove my wife's definition of an optimist. She says that's a woman who puts her shoes back on when I say, "in conclusion." But I want to tell you a little bit about some hearings held in New York some weeks ago by a U.S. Commission on Equal Employment

Opportunities. There were some twenty or so corporate witnesses who testified, and if you would have listened to those executives talk, you'd think that we didn't have any problems, any racial problems in this country whatsoever. For example, Ralph H. Skinner, Vice-President for Personnel at Eastern Airlines, allowed as how his company fully recognized the need for fair employment and he said Eastern had had a very successful year. We have made appreciable strides. And then the commissioners began to ask him some questions, and they elicited information that of Eastern's 816 pilots stationed in New York City, one is a Negro. Of the 703 stewardesses, 42 are Negro. Of the 416 clerical workers, a mere 14 are Negro and 13 are Puerto Rican. Then William C. Fipps, Vice-President of CBS, stepped up and boasted that this broadcasting giant had had an equal opportunity policy since World War II. Questioning revealed that among 2,050 white-collar employees of CBS, 1.25 [percent] are Puerto Rican, and there's not a single Negro in an executive position. Now I mention that 1.25 percent, it's all the more important when you realize that Negroes and Puerto Ricans make up 23 percent of New York's population. Then came John Mortimer of the *New York Times,* and he said the *Times* preaches equal opportunity on its editorial pages and as an employer, we try to practice what we preach. Well, questioning revealed that the *Times* has three Negro reporters on its staff of 200, no Puerto Rican reporters or officials whatsoever, and of the 220 employees at the managerial level, one black man. This produced a rather interesting exchange between Clifford Alexander, the Chairman of the Commission, and Mr. Mortimer:

ALEXANDER: I wonder if you might want to retract item 4 where you say, as an employer we try to practice what we preach.
MORTIMER: No, I certainly would not.
ALEXANDER: Well, I think from what we have heard here today, perhaps you want to put a future tense in there. But there isn't any clear indication in this record you've given us that you are practicing what you preach.
MORTIMER: Well, I would admit that there is plenty of room for improvement. I would like to say that we've been trying. We hope to do better.

Well, I would only wish that the record of that hearing could be read by all those people running around in the labor unions of America saying, "I'm going to vote for George Wallace this year because the black man is taking over the country. I'm going to vote for George Wallace because a white man can't get a job these days. The Government's fixed it so any Negro who walks in is a cinch to get the job." And it amazes me, let me tell you, this is a notion held not just by nitwits or guys out digging ditches. I walked into WTOP in Washington a couple of weeks ago (this is where I tape my television commentary). When I had finished, the young man they call the floor man—that's the fellow who stands at the camera and when somebody upstairs says stand by, he says stand by, when they say go, he drops his finger—but this was a youngster just out of college in a job that is obviously going to lead him to some important position in the television industry. So he said, "Mr. Rowan, would you mind if I asked you a question, I hope you don't think it's personal." I said, "No, there are no embarrassing questions, only answers." He says, "Well, tell me, what do you think about this business where the Negro has the advantage of getting jobs today." I said, "What do you mean?" He said, "I mean, everybody's feeling so guilty about race relations that if a black man and a white man with the same qualifications walk into a company, the black man's going to get the job every time." And I said, "Oh, is this why I see WTOP so overrun by black faces?" And he looked around and of all the people scurrying over this great television station, there wasn't a black man in sight. And I hope that that's the last notion we'll hear from that particular young man.

But, I don't think for a moment that my speech or any column I write, or any other hundred people write, is going to change the notion of a great many Americans for some time to come, because we have a situation in this country where one kind of stupidity is compounded by another kind of stupidity, and we move like that tobaggan sliding down the hill ever closer to racial tragedy. I say to my Negro colleagues, for example, and not always with great popularity, don't think that you've got any claim to greater anger or militancy than I've got. My God! I'm just as angry as any black man who ever breathed from time to time, and don't you kids try to tell me that you invented protest because I was sitting in at the Neil House Hotel in Columbus, Ohio, before they coined the phrase, and when it was a terribly lonely exercise. But let me tell you, there have got to be a hundred different kinds of approaches to resolve this problem and you ask me why I'm not out advocating rioting in the streets and breaking windows and burning buildings; it is because logic tells me that 22,000,000 black people cannot physically take first-class citizenship from 178,000,000 white people. But, there are still some black people who believe that without violence there can be no progress because it takes violence to wake up those white people. But, on the other hand, you now have the growing notion on the part of white people that if they just adopt enough policies of oppression, they can silence even the legitimate protests and aspirations of the black people of this country and that somehow 178,000,000 whites can say to 22,000,000 blacks, shut-up and go back to your place, and they're going to do it. And let me tell you this, it just is not going to happen.

And if there is any responsibility that educated Americans face today, it is to prevent this kind of confrontation in which there can be no winner, because I guarantee you that 22,000,000 black people can't take first-class citizenship, but they can make this country a hell-hole that's not worth living in by anybody. I say this without any intentions of threat whatsoever, but these are the realities of life that have to be faced. You've had about 5% of the black people in the streets in America up 'til now. But I guarantee you, that if you put somebody in the White House who tried to put into practice half of the oppressions that George Wallace has intimated he'd put into effect, you will get a lot more than 5% in the street, and then you're going to get some Carl Rowans out in the street when they start messing with my children's birthright, and I won't be nearly as stupid as those people who stand out in the middle of the street breaking windows in front of the cops and burning down Negro business and destroying the jobs of black people.

So this is an absurdity that we cannot afford to have occur in this country. But how did we get to this point? We got to this point because a great many Americans just did not want to face up to the fact that there were some things they were obligated to do. They just did not want to face up to the fact that we have for many years been on the road to racial calamity. I think I first really began to understand this in 1954 when I went to India at the request of the State Department to lecture on the role of a free press in a free society. To tell you the truth, I said "Yes" with alacrity because I thought it would be a sort of vacation at tax payers' expense. I soon discovered that giving nine or ten speeches a day in torrid summer heat and monsoon humidity was a lot more than I had bargained for. In fact, at the end of the first month, I lost 17 pounds. I can hardly wait for them to ask me back. But I discovered that it didn't matter what I talked about. Eventually they got around to this question of race. Why? Because people looking at two conflicting societies in the world, wondering which to follow, are looking for many qualities of leadership. Strength, yes, reputation of success, yes, integrity, yes, but most of all, a sense of morality, a sense of justice. And they were asking me about race relations in America because most deeply they want to know, does this society offer the world a sense of justice, a sense of compassion.

And I'll never forget the night in Madras when a group of Indian journalists gave a dinner for me. We sat on the floor and ate rice with our fingers and argued about John Foster Dulles' military aid to Pakistan and a recognition of Red China, yes, Vietnam, (that was the year of the Geneva Accords) and, finally, the most distinguished of the journalists stroked his beard and said, "Mr. Rowan, maybe now we can ask you a few questions about something you really know something about." I said, "Yes." He said, "Tell me, is this Minneapolis Tribune that you work for a white newspaper?" I said, "Well, if you mean are the owners and most of the employees white, yes." He said, "I assume your white colleagues give parties now and then." I said, "They do." "Do they ever invite you and your wife?" I said, "Oh, very often." "Do you go?" I said, "Yes." "Do you enjoy yourself?" I said, "Most of the time." And I realized that even in 1954 we had a credibility gap. Drawing on another journalist who said, "Well, Mr. Rowan, let me ask you a question." I said, "Yes." He said, "Does your wife give parties?" I said, "Yes." "Do you ever invite your white colleagues?" I said, "Very often." "Do they come?" I said, "Generally." "Do they enjoy themselves?" I said, "Oh, all the time." And the gap widened. I looked at these faces full of disbelief and I said, "Gentlemen, there's no use our beating around the bush. I can tell that you don't fully believe me. Well, let me tell you something. With those questions about those parties, you put your finger on something that has been tremendously important to me and to the development to whatever philosophy I claim to have." I said, "You see, I walked out of Oberlin College with a pretty strong intellectual commitment to this notion of racial and human equality, but it took these parties to put some meat on the bones of intellectual conviction. And one journalist said, "What the devil are you talking about, meat on the—" I said, "I'll tell you what I'm talking about. I'm talking about the fact that no matter how strong, how deep your intellectual convictions go, there are some lingering doubts until you have the experiences that leave you with no doubt that people are fundamentally the same." And I said, "Where did I really learn it? At these parties. Because it didn't make any difference as to the race of the guest. The parties always ran the same way, starting with the girls clustered over here and the fellows over here, but after a slight libation or two, one of the cute young things walks up, shoes in hand, saying, "You don't mind if I take these off, do you," and makes a beeline for the men, and that would end the sexual segregation. And there was always one fellow to tell a risqué joke at least an hour before that thing was permissible. And it made no difference whatsoever the race of the guest, they all drank more than I was prepared to pay for."

As I sneaked out of that meeting with my hide, I said to myself, "Rowan, you're kind of a sneaky devil, aren't you?" I said, "Oh, you didn't lie to them about your colleagues at the *Minneapolis Tribune* or their parties, or your parties, you told them the truth. But you didn't tell them the whole truth, cause you didn't tell them that while talking about your colleagues at the *Minneapolis Tribune,* you weren't talking about most white Americans. Because you know that most white Americans have never sat down at lunch, cocktails, or dinner with Negroes they considered their cultural, social, intellectual equals. And to that extent, those Americans are uneducated for life in this world of revolution in which we live." And as I let those thoughts turn through my mind on down through the weeks and months and, indeed, years, I've had to say to myself, I didn't even tell them the whole truth about my fellow black Americans because these walls of segregation and the discrimination have been so high and so thick for so long that they have left many an American Negro with doubts himself, about the saneness of mankind and with very little opportunity to do anything about wiping out those doubts. Because they, too, have not had ample opportunity to sit down with white Americans over a glass of jello or a cup of tea or whatever it is that people choose to drink. And to that extent, this nation was permitting to fester the doubts and the old myths and all the old, ugly suspicions that lead to hatred and lead to racial polarization.

But what do we do about it? Well, I'll tell you what I'm doing about it. I'm an integrationist from the word go, and people, oh, they've got all sorts of reasons for trying to talk you away. They say, oh, but I've got a lot of racial pride and I'm not going any place that I'm not wanted. Well, maybe you've got more pride than I've got, I doubt it. But let me tell you this. If I swallowed that nonsense about not going where they don't want me, I'd probably still be walking barefoot in the red clay of McMinnville, Tennessee. Because when I left there in 1943, it was to go to a unit of 337 sailors at Topeka, Kansas, everyone of them white, and you'd better believe there were a lot of them there who didn't want any black kid coming in. And most certainly, when I got to midshipman school, they didn't want me. And God, they'd said, because we've never had a black officer in the history of this country in the Navy, they said it'd be a long day before they'd permit it, a black man to sit down in the ward room with the other Navy officers who, of course, called themselves gentlemen. And I knew I wasn't really wanted there. And you'd better believe that more recently, there were an awful lot of people in Congress and a lot of other places who didn't want a black man running the USIA with 13,000 employees and a budget of some 200 million dollars a year. But I went anyhow, because I felt that I was entitled to go and the country needed to have me go to all of those places. So this is why you may pick up your newspaper every now and then and say, by God, old Rowan's in the news again. Now he's got the country clubs all stirred up down in Washington.

Collateral Readings

Rowan, Carl T., *South of Freedom,* New York, 1952.

————, *The Pitiful and the Proud,* New York, 1956.

————, *Go West to Sorrow,* New York, 1957.

(Read any or all of Carl T. Rowan's numerous magazine and newspaper articles.)

Study Questions and Problems

1. How does Carl Rowan establish initial rapport with his audience in this speech?

2. Illustrate, using this speech, Rowan's technique of making statistical information come alive.

3. Compare Rowan's position of separatism with the view of James Forten. What similarities do you note?

4. How would you describe the organization of this lecture? Is it effective?

5. Does Rowan argue well from statistics? Justify your position by illustrating from this speech.

Floyd McKissick

Floyd B. McKissick was born in Asheville, North Carolina, in 1922. He attended Morehouse College in Atlanta, Georgia, and North Carolina College in Durham, where he first became an active member in the Congress of Racial Equality (CORE). After receiving a B.A. from North Carolina College, McKissick successfully entered the then segregated University of North Carolina Law School and became the first black man to earn an LL.B. at that institution.

As a lawyer McKissick engaged in civil rights trials, desegregating schools and defending the rights of CORE sit-in demonstrators. In June, 1963, McKissick was elected National Chairman of CORE. When James Farmer resigned as National Director of CORE, Floyd McKissick assumed that post and held it until September, 1967. Under McKissick's direction, CORE changed from a nonviolent interracial civil rights group to a militant black power organization. In July, 1966, McKissick stated:

As long as the white man has all the power and money, nothing will happen. The only way to achieve meaningful change is to take power.

McKissick is athletic in appearance, standing six feet tall. According to one account, he speaks with emotion usually bordering on tears or anger. He has been described as having a "sulphurous" style of speaking, which suggests the fire and brimstone Baptist preacher. His voice is varied and it is oriented toward eliciting a response from black auditors, from well educated to bayou and ghetto people.

Floyd McKissick's speech at Coe College, Cedar Rapids, Iowa, illustrates the increasing disenchantment among black leaders with any hope of social change in America. Apparently, McKissick was speaking impromptu, for at one point in this address he refers to speaking strictly ad hoc. His central idea is that contemporary American society is incapable of meeting the needs of the poor, the black, and the young: "The problems of the inability to change; the inability to even hear people, let alone make change after you hear people.

Nonviolence is abhorred by McKissick as a doctrine which reeks of racism. McKissick believes that blacks must have power to solve their own problems and that blacks should not participate in the Vietnam conflict.

The language of this speech is quite unique and is worth examining closely. Floyd McKissick, a college graduate and lawyer, spoke to a predominantly white audience of college students in language similar to that spoken by blacks in the urban ghetto. While one can only speculate about why he chose the language he did, it is conceivable that McKissick was trying to tell his audience indirectly that blacks need not conform to white middle-class standards of speech. The address is full of subtly mispronounced words and jargon like "cat" and "the man." The Negro flavor of the language can be traced to the initial use of such language by Stokely Carmichael and other pioneering militants.

McKissick is quite pessimistic about the future of social change in America. No solutions are offered save the faint hope that the idealism of youth will one day lead to a better society.

The Student and the Ghetto
May, 1969

Thank you very much, it's a pleasure to be here . . . now, we shall start on my purpose for being here. My purpose is to talk about "The College and the Ghetto." It's indeed impossible to cover the range of subjects that we will possibly make allusions to today, it's impossible to really go into the depth of the problem that I would prefer going into, and I can't do it in one hour; I can't educate everybody in one hour; I can't tell you what Malcolm X said in one hour; I can't tell you what W. E. B. Du Bois said in one hour; I can't tell you what Marcus Garvey did in one hour; I can't tell you Roy Wilkins' philosophy in one hour; and neither can I tell you Dr. King's philosophy, or Henry Garnet's or David Walker's. So I'm just going to have to sort of give you a smathering; what they call survey course, and you've been getting them kind of mixed-up educational experiences anyway, so I'm going to have to give you that kind of thing. Then, I'm going to make a recommendation. We have just completed a book called *Three Fifths of a Man;* three fifths, as you know, comes from the Constitution of the United States. The first recognition, well it's not the first recognition, but it is the first constitutional recognition of black men in this country, when they regarded them as three fifths of a man. Our country is a very racist country. I don't think we have to belabor that point! And the great cats who wrote the federalist papers—Jefferson, James Madison, and all of them people—and they wrote the pious language which makes up the Constitution all on slaves, and George Washington, the great father of this society, was indeed the father of this country, cause he sired about thirteen black children. He believed in integration by night, and yet he believed in slavery by day! This is the kind of inconsistency that exists in American history, and I want to go on further and say that because of the constitutional dogma that black people are no more than three fifths of a man is the plague of many of the problems that we have today.

Floyd McKissick   *Los Angeles Times Photo*

Let's look at one or two basic things. We are trying to talk about
the campuses today. Right now on the campuses I think if you turn
on your radio or TV today, you'll find that there's some folks that are
dissatisfied with a lot of college campuses. And I don't think the New
York where I just left it was five campuses that were discussing these
things in a very, ah, very meaningful way, shall we say—more than just
literal discussions. I think we have to recognize today that the campus
demonstration is symptomatic of what is larger with the greater society.
It's symptomatic that the system, the capitalistic system under which
we live, has really reached a stage in its deterioration and what used
to be capitalism ain't no more capitalism. What we call capitalism today
will never be it again and what we are really concerned with is the
failure of American society to deal with its basic problems. And those
problems are not only black people: the problems of the inability to
change; the inability to even hear people, let alone make change after
you hear people. And one of the misgivings I got about being here
is really that I've been around to some forty-some schools this year,
and I'm about tired. And I'm tired simply trying to tell white people
what to do, because I really don't believe that white people are going
to ever change. I don't believe that they got the capacity to even listen
to black people on an equal basis. They still believe that they are superior.
They still believe that anything that a black man thinks, anything that
the black man thinks, has got to be approved by him. The next thing,
he can't even listen. He has not the capacity to even listen! He has
not the capacity—he has not the capacity to even be courteous! He has
not the humanity that's left in him that can identify him with the other
people in this society. He has not the humanity to actually communicate,
negotiate, or even respect other people. He can't respect yellow people;
right now, he's going to tell black people—you stay over here and be
nonviolent—that cat got a great big set going over here in a little country
called Vietnam with a bunch of yellow people that ain't never called
us a nigger, and he's going to take us and put us in an army, and
in thirty days put a machine-gun in your hand, take you way over
somewhere and tell you to shoot down them people over there. And
yet he's going to tell you at home, to be nonviolent. This is what you
call pure racism in its vilest form. Nonviolence is a doctrine that reeks
with racism. Black people ain't never had no business accepting it in
the first place—and in the second place, the only thing that nonviolence
is is setting up dual standards contrary to all psychological concepts.
How come I'm going to be nonviolent with somebody that's beating
up against my head! We're the only people in the world asked to be
nonviolent. And the only reason they want you to be nonviolent is

because they don't intend to make any changes. The cat's got his foot on your neck, black people's neck, and when you tell him—look, take your foot off of my neck—the good liberals, the good liberal white friends say—wait a minute, they tell me, wait a minute, you're moving too fast, let us gradually take our foot off of your neck, because, after all, we had it on there for four-hundred years, and if we jerk it off we make it whiplash! The only way you can communicate with the man you can't sit down and talk with; you can take him into a room and you can say—look man, we don't like the way you're treating us, you're painting that sausage in that counter, or that hamburger, you're painting it red and pouring new blood over it every day, underneath it's rotten! Quit doing that! Cat tell you—I'm not doing that, or, I'm your friend, I love you, you know, and the next day he's pulling the same old stuff! One day, the brothers going to go down there and take care of some business at his place! Then the fellow, then the fellow says that something's wrong with these niggers! I don't know, you can't communicate with this society, and I'm going to tell you, I don't know.

The only reason I'm here today, I'm going to tell you, I hope, I got faith in young people in this society, but I have very little faith in the old people in this society. I have counseled, let me tell you, I'm speaking strictly ad hoc tonight—I have counseled people in this country; some of the best men, they call you in, they want to pay you, I say hell no, I don't want your money cause I don't want you to go around and tell nobody that you gave me some money. I had my bread before I came up here and I'll have it when I'm gone. I know how to deal with it, I don't want your money. College presidents, you set them down at a table, I say look, the cats on your campus are mad, they're going to mess up everything. I say look man, I came up here to sit down and talk and you wanted to listen to me. I said, now I tell you, that's wrong. Well, this executive committee's sitting here, and here's a great university, and I won't call his name cause I'm bound by ethics. It probably won't matter worth a damn, but I am bound by some ethics that I'm going to extend. One of the big universities in this country, that's the reason I don't care what happens to them. The students need to take it over. They need to take it over. That's the only way it's going to get any change. They ain't going to get no change no other wise. And they start talking about a minority of black students taking over a majority. How can some thirty-something black kids take over a university without the explicit cooperation of the white kids there who want to see some change happen too! See! And then, they go on to talk about, talk about a minority. Why hell, that's the only kind of change you're ever going to get with a minority. Look what Christ did, and he didn't have but twelve, and three of them was questionable! Next thing—now here's the kind of board of trustees that you had at this place. Four cats on the executive committee. One come in, one come in, and he sets up his batteries, tunes up his ears—I say, good morning, he say, "Huh, Huh," can't even hear, can't even hear! Then, the next thing, one of them starts coming in, "Uh-huh, I heard it, yea, she had her dress all the way up to here." Talking about mini-skirts. He says—"what's your impression of mini-skirts?" I say, they look real good to me, they look real good cause they don't hide everything! I like miniskirts! You know what I mean? "I'm opposed to mini-skirts, I'm opposed to the pill, I'm opposed to everything"—everything somebody came up with. These are the kind of cats that are running the great big university—four cats on the executive committee. And then, he comes in there, now this is the old one, come in there—"All the music that these young people playing today—rotten, and it's vulgar." I say, look man, did you ever listen to that music today? I said, did you ever listen to it today? I said, did you ever listen to Simon and Garfunkel? "Who are they?" I say, you never listen to Simon and Garfunkel talk about Miss Robinson? You know what Miss Robinson did? "No, who is she?" These are the kind of cats that are running the university—supposed to relate to you, you know! I say, well look, Miss Robinson is this woman who seduced her daughter's boyfriend. "Did what?" You know! I'm telling you! I said, look here, ah, at the cats who are widowed, and I said, look, do you hear the music that these young people are talking about today?

It ain't only with the failure to change affects white people as well as black people. And that's the reason that unless you get him this education, they don't know nothing about black folk, and black folk don't know nothing about you, cause these white folks been thinking they're superior all the time, and they've been keeping away the history about what I've been thinking. And they've been telling you I love you, and that's a damn lie, I ain't never loved you, cause you're too much like them! You see, it ain't been that much love involved in the first place. There's been a false concept. We got too many false concepts and we've got to get down to some basic honesty about what we are doing in this society. We've been off with another false concept, and what I was going to talk about earlier—we talk about the semantics of racism—and I want to go back to them four old cats sitting in that room at the university, but they're still sitting there. And they're still arguing with themselves that you can't bother our great university. It's got more ivy on it then any other building, this building here, and it's been here since the Reconstruction, and this is the great halls great men marched through. Don't nobody give a damn about that! This is the inability in this society to change, some false concepts I want to get to.

Right now, instead of dealing with the problem, you hear everybody come up here to talk about—talk about all we got. The President's report—they spent a million dollars. And these cats went out for a year. They wrote and read a bunch of stuff, and they came back here and they made the great big pronouncement, "We are now living in two societies. One black, and one white." A million dollars! Tax money! Any cat, any cat in the city of Chicago, New York, in Harlem, who ain't never been to school could have told him the same thing. Just like some gals came down there to Harlem the other day. "We are hunting for a location, Mr. McKissick, can you help us?" I say, well what you all doing? "We're opening this class. We are teaching a group of fourteen year old girls." What are you going to teach them? "We are going to teach them elementary sex education." A fourteen-year-old girl in Harlem can teach you education about sex! And these are the false conceptions that we deal with every day.

Now, I want to get back to one other, and this is on this thing called love. Love. Now, let me tell you—if somebody loves me, if a beautiful girl walks down here and says, I love you daddy, and I got two forty-five's on my hip, you know, I ain't thinking about shooting that girl. I'm thinking about talking to her and throwing away the forty-five's! But if some cat walked down here and is real boisterous and slaps up against my head, then I'm going to have to appropriately defend myself. And I found out that if a cat is beating on you, and you tell him, I love you, I love you, he keeps beating on you! And somehow or another, he doesn't get the message that his fists or his brick hurts. And I've been through this in 1947. I was on a freedom ride and I got beat, I seen my wife get beat, I seen my daughter get beat, I've seen all these people. And love is the thing that if you don't just do it unilaterally, that is, you just don't ask black folks to love white folks without white folks loving black folks back. And if you just love unilaterally, you don't get nothing in return. Love is something that always has to have a response. So I'm not asking for anybody's love. All I'm asking for is just a little bit of respect, and I think old Aretha Franklin sort of sings that thing and breaking ground, talking about just a little bit of respect is what black people want. And not so much of this love, because I ain't never seen it work in a very suitable way. The next thing is, I don't believe in this, as I said, this love and this nonviolence is tied up in one concept, and I believe that if anybody comes up, the good book says, you turn the cheek. I follow the good book. I turn the cheek to the left side, then I turn the cheek to the right side, then I pick up a two-by-four. All it is, psychologically; no man has ought to endure anything that another man—no, we can't have dual standards in this society.

And the other thing, the next concept that we are hearing around here all the time now, is separatism, and integration, and desegregation. And they say, Floyd McKissick is a separatist cause he is going to build a city called Soul City and he's building it, he said, it's going to be a black town. Well, let me clear the record up. I don't care what they say, just like right now, you hear the great big argument—black folks ain't got time to argue no more. They ain't got time to argue no more. When right now you hear the phrase, "black capitalism," and you hear the phrase, "economic black power," it don't make no difference cause right now this man has been talking integration, and integration for years, and the one thing he ain't never integrated is Wall Street. He ain't never integrated his Wall Street. And he can talk about integration all he wants to, it's a false concept cause it ain't never been practiced, it's not intended to be practiced. Wall Street, which is the citadel of all the money in this country, has never yet been integrated, which means that black people are the only people living in a capitalistic system without any capital. The only part that they are doing here in the first place is providing the margin of profits, and we are just merely consuming for the benefit of the greater society. The second thing; the real separatists in this society, going back to the President's report, was done ten and fifteen years ago. How do you think Harlem got all black? How do you think the Southside of Chicago got all black? How do you think Roxbury in Boston got all black? How do you think the second ward in Newark got all black? It ain't cause black people had all the power to make it all black. It was because white people decided that they were going to move to the suburbs. And they moved to the suburbs. Thousands moved to the suburbs within the last twenty years. They moved out and built new towns all between Washington and New York. Some fourteen new towns been built between Washington and New York, cause white folks didn't want to live with black folks. You see that the real power to determine whether Harlem is going to be an all-black community or whether Bedford-Stuyvesant is an all black community is not to be determined by the black people in the first place. All the white people moved out of Brooklyn. That's the reason all black folks control it. All the white people moving out of Washington now and it's about seventy-five to eighty percent black. Harlem's black cause all of the generations, each one of them, moved out. The real separatists in this society, the real separatists are the white folks. White folks who move to the suburbs now, and stand out on the suburbs and say, "I believe in integration," and they do, they got their nigger in that school out there! They got one and they show him all the time, the business and industrial world, they got one. They get her and sit her up front with her natural and say, "Here's our nigger, here she is, we believe in integration." How many employees have you got? "Ten thousand, nine-hundred and twenty-seven." How many black? "We got one. Here she sits." And this is the whole concept.

Next thing on this separatism, see, we're living in a pluralistic society in this country. Pluralistic society. And I'm sick of having white people always blame black people about something, because nobody ever complained when the Italians came over here, when the Italians got themselves together. In Italy, Giuseppe Garibaldi got them organized and they formed a thing called Italy, and they started speaking Italian, and they came over to this country and they started wearing black shirts, you know, and they got a monopoly on pizza houses all over the country. Nobody ever calls them separatists. Nobody ever called them Sicilians. The Sicilians came over. Not only did they get them a Cosa Nostro, they got them a Mafia. You know, ain't nobody ever called them separatists. The Chinese came over. The Chinese came over and they organized, got themselves together. In New York they own all the way from Canal Street all the way down to the Brooklyn Bridge. They speak Chinese, got Chinese banks, and got a monopoly on the Chinese dragon that moves through that street on Chinese New Year, and ain't nobody ever called them separatists. Every nationality in the world comes over here bringing a smorgasbord, or something, and they get organized and get themselves together and get a monopoly on their culture pattern and their cultural artifacts, and nobody ever calls them separatists. But the minute black folks decide that they're going to get something together, nobody ever says, let us integrate with you up here. The people came up to Wisconsin and got the cheese industry. Every nationality came here and got organized along racial lines. John Kennedy came over from Ireland. The Kennedy family, not only did they get organized, they got the heiress thing going and then got the religious thing going with them too. Both things to get organized to get political power. Every nationality that ever came over! You look and you'll see. Every nationality brought his thing, and one of the sad tragedies in this country is that you got to recognize the black man in this new day because the black man is now talking about a nationalistic spirit. A nationalistic spirit. That means that he himself ain't no Negro, and ain't nobody got no right to name him no Negro. A man is the nationality that he chooses himself. I ain't no Negro. Everybody—you can look at the Chinese. Where do they come from? China! Look at the Italians. They come from Italy! Look at the Russians. They come from Russia! Look at the French. They come from France! Now where is any country called Negro! Ain't no country called Negro nowhere! The only thing Negro is is a designation given to a group of people that you first regarded as three fifths of a man, and you still regard him that way. And you still treat him that way. I ain't no Negro, don't want to be none, and the sad thing about it my good friends, when I was fighting for integration, my concept of integration ain't what white people thought it was. All I wanted to do was to sit on that bus where anybody else sits, and I didn't give a damn who sat next to me. Whether they were purple, green, or polka-dot, or striped like a zebra. It didn't make much difference. I just wanted to sit on that bus, because if you had a law that said all people had a right to sit on a bus, any seat, I'm going to sit on any seat, and who I sit next to was inconsequential. And some people attached that I had to sit on there cause I had to sit by some white, like some white is going to make me any brighter or any purer. I have more damn sense that I'm going to have anyhow. Sitting next to white people ain't going to do me no good. These are some false concepts you got. And let me tell you something—I ain't never wanted to be white. I ain't trying to be white, and one of the worse things could ever happen to me is if I woke up tomorrow morning and found out that I was white. I ain't trying to be white. And it ain't no need white people thinking we all want to be middle class and hung up like them. We don't. And if I took the realistic thing of it, if I took your Ivory, soap, which is one-hundred percent pure, and bathed myself for twenty-five days, on the twenty-sixth day I'd still be the same black cat that I am now.

And you give me a concept of integration, how can I ever get totally assimilated with you in the first place? It won't happen in this century and any others. Races have always been on the face of the earth. We're going to always be there, and you're going to have to accept us as we are. And ain't no need of thinking that I'm going to change. I'm going to be black and you're going to have to respect black. And if I don't eat with a knife, fork, and spoon, the Constitution doesn't require me to eat with a knife, fork, and spoon. I can be born here syphilitic, blind, or crazy, that's all it is, and I ain't going to be changing and trying to jump through a bunch of hula-hoops trying to be white, and trying to play like I'm something I'm not just to satisfy some white people to integrate me. That's not what I'm trying to do.

I say that white people got to understand now! So we, so this society is hung up. I don't know, society is hung up in so many respects. I don't know whether society can ever change, cause I've reached a stage in my life where I question the ability, our ability, to get along together. I question that ability to get along together sincerely. I question that ability not so much in young people, but I question the ability of the old people who are really in the power of this country. It's about sixty-five of them that control the welfare of this country. Only sixty-five. And a good sixty percent of them are women. And they control the welfare of this country. And I'm sick, I don't believe that any black man ought to go fight any war in this country. I don't believe, and I don't advocate that any black cat get in the Army or the Navy, the Marines, or nothing. I don't advocate that.

And I want to make my position clear on one or two things. The country is hung up. We are headed down, unfortunately, one hell-of-a street. And it ain't going to be this university that really ain't going to play no damn part in this society, it ain't going to play no part. It's going to be one of your stupid white supremacist cops who walks down a beat in San Francisco or Los Angeles, or Atlanta, Georgia, and slaps a black cat upside the head. The black cat done had enough for the day and he ain't going to take it, and they're going to start waltzing in the street, and some other white cat is going to come up, and about ten black cats are going to come up, and a thing is going to be on. A thing is going to be on. You can sit here, and you can talk, talk about the changes in society, talk about the logic of change, talk about music appreciation, talk about all that kind of crap, but colleges better get on the ball that they're going to deal with the basic realities of this society. The basic realities of this society is that there ain't no question of whether society is sick, it's a question of how sick it is. And I don't want to spend my time measuring. I don't even know whether I want to stay too long, and one of the reasons why I want to build Soul City is because I already decided, I done already decided that I don't know whether I want to really be bothered too much more. I want to go on out. I ain't asking nobody to love me no more, didn't ask it ever, but I'm telling you, I've been through it. I've tried to sit down and talk, and I understand how the brothers feel all over the country. I've talked to them, I've met them in CORE, and when I was with CORE I met with them and talked to them all over the United States. They've been trying to talk. The President's talking junk. Everybody's talking out both sides of their mouth. Black folks out here are hungry. They're talking about giving India a bunch of wheat and folks are starving in Mississippi. The President came out the other day, said he's got a program to sponsor starvation. And I said, that's commendable. Every Sunday school teacher's always said that. You know. The churches ain't doing their part. The government's not doing its part. The universities not doing their part. And everybody's looking back and saying, "Society, this great American society." And they stand up here and all they're doing is painting signs. I was in Washington the other day, and they're spending millions of dollars washing off Lincoln's monument, and you know, Statue of Liberty, polishing all that bull up, you know. It's got a sign up there, "Give me your tired, and your hungry, and your poor." That's a damn lie! They don't want nobody coming over here from Africa, and the yellow people, or the people from South America. Oh, cut out that bull! The Statue of Liberty with all this Lincoln up there sitting real noble in the chair, you know. Great man. He freed the slaves. He didn't free no slaves in the last announcement. All he did was fire them! It's technical revolution. He didn't free no slaves. My friends, in all these things, all these things are enough to make people who were sincerely dedicated about the society in which we live and about the changes which need to be made in this society, many people are extremely tired.

Once again, once again, everywhere you go right now, somebody ask you, "What's going to happen this summer?" "Is it a long, hot summer ahead?" And I look at him and I say, fool. I mean, why are you going to ask me such stupid questions? What have you done that you didn't do last summer? What has been done? You can't just keep pushing people around. Maybe I'm a bit quieter. This is the last generation of me, cause in two or three more years, they'll be calling me an Uncle Tom. Let me tell you this, cause the youngsters ain't taking it. And when I talk to my kids right now, they ain't going to take what I took. I think I really don't know what it's going to take to make this society develop the capacity to hear. I'm much convinced that this society doesn't want to hear because it knows what it has to hear and it's not ready to make any changes. I believe this society would rather shoot down every black man in the country than to stand forward on the basis of a Constitution that they've got in Washington. And right now, this Administration is already got an attorney general fixed up, and a McCarran Act, and they've got concentration camps ready. I believe that's what this country wants to do, in fact. And I believe that most of the white people in this country, saving except a few, would sit idly and docilely by and do not a damn thing. And that's about the way I feel tonight. And thank you very much. We depend upon you to change this society.

Collateral Reading

Barbour, Floyd B., ed., *The Black Power Revolt.* Boston, 1968.

"CORE: Wild Child of Civil Rights," *Ebony,* XXII (October, 1965), 35-38.

McKissick, Floyd, "Black Power," *Interracial Review,* (July, 1966).
—————, *Three Fifths of a Man.* New York, 1969.

Rich, Marvin, "CORE and its Strategy," *The Annals of the American Academy of Political and Social Science,* CCCLVII (January, 1965), 113-117.

Study Questions and Problems

1. What is McKissick's basic position on relations between the races?

2. Identify slang expressions in McKissick's speech used by many blacks. Why do you think McKissick, a lawyer, used these terms?

3. What can you say about the organization of this speech?

4. Read McKissick's *Three Fifths of a Man* for a more complete understanding of the speaker's ideas.

5. What similarities and differences do you observe between the views of McKissick and Powell?

6. Do you agree with Floyd McKissick's pessimistic view toward the resolution of the race problem in America? Justify your position.

Eldridge Cleaver

Eldridge Cleaver was born in 1934. He spent many of his young adult years in prison. Cleaver became a staff writer for Ramparts *magazine in San Francisco, where he joined the Black Panther Party and edited the Party's newspaper,* The Black Panther. *Cleaver's book,* Soul on Ice, *published in 1967, was voted one of the ten outstanding books of the year by the* New York Times. *At present, Cleaver is a fugitive (accused of violating parole) living in exile.*

This short eulogy by Eldridge Cleaver presents the thesis that Dr. Martin Luther King's murder represented the death of King's "dream" of peace, brotherhood, and equality of opportunity between blacks and whites in American society. The meditation is a jeremiad prophesying the coming of a terrible and bloody holocaust and likening the corruption of America to the corruption of Babylon of old. To Cleaver, King's death represented an end to the era of nonviolent protest and attempts at conciliation of the races. In Cleaver's opinion the time of the black liberation struggle had begun. Now all black people were Black Panthers in spirit.

The language of the eulogy is poignant throughout, perhaps reaching its emotional depth with the speaker's observation:

And it is strange to see how, with each significant shot that is fired, time is speeded up. How the dreadful days that we all somehow knew were coming seem to cascade down upon us immediately, and the dreadful hours that we thought were years away are immediately upon us, immediately before us. And all eternity is gone, blown away, washed away in the blood of martyrs.

The excerpt contains rare eloquence as a eulogy not to Dr. King but to the notion of passive resistance to evil. It is brief because "words are no longer relevant. Action is all that counts now."

Meditation on the Assassination of Martin Luther King, Jr.

April, 1968

The murder of Dr. Martin Luther King came as a surprise—and surprisingly it also came as a shock. Many people, particularly those in the black community who long ago abandoned nonviolence and opted to implement the slogan of Malcolm X—"black liberation by any means necessary"—have been expecting to hear of Dr. King's death for a long time. Many even became tired of waiting. For here was a man who refused to abandon the philosophy and the principle of nonviolence in face of a hostile and racist nation which has made it indisputably clear that it has no intention and no desire to grant a redress of the grievances of the black colonial subjects who are held in bondage.

To black militants, Dr. King represented a stubborn and persistent stumbling block in the path of the methods that had to be implemented to bring about a revolution in the present situation. And so, therefore, much hatred, much venom and much criticism was focused upon Dr. King by the black militants. And the contradiction in which he was caught up cast him in the role of one who was hated and held in contempt, both by the whites in America who did not want to free black people, and by black people who recognized the attitude of white America and who wanted to be rid of the self-deceiving doctrine of nonviolence. Still, black militants were willing to sit back and watch, and allow Dr. King to play out his role. And his role has now been played out.

The assassin's bullet not only killed Dr. King, it killed a period of history. It killed a hope, and it killed a dream.

That white America could produce the assassin of Dr. Martin Luther King is looked upon by black people—and not just those identified as black militants—as a final repudiation by white America of any hope of reconciliation, of any hope of change by peaceful and nonviolent means. So that it becomes clear that the only way for black people in this country to get the things that they want—and the things that they have a right to and that they deserve—is to meet fire with fire.

In the last few months, while Dr. King was trying to build support for his projected poor people's march on Washington, he already resembled something of a dead man. Of a dead symbol, one might say more correctly. Hated on both sides, denounced on both sides—yet he persisted.

And now his blood has been spilled. The death of Dr. King signals the end of an era and the beginning of a terrible and bloody chapter that may remain unwritten, because there may be no scribe left to capture on paper the holocaust to come.

That there is a holocaust coming I have no doubt at all. I have been talking to people around the country by telephone, people intimately involved in the black liberation struggle—and their reaction to Dr. King's murder has been unanimous: the war has begun. The violent phase of the black liberation struggle is here, and it will spread. From that shot, from that blood. America will be painted red. Dead bodies will litter the streets and the scenes will be reminiscent of the disgusting, terrifying, nightmarish news reports coming out of Algeria during the height of the general violence right before the final breakdown of the French colonial regime.

America has said "No" to the black man's demand for liberation, and this "No" is unacceptable to black people. They are going to strike back, they are going to reply to the escalation of this racist government, this racist society. They are going to escalate their retaliation. And the responsibility for all this blood, for all this death, for all this suffering . . . well, it's beyond the stage of assigning blame. Black people are no longer interested in adjudicating the situation, in negotiating the situation, in arbitrating the situation. Their only interest now is in being able to summon up whatever it will take to wreak the havoc upon Babylon that will force Babylon to let the black people go. For all other avenues have been closed.

The assassin's bullet which struck down Dr. King closed a door that to the majority of black people seemed closed long ago. To many of us it was clear that that door had never been open. But we were willing to allow the hopeful others to bang upon that door for entry, we were willing to sit back and let them do this. Indeed, we had no other choice. But now all black people in America have become Black Panthers in spirit. There will, of course, be those who stand up before the masses and echo the eloquent pleas of Dr. King for a continuation of the nonviolent tactic. They will be listened to by many, but from another perspective: people will look back upon Dr. King and upon his successors with something of the emotions one feels when one looks upon the corpse of a loved one. But it is all dead now. It's all dead now. Now there is the gun and the bomb, dynamite and the knife, and they will be used liberally in America. America will bleed. America will suffer.

And it is strange to see how, with each significant shot that is fired, time is speeded up. How the dreadful days that we all somehow knew were coming seem to cascade down upon us immediately, and the dreadful hours that we thought were years away are immediately upon us, immediately before us. And all eternity is gone, blown away, washed away in the blood of martyrs.

Is the death of Dr. King a sad day for America? No. It is a day consistent with what America demands by its actions. The death of Dr. King was not a tragedy for America. America should be happy that Dr. King is dead, because America worked so hard to bring it about. And now all the hypocritical, vicious madmen who pollute the government of this country and who befoul the police agencies of this country, all of the hypocritical public announcements following the death of Dr. King are being repudiated and held in contempt, not only by black people but by millions of white people who know that had these same treacherous, political gangsters made the moves that clearly lay within their power to make, Dr. King would not be dead, nonviolence would prevail and the terror would not be upon us. These people, the police departments, the legislatures, the government, the Democratic Party, the Republican Party, those commonly referred to as the Establishment or the power structure, they can be looked upon as immediate targets and symbols of blame.

But it has been said that a people or a country gets the leaders and the government that it deserves. And here we have at the death of Dr. King a president by the name of Lyndon Baines Johnson who has the audacity to stand before this nation and mourn Dr. King and to praise his leadership and the nonviolence he espoused, while he has the blood of hundreds of thousands of people and the slaughtered conscience of America upon his hands. If any one man could be singled out as bearing responsibility for bringing about the bloodshed and violence to come, it would be Lyndon Baines Johnson. But not just Lyndon Baines Johnson. All of the greedy, profit-seeking businessmen in America, all of the conniving, unscrupulous labor leaders of America, all of the unspeakable bootlickers, the big businessmen of the civil rights movement and the average man on the streets who feels hatred instilled in his heart by this vicious and disgusting system—the blame is everywhere and nowhere.

Washington, D.C., is burning. My only thought at that is: I hope Stokely Carmichael survives Washington. Chicago is burning, Detroit is burning and there is fire and the sound of guns from one end of Babylon to the other.

Last night I heard Lyndon Baines Johnson admonishing his people, admonishing black people to turn away from violence, and not to follow the path of the assassins. And of all the corn pone that he spouted forth, one thing struck me and I felt insulted by it. He was ringing changes on a famous statement made by Malcolm X in his speech, "The Ballot or the Bullet." Malcolm X had prophesied that if the ballot did not prevail in gaining black people their liberation, then the bullet would be made to prevail. And Lyndon Johnson said last night that he was going to prove to the nation and to the American people that the ballot and not the bullet would prevail. Coming from him, it was a pure insult.

Those of us in the Black Panther Party who have been reading events and looking to the future have said that this will be the Year of the Panther, that this will be the Year of the Black Panther. And now everything that I can see leaves no doubt of that. And now there is Stokely Carmichael, Rap Brown, and above all there is Huey P. Newton. Malcolm X prophesied the coming of the gun, and Huey Newton picked up the gun, and now there is gun against gun. Malcolm X gunned down. Martin Luther King gunned down.

I am trying to put a few words on tape because I was asked to do so by the editor of this magazine, to try to give my thoughts on what the assassination of Dr. King means for the future, what is likely to follow and who is likely to emerge as a new or a prevailing leader of black people. It is hard to put words on this tape because words are no longer relevant. Action is all that counts now. And maybe America will understand that. I doubt it. I think that America is incapable of understanding *anything* relevant to human rights. I think that America has already committed suicide and we who now thrash within its dead body are also dead in part and parcel of the corpse. America is truly a disgusting burden upon this planet. A burden upon all humanity. And if we here in America . . .

Collateral Reading

Cleaver, Eldridge, *Post-Prison Writings and Speeches.* Edited by Robert Scheer. New York, 1969.

———, *Soul on Ice.* New York, 1968.

Cleaver, Kathleen, "On Eldridge Cleaver," *Ramparts,* VII (June, 1969), p. 4.

Marine, G., *The Black Panthers.* New York, 1969.

Swain, L., "Eldridge Cleaver," *North American Review,* (July, 1968).

Study Questions and Problems

1. What does the symbol of the Black Panther represent? Do you think the name was well chosen?

2. Do you agree with Cleaver's thesis that nonviolence died with the assassination of Dr. King?

3. Read the speeches contained in Eldridge Cleaver, *Post-Prison Writings and Speeches,* edited by Robert Scheer. New York: 1969. What basic weaknesses do you notice in Cleaver's speaking ability?

4. Read Cleaver's *Soul on Ice* for a more complete understanding of the mind of the speaker.

5. How were the Black Panthers created? What was their original purpose? What is their present program?

James Forman

James Forman was born in Chicago in 1930. He received a B.A. from Roosevelt University in Chicago and also studied at the Institute of African Affairs at Boston University. He served as the Executive Director of SNCC from 1961 to 1966.

The "Black Manifesto" was adopted at the National Black Economic Development Conference in Detroit, Michigan, on April 26, 1969. In May, James Forman delivered a speech in front of the Riverside Church in New York City, interrupting a Sunday worship service to demand reparations for discrimination practiced by white America over the centuries. This later occasion provoked a heated debate over the merits of Forman's proposal and whether or not the interruption of a church service violated social decorum.

In the introduction to the "Black Manifesto," James Forman articulates a Marxist-inspired revolutionary rhetoric. He contends that capitalism must be abolished in order to rid the nation of economic exploitation and racism. The argument follows that blacks are the most oppressed class and therefore they must (according to the "laws of revolution") assume leadership and control of the revolution. Forman, in traditional Marxist language, condemned alleged U.S. imperialistic interests in Africa, Latin America, and Asia. He called for eventual armed confrontation and long years of guerilla warfare. He urged that blacks build a new society. "We must commit ourselves to a society where the total means of production are taken from the rich people and placed into the hands of the state for the welfare of all the people." According to Forman, only an armed, well-disciplined, black-controlled government can eliminate racism in the United States.

The program for the seizure of power is presented in a twelve-point "Manifesto." The speech is organized in a problem-solution pattern with the solution portion contained in the twelve demands of the Black Economic Conference to the white Christian churches and synagogues of America. Essentially, the conference was on record for demanding $500,000,000 in reparations from the churches and synagogues of America. Forman con-

cluded by noting, "Our demands are negotiable, but they cannot be mini-mized, they can only be increased and the Church is asked to come up with larger sums of money than we are asking."

James Forman's audience consisted of a number of black leaders, includ-ing Julian Bond and Fannie Lou Hamer, together with members of Chris-tian churches representing that element of the Christian faith which ex-pressed concern and involvement in economic, social, and political problems of the day.

Black Manifesto

April 26, 1969

Total Control as the Only Solution to the Economic Problems of Black People

BROTHERS AND SISTERS:

We have come from all over the country, burning with anger and despair not only with the miserable economic plight of our people, but fully aware that the racism on which the Western World was built domi-nates our lives. There can be no separation of the problems of racism from the problems of our economic, political, and cultural degradation. To any black man, this is clear.

But there are still some of our people who are clinging to the rhetoric of the Negro and we must separate ourselves from those Negroes who go around the country promoting all types of schemes for black capital-ism.

Ironically, some of the most militant Black Nationalists, as they call themselves, have been the first to jump on the bandwagon of black capitalism. They are pimps: Black Power pimps and fraudulent leaders and the people must be educated to understand that any black man or Negro who is advocating a perpetuation of capitalism inside the United States is in fact seeking not only his ultimate destruction and death, but is contributing to the continuous exploitation of black people all around the world. For it is the power of the United States Government, this racist, imperialist government that is choking the life of all people around the world.

We are an African people. We sit back and watch the Jews in this country make Israel a powerful conservative state in the Middle East, but we are not concerned actively about the plight of our brothers in

Africa. We are the most advanced technological group of black people
in the world, and there are many skills that could be offered to Africa.
At the same time, it must be publicly stated that many African leaders
are in disarray themselves, having been duped into following the lines
as laid out by the Western imperialist governments.

Africans themselves succumbed to and are victims of the power of
the United States. For instance, during the summer of 1967, as the
representatives of SNCC, Howard Moore and I traveled extensively in
Tanzania and Zambia. We talked to high, very high, governmental
officials. We told them there were many black people in the United
States who were willing to come and work in Africa. All these government
officials who were part of the leadership in their respective governments,
said they wanted us to send as many skilled people as we could contact.
But this program never came into fruition and we do not know the
exact reasons, for I assure you that we talked and were committed to
making this a successful program. It is our guess that the United States
put the squeeze on these countries, for such a program directed by SNCC
would have been too dangerous to the international prestige of the U.S.
It is also possible that some of the wild statements by some black leaders
frightened the Africans.

In Africa today, there is a great suspicion of black people in this
country. This is a correct suspicion since most of the Negroes who have
left the States for work in Africa usually work for the Central Intelligence
Agency (CIA) or the State Department. But the respect for us as a people
continues to mount and the day will come when we can return to our
homeland as brothers and sisters. But we should not think of going
back to Africa today, for we are located in a strategic position. We
live inside the U.S. which is the most barbaric country in the world
and we have a chance to help bring this government down.

Time is short and we do not have much time and it is time we stop
mincing words. Caution is fine, but no oppressed people ever gained
their liberation until they were ready to fight, to use whatever means
necessary, including the use of force and power of the gun to bring
down the colonizer.

We have heard the rhetoric, but we have not heard the rhetoric which
says that black people in this country must understand that we are the
Vanguard Force. We shall liberate all the people in the U.S. and we
will be instrumental in the liberation of colored people the world around.
We must understand this point very clearly so that we are not trapped
into diversionary and reactionary movements. Any class analysis of the
U.S. shows very clearly that black people are the most oppressed group
of people inside the United States. We have suffered the most from

racism and exploitation, cultural degradation and lack of political power. It follows from the laws of revolution that the most oppressed will make the revolution, but we are not talking about just making the revolution. All the parties on the left who consider themselves revolutionary will say that blacks are the Vanguard, but we are saying that not only are we the Vanguard, but we must assume leadership, total control and we must exercise the humanity which is inherent in us. We are the most humane people within the U.S. We have suffered and we understand suffering. Our hearts go out to the Vietnamese for we know what it is to suffer under the domination of racist America. Our hearts, our souls and all the compassion we can mount goes out to our brothers in Africa, Santa Domingo, Latin America and Asia who are being tricked by the power structure of the U.S. which is dominating the world today. These ruthless, barbaric men have systematically tried to kill all people and organizations opposed to its imperialism. We no longer can just get by with the use of the word capitalism to describe the U.S., for it is an imperial power, sending money, missionaries and the army throughout the world to protect this government and the few rich whites who control it. General Motors and all the major auto industries are operating in South Africa, yet the white-dominated leadership of the United Auto Workers sees no relationship to the exploitation of black people in South Africa and the exploitation of black people in the U.S. If they understand it, they certainly do not put it into practice, which is the actual test. We as black people must be concerned with the total conditions of all black people in the world.

But while we talk of revolution which will be an armed confrontation and long years of sustained guerilla warfare inside this country, we must also talk of the type of world we want to live in. We must commit ourselves to a society where the total means of production are taken from the rich people and placed into the hands of the state for the welfare of all the people. This is what we mean when we say total control. And we mean that black people who have suffered the most from exploitation and racism must move to protect their black interest by assuming leadership inside of the United States of everything that exists. The time has passed when we are second in command and the white boy stands on top. This is especially true of the Welfare Agencies in this country, but it is not enough to say that a black man is on top. He must be committed to building the new society, to taking the wealth away from the rich people such as General Motors, Ford, Chrysler, the DuPonts, the Rockefellers, the Mellons, and all the other rich white exploiters and racists who run this world.

Where do we begin? We have already started. We started the moment we were brought to this country. In fact, we started on the shores of Africa, for we have always resisted attempts to make us slaves and now we must resist the attempts to make us capitalists. It is in the financial interest of the U.S. to make us capitalists, for this will be the same line as that of integration into the mainstream of American life. Therefore, brothers and sisters, there is no need to fall into the trap that we have to get an ideology. We *have* an ideology. Our fight is against racism, capitalism and imperialism and we are dedicated to building a socialist society inside the United States where the total means of production and distribution are in the hands of the State and that must be led by black people, by revolutionary blacks who are concerned about the total humanity of this world. And, therefore, we obviously are different from some of those who seek a black nation in the United States, for there is no way for that nation to be viable if in fact the United States remains in the hands of white racists. Then too, let us deal with some arguments that we should share power with whites. We say that there must be a revolutionary black vanguard and that white people in this country must be willing to accept black leadership, for that is the only protection that black people have to protect ourselves from racism rising again in this country.

Racism in the U.S. is so pervasive in the mentality of whites that only an armed, well-disciplined, black-controlled government can insure the stamping out of racism in this country. And that is why we plead with black people not to be talking about a few crumbs, a few thousand dollars for this cooperative, or a thousand dollars which splits black people into fighting over the dollar. That is the intention of the government. We say . . . think in terms of total control of the U.S. Prepare ourselves to seize state power. Do not hedge, for time is short and all around the world, the forces of liberation are directing their attacks against the U.S. It is a powerful country, but that power is not greater than that of black people. We work the chief industries in this country and we could cripple the economy while the brothers fought guerrilla warfare in the streets. This will take some long-range planning, but whether it happens in a thousand years is of no consequence. It cannot happen unless we start. How then is all of this related to this conference?

First of all, this conference is called by a set of religious people, Christians, who have been involved in the exploitation and rape of black people since the country was founded. The missionary goes hand in hand with the power of the states. We must begin seizing power wherever we are and we must say to the planners of this conference that you are no longer in charge. We the people who have assembled here thank you for getting us here, but we are going to assume power over the conference and determine from this moment on the direction in which we want it to go. We are not saying that the conference was planned badly. The staff of the conference has worked hard and have done a magnificent job in bringing all of us together and we must include them in the new leadership which must surface from this point on. The conference is now the property of the people who are assembled here. This we proclaim as fact and not rhetoric and there are demands that we are going to make and we insist that the planners of this conference help us implement them.

We maintain we have the revolutionary right to do this. We have the same rights, if you will, as the Christians had in going into Africa and raping our Motherland and bringing us away from our continent of peace and into this hostile and alien environment where we have been living in perpetual warfare since 1619.

Our seizure of power at this conference is based on a program and our program is contained in the following *Manifesto:*

Black Manifesto

To the White Christian Churches and the Jewish Synagogues in the United States of America and All Other Racist Institutions:

We the black people assembled in Detroit, Michigan, for the National Black Economic Development Conference are fully aware that we have been forced to come together because racist white America has exploited our resources, our minds, our bodies, our labor. For centuries we have been forced to live as colonized people inside the United States, victimized by the most vicious, racist system in the world. We have helped to build the most industrial country in the world.

We are therefore demanding of the white Christian churches and Jewish synogogues which are part and parcel of the system of capitalism, that they begin to pay reparations to black people in this country. We are demanding $500,000,000 from the Christian white churches and the Jewish synagogues. This total comes to 15 dollars per nigger. This is a low estimate, for we maintain there are probably more than 30,000,000 black people in this country. Fifteen dollars a nigger is not a large sum of money and we know that the churches and synagogues have a tremendous wealth and its membership, white America, has profited and still exploits black people. We are also not unaware that the exploitation of colored peoples around the world is aided and abetted by the white Christian churches and synagogues. This demand for $500,000,000 is not an idle resolution or empty words. Fifteen dollars for every black brother and sister in the United States is only a beginning of the reparations due us as people who have been exploited and degraded, brutalized, killed and persecuted. Underneath all of this exploitation, the racism of this country has produced a psychological effect upon us that we are beginning to shake off. We are no longer afraid to demand our full rights as a people in this decadent society.

We are demanding $500,000,000 to be spent in the following way:

1. We call for the establishment of a Southern land bank to help our brothers and sisters who have to leave their land because of racist pressure, for people who want to establish cooperative farms, but who have no funds. We have seen too many farmers evicted from their homes because they have dared to defy the white racism of this country. We need money for land. We must fight for massive sums of money for this Southern Land Bank. We call for $200,000,000 to implement this program.

2. We call for the establishment of four major publishing and printing industries in the United States to be funded with ten million dollars each. These publishing houses are to be located in Detroit, Atlanta, Los Angeles, and New York. They will help to generate capital for further cooperative investments in the black community, provide jobs and an alternative to the white-dominated and controlled printing field.

3. We call for the establishment of four of the most advanced scientific and futuristic audio-visual networks to be located in Detroit, Chicago, Cleveland, and Washington, D.C. These TV networks will provide an alternative to the racist propaganda that fills the current television networks. Each of these TV networks will be funded by ten million dollars each.

4. We call for a research skills center which will provide research on the problems of black people. This center must be funded with no less than 30 million dollars.

5. We call for the establishment of a training center for the teaching of skills in community organization, photography, movie making, television making and repair, radio building and repair and all other skills needed in communication. This training center shall be funded with no less than ten million dollars.

6. We recognize the role of the National Welfare Rights Organization

and we intend to work with them. We call for ten million dollars to assist in the organization of welfare recipients. We want to organize the welfare workers in this country so that they may demand more money from the government and better administration of the welfare system of this country.

7. We call for $20,000,000 to establish a National Black Labor Strike and Defense Fund. This is necessary for the protection of black workers and their families who are fighting racist working conditions in this country.

*8. We call for the establishment of the International Black Appeal (IBA). This International Black Appeal will be funded with no less than $20,000,000. The IBA is charged with producing more capital for the establishment of cooperative businesses in the United States and in Africa, our Motherland. The International Black Appeal is one of the most important demands that we are making for we know that it can generate and raise funds throughout the United States and help our African brothers. The IBA is charged with three functions and shall be headed by James Forman:

(a) Raising money for the program of the National Black Economic Development Conference.

(b) The development of cooperatives in African countries and support of African Liberation movements.

(c) Establishment of a Black Anti-Defamation League which will protect our African image.

9. We call for the establishment of a Black University to be funded with $130,000,000 to be located in the South. Negotiations are presently under way with a Southern university.

10. We demand that IFCO allocate all unused funds in the planning budget to implement the demands of this conference.

In order to win our demands, we are aware that we will have to have massive support. Therefore:

1. We call upon all black people throughout the United States to consider themselves as members of the National Black Economic Development Conference and to act in unity to help force the racist white Christian churches and Jewish synogogues to implement these demands.

2. We call upon all the concerned black people across the country to contact black workers, black women, black students and the black

---

*Revised and approved by Steering Committee.

unemployed, community groups, welfare organizations, teachers organizations, church leaders and organizations explaining how these demands are vital to the black community of the U.S. Pressure by whatever means necessary should be applied to the white power structure of the racist white Christian churches and Jewish synagogues. All black people should act boldly in confronting our white oppressors and demanding this modest reparation of 15 dollars per black man.

3. Delegates and members of the National Black Economic Development Conference are urged to call press conferences in the cities and to attempt to get as many black organizations as possible to support the demands of the conference. The quick use of the press in the local areas will heighten the tension and these demands must be attempted to be won in a short period of time, although we are prepared for protracted and long-range struggle.

4. We call for the total disruption of selected church sponsored agencies operating anywhere in the U.S. and the world. Black workers, black women, black students, and the black unemployed are encouraged to seize the offices, telephones, and printing apparatus of all church sponsored agencies and to hold these in trusteeship until our demands are met.

5. We call upon all delegates and members of the National Black Economic Development Conference to stage sit-in demonstrations at selected black and white churches. This is not to be interpreted as a continuation of the sit-in movement of the early sixties but we know that active confrontation inside white churches is possible and will strengthen the possibility of meeting our demands. Such confrontation can take the form of reading the Black Manifesto instead of a sermon or passing it out to church members. The principle of self-defense should be applied if attacked.

6. On May 4, 1969, or a date thereafter, depending upon local conditions, we call upon black people to commence the disruption of the racist churches and synogogues throughout the United States.

7. We call upon IFCO to serve as a central staff to coordinate the mandate of the conference and to reproduce and distribute en mass literature, leaflets, news items, press releases and other material.

8. We call upon all delegates to find within the white community those forces which will work under the leadership of blacks to implement these demands by whatever means necessary. By taking such actions, white Americans will demonstrate concretely that they are willing to

fight the white skin privilege and the white supremacy and racism which has forced us as black people to make these demands.

9. We call upon all white Christians and Jews to practice patience, tolerance, understanding and nonviolence as they have encouraged, advised and demanded that we as black people should do throughout our entire enforced slavery in the United States. The true test of their faith and belief in the Cross and the words of the prophets will certainly be put to a test as we seek legitimate and extremely modest reparations for our role in developing the industrial base of the Western world through our slave labor. But we are no longer slaves, we are men and women, proud of our African heritage, determined to have our dignity.

10. We are so proud of our African heritage and realize concretely that our struggle is not only to make revolution in the United States, but to protect our brothers and sisters in Africa and to help them rid themselves of racism, capitalism, and imperialism by whatever means necessary, including armed struggle. We are and must be willing to fight the defamation of our African image wherever it rears its ugly head. We are therefore charging the Steering Committee to create a Black Anti-Defamation League to be funded by money raised from the International Black Appeal.

11. We fully recognize that revolution in the United States and Africa, our Motherland, is more than a one-dimensional operation. It will require the total integration of the political, economic, and military components and therefore, we call upon all our brothers and sisters who have acquired training and expertise in the fields of engineering, electronics, research, community organization, physics, biology, chemistry, mathematics, medicine, military science and warfare to assist the National Black Economic Development Conference in the implementation of its program.

12. To implement these demands we must have a fearless leadership. We must have a leadership which is willing to battle the church establishment to implement these demands. To win our demands we will have to declare war on the white Christian churches and synogogues and this means we may have to fight the total government structure of this country. Let no one here think that these demands will be met by our mere stating them. For the sake of the churches and synagogues, we hope that they have the wisdom to understand that these demands are modest and reasonable. But if the white Christians and Jews are not willing to meet our demands through peace and good will, then we declare war and we are prepared to fight by whatever means necessary. We are, therefore, proposing the election of the following Steering Committee:

Lucious Walker   Mark Comfort
Renny Freeman   Earl Allen
Luke Tripp   Robert Browne
Howard Fuller   Vincent Harding
James Forman   Mike Hamlin
John Watson   Len Holt
Dan Aldridge   Peter Bernard
John Williams   Michael Wright
Ken Cockrel   Muhammed Kenyatta
Chuck Wooten   Mel Jackson
Fannie Lou Hamer   Howard Moore
Julian Bond   Harold Holmes

Brothers and sisters, we no longer are shuffling our feet and scratching our heads. We are tall, black, and proud.

And we say to the white Christian churches and Jewish synagogues, to the government of this country and to all the white racist imperialists who compose it, there is only one thing left that you can do to further degrade black people and that is to kill us. But we have been dying too long for this country. We have died in every war. We are dying in Vietnam today fighting the wrong enemy.

The new black man wants to live and to live means that we must not become static or merely believe in self-defense. We must boldly go out and attack the white Western world at its power centers. The white Christian churches are another form of government in this country and they are used by the government of this country to exploit the people of Latin America, Asia and Africa, but the day is soon coming to an end. Therefore, brothers and sisters, the demands we make upon the white Christian churches and the Jewish synagogues are small demands. They represent 15 dollars per black person in these United States. We can legitimately demand this from the church power structure. We must demand more from the United States Government.

But to win our demands from the Church which is linked up with the United States Government, we must not forget that it will ultimately be by force and power that we will win.

We are not threatening the churches. We are saying that we know the churches came with the military might of the colonizers and have been sustained by the military might of the colonizers. Hence, if the churches in colonial territories were established by military might, we know deep within our hearts that we must be prepared to use force to get our demands. We are not saying that this is the road we want to take. It is not, but let us be very clear that we are not opposed to force and we are not opposed to violence. We were captured in Africa by violence. We were kept in bondage and political servitude and forced to work as slaves by the military machinery and the Christian Church working hand in hand.

We recognize that in issuing this manifesto we must prepare for a long range educational campaign in all communities of this country, but we know that the Christian churches have contributed to our oppression in white America. We do not intend to abuse our black brothers and sisters in black churches who have uncritically accepted Christianity. We want them to understand how the racist white Christian Church with its hypocritical declarations and doctrines of brotherhood has abused our trust and faith. An attack on the religious beliefs of black people is not our major objective, even though we know that we were not Christians when we were brought to this country, but that Christianity was used to help enslave us. Our objective in issuing this Manifesto is to force the racist white Christian Church to begin the payment of reparations which are due to all black people, not only by the Church but also by private business and the U.S. Government. We see this focus on the Christian Church as an effort around which all black people can unite.

Our demands are negotiable, but they cannot be minimized, they can only be increased and the Church is asked to come up with larger sums of money than we are asking. Our slogans are:

ALL ROADS MUST LEAD TO REVOLUTION
UNITE WITH WHOMEVER YOU CAN UNITE
NEUTRALIZE WHEREVER POSSIBLE
FIGHT OUR ENEMIES RELENTLESSLY
VICTORY TO THE PEOPLE
LIFE AND GOOD HEALTH TO MANKIND
RESISTANCE TO DOMINATION BY THE WHITE CHRISTIAN CHURCHES
   AND THE JEWISH SYNAGOGUES
REVOLUTIONARY BLACK POWER
WE SHALL WIN WITHOUT A DOUBT

Collateral Reading

"Black's Manifesto Declares War on Churches," *Churches Today* (May 23, 1969), 29.

"Churches and James Forman," *Christian Today* (June 6, 1969), 27.

Warren, Robert Penn, *Who Speaks for the Negro?* New York, 1965.

Westin, Alan E., ed., *Freedom Now! The Civil Rights Struggle in America.* New York, 1964.

Study Questions and Problems

1. What is James Forman's general purpose in this speech? What is his specific purpose?

2. Compare Forman's "Black Manifesto" to Garnet's "Address to the Slaves of America." What similarities do you observe?

3. What long-range effects may result from the reparation demands? In your opinion, how will organized religion in America react to this issue?

4. What elements of classical Marxism do you observe in Forman's speech?

5. Evaluate Forman's reparations program. What aspects of the program appear plausible and what parts appear impractical?

James Farmer
and
Malcolm X

James Farmer was born in Marshall, Texas, on January 12, 1920. He received a B.D. from Howard University in 1941. In 1942 he helped organize the Congress of Racial Equality (CORE), an organization based on the principle of nonviolent protest for civil liberties. Farmer became CORE's National Director from 1961 to 1966 and originated the concept of the "Freedom Ride," which led to the successful integration of transportation facilities in the South. Farmer also served as an Assistant Secretary in the Department of Health, Education, and Welfare.

Malcolm X was born Malcolm Little in Omaha, Nebraska, on May 19, 1925. He converted to the religious sect of Black Muslims at the age of 21 while serving a prison sentence for burglary. Malcolm X broke away from the Black Muslims group headed by Elijah Muhammed in 1964 to form the Muslim Mosque, Inc., and later the nonreligious organization of Afro-American Unity. He was assassinated in 1965.

James Farmer and Malcolm X debated the solution to the race problem at Cornell University in Ithaca, New York, on March 7, 1962, before an audience of predominantly white upper-middle-class university students. Each speaker presented an initial speech followed by a somewhat shorter rebuttal speech.

Both speakers assumed that racism did exist in American society, so that in a sense both speakers acknowledged the need to put an end to racial discrimination. Thus, the debate focused upon which speaker's solution or plan was workable and more advantageous. Farmer pointed out that race prejudice damaged Negroes psychologically, economically, and politically. The CORE leader advocated continued use of nonviolent direct action protest as a means of ending segregation. He cited numerous examples of successful direct action protests as evidence of the power of this form of demonstration. Thus, James Farmer advocated integration of American society as a means of repudiating the racist theories and practices of the past.

Malcolm X's central thesis was that nonwhites throughout the world want freedom, justice, and equality. "It is not a case of wanting integration or separation, it is a case of wanting freedom, justice, and equality." He argued that integration-minded Negroes were a minority of middle- and upper-middle-class Negroes who were not representative of the disillusioned masses. He contended that integration was a practical failure and that it had not overcome the inherently racist nature of American society. He therefore advocated separation and identification with the Muslims on the earth and the setting aside of a part of America for all black Americans.

Debate on the Solution
to America's Race Problem

March 7, 1962

JAMES FARMER: When the Freedom Riders left from Montgomery, Alabama, to ride into the conscience of America and into Jackson, Mississippi, there were many persons who said to us, "Don't go into Mississippi, go any place you like, go to the Union of South Africa, but stay out of Mississippi." They said, "What you found in Alabama will be nothing compared to what you will meet in Mississippi." I remember being told a story by one minister who urged us not to go. He said, "Once upon a time there was a Negro who had lived in Mississippi, lived for a long time running from county to county. Finally he left the state, and left it pretty fast, as Dick Gregory would put it, not by Greyhound, but by bloodhound, and he went to Illinois to live, in Chicago. And unable to find a job there, after several weeks of walking the street unemployed, he sat down and asked God what he should do. God said, 'Go back to Mississippi.' He said, 'Lord, you surely don't mean it, you're jesting. You don't mean for me to go back to Mississippi. There is segregation there!' The Lord said, 'Go back to Mississippi.' The man looked up and said, 'Very well, Lord, if you insist, I will do it, I will go. But will you go with me?' The Lord said, 'As far as Cincinnati.'"

The Freedom Riders felt that they should go all the way because there is something wrong with our nation and we wanted to try to set it right. As one of the nation's scholars wrote at the turn of the century, "The problem of the twentieth century will be the problem of the color-line, of the relations between the lighter and the darker peoples of the earth, Asia and Africa, in America, and in the islands of the sea." What prophetic words, indeed. We have seen the struggle for freedom all over the world. We have seen it in Asia; we have seen it in the island of the sea; we have seen it in Africa; and we are seeing it in America now. I think the racist theories of Count DeGobineu, Lothrop Stoddard, and the others have set the pattern for a racism that exists within our country. There are theories that are held today, not only by those men and their followers and successors, but by Ross Barnett, John Patterson devotees and followers of the Klan and the White Citizens Councils, and Lincoln Rockwell of the American Nazi Party.

These vicious racist theories hold that Negroes are inferior and whites are superior innately. Ordained by God, so to speak. No more vicious theory has existed in the history of mankind. I would suggest to you that no theory has provided as much human misery throughout the

James Farmer   *Los Angeles Times Photo*

centuries as the theory of races—the theories that say some people are innately inferior and that others are innately superior. Although we have some of those theories in our country, we also have a creed of freedom and of democracy. As Pearl Buck put it, "Many Americans suffer from a split personality. One side of that personality is believing in democracy and freedom, as much as it is possible for a man so to believe. The other side of this personality is refusing, just as doggedly, to practice that democracy and that freedom, in which he believes." That was the split personality. Gunnar Myrdal, in his book, *The American Dilemma*, indicated that this was basically a moral problem, and that we have this credo which Americans hold to, of freedom, and democracy, and equality, but still we refuse to practice it. Gunnar Myrdal indicated that this is sorely troubling the American conscience.

All of us are a part of this system, *all* a part of it. We have all developed certain prejudices, I have mine, you have yours. It seems to me that it is extremely dangerous when any individual claims to be without prejudice, when he really does have it. I'm prejudiced against women drivers. I think they are a menace to civilization, and the sooner they are removed from the highways, the safer we will all be, but I know that's nothing but a prejudice. I have seen women drivers who are better drivers than I am, but does that destroy my prejudice? No. What I do then is to separate her from the group of women drivers and say, "Why she is an exception." Or maybe I say she is driving very well because she feels guilty. She knows that other women in the past have had accidents, and so she drives cautiously.

I remember several years ago when I was a youth, attending a church youth conference, and a young fellow from Mississippi and I became very good friends. The last day of the conference as we walked along the road he put his arm on my shoulder and said, "Jim, I have no race prejudice." "No," said I. "Absolutely not," said he. I raised my eyebrows. "As a matter of fact," he went on, "I was thirteen years old before I knew I was any better than a Negro." Well sometimes a supposed absence of racial prejudice runs quite along those lines. Now prejudice is a damaging thing to Negroes. We have suffered under it tremendously. It damages the lives of little children. I remember when I first came into contact with segregation; it was when I was a child in Mississippi when my mother took me downtown, and on the way back this hot July day I wanted to stop and get a Coke, and she told me I couldn't get a Coke, I had to wait until I got home. "Well why can't I, there's a little boy going in," said I. "I bet he's going to get a Coke." He was. "Well why can't I go?" "Because he's white," she said, "and you're colored." It's not important what happened to me, the fact is that the same thing over and over again happens to every mother's child whose skin happens to be dark.

If the damage that is done to Negroes is obvious, the damage that is done to whites in America is equally obvious, for they're prejudiced. I lived in Texas a large part of my life; [I] remember driving through the state, and after dusk had fallen being followed by cars of whites who forced me off the road and said to me, "Don't you know that your kind is not supposed to be in this town after sundown." I wondered what was happening to these people; how their minds were being twisted, as mine and others like me had had our minds twisted by this double-edged sword of prejudice. It is a disease indeed. It is an American disease. It is an American dilemma.

The Nation Suffers for Segregation

The damage to Negroes is psychological; it is also economic. Negroes occupy the bottom of the economic ladder, the poorest jobs, the lowest paying jobs. Last to be hired, and first to be fired, so that today the percentage of unemployed Negroes is twice as high as that of whites. There has been political damage as well. In the South we find that comparatively few Negroes are registered to vote. Many are apathetic even when they could register. The percentage who are registered in the North is almost equally as low. As a result, comparatively few Negroes are elected to political office. Thus, the damage to the Negroes, as a result of the disease of segregation, has been psychological, economic, social, and political. I would suggest to you that the same damages have occurred to whites. Psychological damages are obvious. Economic—the nation itself suffers economically, as a result of denying the right of full development to one-tenth of its population. Skills, talents, and abilities are crushed in their cradle, are not allowed to develop. Snuffed out. Thus, the nation's economy has suffered. People who could be producing are instead walking the streets. People who could be producing in better jobs and producing more are kept in the lower jobs, sweeping the floors and serving other persons. The whole nation has been damaged by segregation. Now, all of us share the guilt too. I myself am guilty. I am guilty because I spent half my life in the South. During those years I participated in segregation, cooperated with it, and supported it.

We are all intricately involved in the system of segregation. We have not yet extricated ourselves. Negroes are involved, and guilty, and share the blame to the extent they themselves have, by their deeds and their acts, allowed segregation to go on for so long. I do not believe that guilt is a part of my genes or your genes. It hinges upon the deeds that you have done. If you have supported segregation, then you are guilty. If you continue to support it, then your guilt is multiplied. But that is your guilt, that is mine. We share the guilt for the disease of segregation, and its continued existence. All too long, Negro Americans have put up with the system of segregation, North and South. Incidentally, it is not a Southern problem, it is a Northern one as well. Segregation exists in housing and in jobs and in schools. We have put up with it, have done nothing about it.

The day before the Freedom Riders left Washington, D. C., to ride into the South, I visited my father who was in the hospital on what proved to be his deathbed. I told him I was going on a Freedom Ride into the South. He wanted to know what it was and I told him. "Where are you going?" he asked, and I told him. He said, "Well, I'm glad that you're going, son, and I hope you survive. I realize you may not return, but," said he, "I'm glad you're going because when I was a child in South Carolina and Georgia, we didn't like segregation either, but we thought that's the way things always had to be and the way they always would be, so we put up with it, took part in it, decided to exist and to stay alive. I am glad," said he, "that there are lots of people today who are no longer willing to put up with the evil of segregation, but want to do something about it and know that something can be done." How right he was indeed.

The masses of Negroes are through putting up with segregation; they are tired of it. They are tired of being pushed around in a democracy which fails to practice what it preaches. The Negro students of the South who have read the Constitution, and studied it, have read the amendments to the Constitution, and know the rights that are supposed to be theirs—they are coming to the point where they themselves want to do something about achieving these rights, not [to] depend on somebody else. The time has passed when we can look for pie in the sky, when we can depend upon someone else on high to solve the problem for us. The Negro students want to solve the problem themselves. Masses of older Negroes want to join them in that. We can't wait for the law. The Supreme Court decision in 1954 banning segregated schools has had almost eight years of existence, yet less than 8 percent of the Negro kids are in integrated schools. That is far too slow. Now the people themselves want to get involved, and they are. I was talking with one of the student leaders of the South only last week; he said, "I myself desegregated a lunch counter, not somebody else, not some big man, some powerful man, but me, little me. I walked the picket line and I sat in and the walls of segregation toppled. Now all people can eat there." One young prize fighter was a cell-mate of mine in the prisons of Mississippi as a Freedom Rider; he had won his last fight and had a promising career. I saw him three weeks ago and asked him, "How are you coming along?" He said, "Not very well, I lost the last fight and I am through with the prize ring. I have no more interest in it. The only fight I want now," said he, "is the freedom fight. Because I, a little man, can become involved in it, and can help to win freedom." So that's what's happening; you see, we are going to do something about freedom now, we are not waiting for other people to do it. The student sit-ins have shown it; we are winning. As a result of one year of the student sit-ins, the lunch counters were desegregated in more than 150 cities. The walls are tumbling down.

Direct Action Brings Results

Who will say that lunch counters, which are scattered all over the country, are not important? Are we not to travel? Picket lines and boycotts brought Woolworth's to its knees. In its annual report of last year, Woolworth's indicated that profits had dropped and one reason for the drop was the nationwide boycott in which many Northern students, including Cornellians, participated. The picketing and the nationwide demonstrations are the reason that the walls came down in the South, because people were in motion with their own bodies, marching with picket signs, sitting in, boycotting, withholding their patronage. In Savannah, Georgia, there was a boycott, in which 99 percent of the Negroes participated. They stayed out of the stores. They registered to vote. The store owners then got together and said, "We want to sit down and talk; gentlemen, you have proved your point. You have proved that you can control Negroes' purchasing power and that you can control their votes. We need no more proof, we are ready to hire the people that you send." Negroes are hired in those stores now as a result of this community-wide campaign. In Lexington, Kentucky, the theaters were opened up by CORE as a result of picketing and boycotting. Some of the theaters refused to admit Negroes, others would let Negroes sit up in the balcony. They boycotted one, picketed the others. In a short period of time, the theater owners sat down to negotiate. All of the theaters there are open now. Using the same technique, they provided scores of jobs in department stores, grocery stores, and more recently as city bus drivers.

Then came the Freedom Rides. Three hundred and twenty-five people were jailed in Jackson, Mississippi, others beaten, fighting for freedom nonviolently. They brought down many, many barriers. They helped to create desegregation in cities throughout the South. The ICC [Interstate Commerce Commission] order was forthcoming as a result of the Freedom Rides and a more recent Supreme Court ruling. CORE sent test teams throughout the South after the ICC order went into effect. The test teams found that in hundreds of cities throughout the South, where terminals had been previously segregated, they now were desegregated and Negroes were using them. Mississippi is an exception, except for two cities; Louisiana is an exception, except for one pocket of the state; but by and large the Rides were successful. And then on Route 40. How many Negroes and interracial groups have driven Route 40 to Washington or to New York and carried their sandwiches, knowing that they could not eat between Wilmington and Baltimore. The Freedom Rides there, and some Cornell students participated in those Freedom Rides, brought down the barriers in more than half of those restaurants and each weekend, rides are taking place aimed at the others. By Easter we will have our Easter dinner in any place we choose on Route 40. At least fifty-three out of the eighty are now desegregated. In voter registration projects, we have registered seventeen thousand Negroes in South Carolina, previously unregistered. The politicians, segregationists, it's true, now call up our leaders and say, "I would like to talk to you because I don't believe in segregation as much as my opponent," or, "We would like to sit down and talk," or, "Can you come by my house and let's talk about this thing." Because they are realizing that now they have to be responsible to the votes of Negroes as well as the handful of whites, these are the things that are being done by people themselves in motion. Not waiting for someone else to do it, not looking forward to pie in the sky at some later date, not expecting a power on high to solve the problem for them, but working to solve it themselves and winning.

Integration Repudiates Racist Theories

What are our objectives: segregation, separation? Absolutely not! The disease and the evils that we have pointed to in our American culture have grown out of segregation and its partner, prejudice. We are for integration, which is the repudiation of the evil of segregation. It is a rejection of the racist theories of DeGobineu, Lothrop Stoddard, and all the others. It matters not whether they say that whites are superior to Negroes and Negroes are inferior, or if they reverse the coin and say that Negroes are superior and whites are inferior. The theory is just as wrong, just as much a defiance of history. We reject those theories. We are working for the right of Negroes to enter all fields of activity in American life. To enter business if they choose, to enter the professions, to enter the sciences, to enter the arts, to enter the academic world. To be workers, to be laborers if they choose. Our objective is to have each individual accepted on the basis of his individual merit and not on the basis of his color. On the basis of what he is worth himself.

This has given a new pride to [a] large number of people. A pride to the people in Mississippi, who themselves saw others, white and Negro, joining them in the fight for freedom; forty-one local citizens went into the jails of Mississippi joining the Freedom Riders. They have come out now and they have started their own nonviolent Jackson movement for freedom. They are sitting in. They are picketing, they are boycotting, and it is working. In Macomb, Mississippi, local citizens are now seeking to register to vote, some of them registering. In Huntsville, Alabama, as a result of CORE's campaign there (and we are now under injunction), for the past six weeks local Negro citizens have been sitting in every day at lunch counters. One of the white CORE leaders there in Huntsville was taken out of his house at gunpoint, undressed, and sprayed with mustard oil. That's the kind of treatment they have faced, but they will not give up because they know they are right and they see the effects of their efforts; they see it in the crumbling walls in interstate transportation and in other public facilities.

We are seeking an open society, an open society of freedom where people will be accepted for what they are worth, will be able to contribute fully to the total culture and the total life of the nation.

Now we know the disease, we know what is wrong with America, we know now that the CORE position is trying to right it. We must do it in interracial groups because we do not think it is possible to fight against caste in a vehicle which in itself is a representative of caste. We know that the students are still sitting in, they are still fighting for freedom. What we want, Mr. X, [as] the representative of the Black Muslims and Elijah Muhammad, to tell us today, is what his program is, what he proposes to do about killing this disease. We know the disease, physician, what is your cure? What is your program and how do you hope to bring it into effect? How will you achieve it? It is not enough to tell us that it may be a program of a black state. The Communists had such a program in the thirties and part of the forties, and they dropped it before the fifties as being impractical. So we are not only interested in the terminology. We need to have it spelled out; if we are being asked to follow it, to believe in it, what does it mean? Is it a separate Negro society in each city? As a Harlem, a South Side Chicago? Is it a separate state in one part of the country? Is it a separate nation in Africa, or elsewhere? Then we need to know how is it to be achieved. I assume that before a large part of land could be granted to Negroes or to Jews or to anybody else in the country it would have to be approved by the Senate of the United States.

You must tell us, Mr. X, if you seriously think that the Senate of the United States which has refused or failed for all these years to pass a strong Civil Rights Bill, you must tell us if you really think that this Senate is going to give us, to give you, a black state. I am sure that Senator Eastland would so vote, but the land that he would give us would probably be in the bottom of the sea. After seeing Alabama and Mississippi, if the power were mine, I would give you those states, but the power is not mine, I do not vote in the Senate. Tell us how you expect to achieve this separate black state.

Now it is not enough for us to know that you believe in black businesses, all of us believe that all Americans who wish to go into business should go into business. We must know, we need to know, if we are to appraise your program, the kind of businesses, how they are to be established; will we have a General Motors, a General Electric? Will I be able to manufacture a Farmer Special? Where am I going to get the capital from? You must tell us if we are going to have a separate interstate bus line to take the place of Greyhound and Trailways. You must tell us how this separate interstate bus line is going to operate throughout the country if all of us are confined within one separate state.

You must tell us these things, Mr. X, spell them out. You must tell us also what the relationship will be between the black businesses which you would develop and the total American economy. Will it be a competition? Will it be a rival economy, a dual economy, or will there be cooperation between these two economies?

Our program is clear. We are going to achieve our goals of integration by nonviolent direct action on an interracial level with whites and Negroes jointly cooperating to wipe out a disease which has afflicted and crippled all of them, white and black alike. The proof of the pudding is the eating. We have seen barriers fall as the result of using these techniques. We ask you, Mr. X, what is your program?

MALCOLM X: In the name of Allah, the Beneficent, the Merciful, to whom all praise is due, whom we forever thank for giving America's twenty million so-called Negroes the most honorable Elijah Muhammad as our leader and our teacher and our guide.

I would point out at the beginning that I wasn't born Malcolm Little. Little is the name of the slave master who owned one of my grandparents during slavery, a white man, and the name Little was handed down to my grandfather, to my father, and on to me. But after hearing the teachings of the honorable Elijah Muhammad and realizing that Little is an English name, and I'm not an Englishman, I gave the Englishman back his name; and since my own had been stripped from me, hidden from me, and I don't know it, I use X; and someday, as we are taught by the honorable Elijah Muhammad, every black man, woman, and child in America will get back the same name, the same language, and the same culture that he had before he was kidnapped and brought to this country and stripped of these things.

I would like to point out in a recent column by James Reston on the editorial page of *The New York Times,* December 15, 1961, writing

Malcolm X   *Los Angeles Times Photo*

from London, [that] Mr. Reston, after interviewing several leading European statesmen, pointed out that the people of Europe, or the statesmen in Europe, don't feel that America or Europe has anything to worry about in Russia; that the people in Europe foresee the time when Russia, Europe, and America will have to unite together to ward off the threat of China and the nonwhite world. And if this same statement was made by a Muslim, or by the honorable Elijah Muhammad, it would be classified as racist; but Reston, who is one of the leading correspondents in this country and writing for one of the most respected newspapers, points out that the holocaust that the West is facing is not something from Russia, but threats of the combined forces of the dark world against the white world.

Why do I mention this? Primarily because the most crucial problem facing the white world today is the race problem. And the most crucial problem facing white America today is the race problem. Mr. Farmer pointed out beautifully and quoted one writer actually as saying that the holocaust that America is facing is primarily still based upon race. This doesn't mean that when people point these things out that they are racist; this means that they are facing the facts of life that we are confronted with today. And one need only to look at the world troubles in their international context, national context, or local context, and one will always see the race problem right there, a problem that it is almost impossible to duck around.

It so happens that you and I were born at a time of great change, when changes are taking place. And if we can't react intelligently to these changes, then we are going to be destroyed. When you look into the United Nations set-up, the way it is, we see that there is a change of power taking place, a change of position, a change of influence, a change of control. Whereas, in the past, white people used to exercise unlimited control and authority over dark mankind, today they are losing their ability to dictate unilateral terms to dark mankind. Whereas, yesterday dark nations had no voice in their own affairs, today, the voice that they exercise in their own affairs is increasing, which means in essence that the voice of the white man or the white world is becoming more quiet every day, and the voice of the nonwhite world is becoming more loud every day. These are the facts of life and these are the changes that you and I, this generation, have to face up to on an international level, a national level, or a local level before we can get a solution to the problems that confront not only the white man, but problems that confront also the black man, or the nonwhite man.

When we look at the United Nations and see how these dark nations get their independence—they can out-vote the Western bloc or what is known as the white world—and to the point where up until last year the United Nations was controlled by the white powers, or Western powers, mainly Christian powers, and the secretaryship used to be in the hands of a white European Christian; but now when we look at the general structure of the United Nations we see a man from Asia, from Burma, who is occupying the position of Secretary, who is a Buddhist, by the way, and we find the man who is occupying the seat of President is a Moslem from Africa, namely Tunisia. Just in recent times all of these changes are taking place, and the white man has got to be able to face up to them, and the black man has to be able to face up to them, before we can get our problem solved, on an international level, a national level, as well as on the local level.

In terms of black and white, what this means is that the unlimited power and prestige of the white world is decreasing, while the power and prestige of the nonwhite world is increasing. And just as our African and Asian brothers wanted to have their own land, wanted to have their own country, wanted to exercise control over themselves and govern themselves—they didn't want to be governed by whites or Europeans or outsiders, they wanted control over something among the black masses here in America. I think it would be mighty naive on the part of the white man to think that same feeling that is sweeping through the dark world is not going to leap nine thousand miles across the ocean and come into the black people here in this country, who have been begging you for four hundred years for something that they have yet to get.

In the areas of Asia and Africa where the whites gave freedom to the nonwhites a transition took place, of friendliness and hospitality. In the areas where the nonwhites had to exercise violence, today there is hostility between them and the white man. In this, we learn that the only way to solve a problem that is unjust, if you are wrong, is to take immediate action to correct it. But when the people against whom these actions have been directed have to take matters in their own hands, this creates hostility, and lack of friendliness and good relations between the two.

An Era of Great Change

I emphasize these things to point up the fact that we are living in an era of great change, when dark mankind wants freedom, justice, and equality. It is not a case of wanting integration or separation, it is a case of wanting freedom, justice, and equality.

Now if certain groups think that through integration they are going to get freedom, justice, equality, and human dignity, then well and good, we will go along with the integrationists. But if integration is not going to return human dignity to dark mankind, then integration is not the solution to the problem. And ofttimes we make the mistake of confusing the objective with the means by which the objective is to be obtained. It is not integration that Negroes in America want, it is human dignity. They want to be recognized as human beings. And if integration is going to bring us recognition as human beings, then we will integrate. But if integration is not going to bring us recognition as human beings, then integration [is] "out the window," and we have to find another means or method and try that to get our objectives reached.

The same hand that has been writing on the wall in Africa and Asia is also writing on the wall right here in America. The same rebellion, the same impatience, the same anger that exists in the hearts of the dark people in Africa and Asia is existing in the hearts and minds of twenty million black people in this country who have been just as thoroughly colonized as the people in Africa and Asia. Only the black man in America has been colonized mentally, his mind has been destroyed. And today, even though he goes to college, he comes out and still doesn't even know he is a black man; he is ashamed of what he is, because his culture has been destroyed, his identity has been destroyed; he has been made to hate his black skin, he has been made to hate the texture of his hair, he has been made to hate the features that God gave him. Because the honorable Elijah Muhammad is coming along today and teaching us the truth about black people to make us love ourselves, instead of realizing that it is you who taught us to hate ourselves and our own kind, you accuse the honorable Elijah Muhammad of being a hate teacher and accuse him of being a racist. He is only trying to undo the white supremacy that you have indoctrinated the entire world with.

I might point out that it makes America look ridiculous to stand up in world conferences and refer to herself as the leader of the free world. Here is a country, Uncle Sam, standing up and pointing a finger at the Portuguese, and at the French, and at other colonizers, and there are twenty million black people in this country who are still confined to second-class citizenship, twenty million black people in this country who are still segregated and Jim-Crowed, as my friend, Dr. Farmer, has already pointed out. And despite the fact that twenty million black people here yet don't have freedom, justice, and equality, Adlai Stevenson has nerve enough to stand up in the United Nations and point the finger at South Africa, and at Portugal, and at some of these other countries. All we say is that South Africa preaches what it practices and practices what it preaches; America preaches one thing and practices another.

And we don't want to integrate with hypocrites who preach one thing and practice another.

The good point in all of this is that there is an awakening going on among whites in America today, and this awakening is manifested in this way: two years ago you didn't know that there were black people in this country who didn't want to integrate with you; two years ago the white public had been brainwashed into thinking that every black man in this country wanted to force his way into your community, force his way into your schools, or force his way into your factories; two years ago you thought that all you would have to do is give us a little token integration and the race problem would be solved. Why? Because the people in the black community who didn't want integration were never given a voice, were never given a platform, were never given an opportunity to shout out the fact that integration would never solve the problem. And it has only been during the past year that the white public has begun to realize that the problem will never be solved unless a solution is devised acceptable to the black masses, as well as the black bourgeoisie—the upper-class or middle-class Negro. And when the whites began to realize that these integration-minded Negroes were in the minority, rather than in the majority, then they began to offer an open forum and give those who want separation an opportunity to speak their mind too.

Middle-Class Settles for Integration

We who are black in the black belt, or black community, or black neighborhood, can easily see that our people who settle for integration are usually the middle-class so-called Negroes, who are in the minority. Why? Because they have confidence in the white man; they have absolute confidence that you will change. They believe that they can change you, they believe that there is still hope in the American dream. But what to them is an American dream to us is an American nightmare, and we don't think that it is possible for the American white man in sincerity to take the action necessary to correct the unjust conditions that twenty million black people here are made to suffer morning, noon, and night. And because we don't have any hope or confidence or faith in the American white man's ability to bring about a change in the injustices that exist, instead of asking or seeking to integrate into the American society we want to face the facts of the problem the way they are, and separate ourselves. And in separating ourselves this doesn't mean that we are anti-white, or anti-American, or anti-anything. We feel that if integration all these years hasn't solved the problem yet, then we want to try something new, something different, and something that is in accord with the conditions as they actually exist.

The honorable Elijah Muhammad teaches us that there are over 725 million Moslems or Muslims on this earth. I use both words interchangeably. I use the word Moslem for those who can't undergo the change, and I use the word Muslim for those who can. He teaches us that the world of Islam stretches from the China Seas to the shores of West Africa and that the twenty million black people in this country are the lost-found members of the nation of Islam. He teaches us that before we were kidnapped by your grandfathers and brought to this country and put in chains, our religion was Islam, our culture was Islamic, we came from the Muslim world, we were kidnapped and brought here out of the Muslim world. And after being brought here we were stripped of our language, stripped of our ability to speak our mother tongue, and it's a crime today to have to admit that there are twenty million black people in this country who not only can't speak their mother tongue, but don't even know they ever had one. This points up the crime of how thoroughly and completely the black man in America has been robbed by the white man of his culture, of his identity, of his soul, of his self. And because he has been robbed of his self, he is trying to accept your self. Because he doesn't know who he is, now he wants to be who you are. Because he doesn't know what belongs to him, he is trying to lay claim to what belongs to you. You have brain-washed him and made him a monster. He is black on the outside, but you have made him white on the inside. Now he has a white heart and a white brain, and he's breathing down your throat and down your neck because he thinks he's a white man the same as you are. He thinks that he should have your house, that he should have your factory, he thinks that he should even have your school, and most of them even think that they should have your woman, and most of them are after your woman.

So-Called Negroes Are Lost Sheep

The honorable Elijah Muhammad teaches us that the black people in America, the so-called Negroes, are the people who are referred to in the Bible as the lost sheep, who are to be returned to their own in the last days. He says that we are also referred to in the Bible, symbolically, as the lost tribe. He teaches us in our religion that we are those people whom the Bible refers to who would be lost until the end of time—lost in a house that is not theirs, lost in a land that is not theirs, lost in a country that is not theirs—and who will be found in the last days by the Messiah who will awaken them and enlighten them, and teach them that which they had been stripped of, and then this would give them the desire to come together among their own kind and go back among their own kind.

And this, basically, is why we who are followers of the honorable Elijah Muhammad don't accept integration: we feel that we are living at the end of time; by this, we feel that we are living at the end of the world. Not the end of the earth, but the end of the world. He teaches us that there are many worlds. The planet is an earth, and there is only one earth, but there are many worlds on this earth, the Eastern world and the Western world. There is a dark world and a white world. There is the world of Christianity, and the world of Islam. All of these are worlds and he teaches us that when the book speaks of the end of time, it doesn't mean the end of the earth, but it means the end of time for certain segments of people, or a certain world that is on this earth. Today, we who are here in America who have awakened to the knowledge of ourselves, we believe that there is no God but Allah, and we believe that the religion of Islam is Allah's religion, and we believe that it is Allah's intention to spread his religion throughout the entire earth. We believe that the earth will become all Muslim, all Islam, and because we are in a Christian country we believe that this Christian country will have to accept Allah as God, accept the religion of Islam as God's religion, or otherwise God will come in and wipe it out. And we don't want to be wiped out with the American white man, we don't want to integrate with him, we want to separate from him.

Separation Is the Best Solution

The method by which the honorable Elijah Muhammad is straightening out our problem is not teaching us to force ourselves into your society, or force ourselves even into your political, economic, or any phase of your society, but he teaches us that the best way to solve this problem is for complete separation. He says that since the black man here in America is actually the property that was stolen from the East by the American white man, since you have awakened today and realized that this is what we are, we should be separated from you, and your government should ship us back to where we came from, not at our expense, because we didn't pay to come here. We were brought here in chains. So the honorable Elijah Muhammad and the Muslims who follow him, we want to go back to our own people. We want to be returned to our own people.

But in teaching this among our people and the masses of black people in this country, we discover that the American government is the foremost agency in opposing any move by any large number of black people to leave here and go back among our own kind. The honorable Elijah Muhammad's words and work are harassed daily by the FBI and every other government agency which uses various tactics to make the so-called Negroes in every community think that we are all about to be rounded up, and they will be rounded up too if they will listen to Mr. Muhammad; but what the American government has failed to realize, the best way to open up a black man's head today and make him listen to another black man is to speak against that black man. But when you begin to pat a black man on the back, no black man in his right mind will trust that black man any longer. And it is because of this hostility on the part of the government toward our leaving here that the honorable Elijah Muhammad says then, if the American white man or the American government doesn't want us to leave, and the government has proven its inability to bring about integration or give us freedom, justice, and equality on a basis, equally mixed up with white people, then what are we going to do? If the government doesn't want us to go back among our own people, or to our own people, and at the same time the government has proven its inability to give us justice, the honorable Elijah Muhammad says if you don't want us to go and we can't stay here and live in peace together, then the best solution is separation. And this is what he means when he says that some of the territory here should be set aside, and let our people go off to ourselves and try and solve our own problem.

Some of you may say, Well, why should you give us part of this country? The honorable Elijah Muhammad says that for four hundred years we contributed our slave labor to make the country what it is. If you were to take the individual salary or allowances of each person in this audience it would amount to nothing individually, but when you take it collectively all in one pot you have a heavy load. Just the weekly wage. And if you realize that from anybody who could collect all of the wages from the persons in this audience right here for one month, why they would be so wealthy they couldn't walk. And if you see that, then you can imagine the result of millions of black people working for nothing for 310 years. And that is the contribution that we made to America. Not Jackie Robinson, not Marian Anderson, not George Washington Carver, that's not our contribution; our contribution to American society is 310 years of free slave labor for which we have not been paid one dime. We who are Muslims, followers of the honorable Elijah Muhammad, don't think that an integrated cup of coffee is sufficient payment for 310 years of slave labor.

JAMES FARMER *(Rebuttal):* I think that Mr. X's views are utterly impractical and that his so-called "black state" cannot be achieved. There is no chance of getting it unless it is to be given to us by Allah. We have waited for a long time for God to give us other things and we have found that the God in which most of us happen to believe helps those who help themselves. So we would like you to tell us, Mr. X, just what steps you plan to go through to get this black state. Is it one that is going to be gotten by violence, by force? Is it going to be given to us by the Federal Government? Once a state is allocated, then are the white people who happen to live there to be moved out forcibly, or Negroes who don't want to go to your black state [are they] going to be moved forcibly? And what does this do to their liberty and freedom?

Now Mr. X suggests that we Negroes or so-called Negroes, as he puts it, ought to go back where we came from. You know, this is a very interesting idea. I think the solution to many of the problems, including the economic problem of our country, would be for all of us to go back where we came from and leave the country to the American Indians. As a matter of fact, maybe the American Indian can go back to Asia, where I understand the anthropologists tell us he came from, and I don't know who preceded him there. But if we search back far enough I am sure that we can find some people to people or populate this nation. Now the overwhelming number of Negroes in this country consider it to be their country; their country more than Africa: I was in Africa three years ago, and while I admire and respect what is being done there, while there is certainly a definite sense of identification and sympathy with what is going on there, the fact is that the cultures are so very different. Mr. X, I am sure that you have much more in common with me or with several people whom I see sitting here than you do with the Africans, than you do with Tom Mboya. Most of them could not understand you, or you they, because they speak Swahili or some other language and you would have to learn those languages.

I tell you that we are Americans. This is our country as much as it is white American. Negroes came as slaves, most of us did. Many white people came as indentured servants; indentured servants are not free. Don't forget it wasn't all of you who were on that ship, the Mayflower.

Now separation of course has been proposed as the answer to the problem, rather than integration. I am pleased however that Malcolm, oh pardon me, Mr. X, indicated that if integration works, and if it provides dignity, then we are for integration. Apparently he is almost agreeing with us there. He is sort of saying as King Agrippa said to St. Paul, "Almost thou persuadest me." I hope that he will be able to come forth and make the additional step and join me at the integrationist side of this table. In saying that separation really is the answer and the most effective solution to this problem, he draws a distinction between separation and segregation, saying that segregation is forced ghettoism while separation is voluntary ghettoism. Well now, I would like to ask Mr. X whether it would be voluntary for Negroes to be segregated as long as we allow discrimination in housing throughout the country to exist. If you live in a black state and cannot get a house elsewhere, then are you voluntarily separated, or are you forcibly segregated?

Black Men and White Women

Now Mr. X suggests that actually the Negroes of this country want the white man's women. Now this is a view, of course, which is quite familiar to you; I've heard it before, there are some Negroes who are married to white people, and I, just before I came up, was looking for a back issue of the paper of the Muslims and saw in there an indication that I myself have a white wife. And it was suggested that therefore I have betrayed my people in marrying a white woman. Well you know I happen to have a great deal of faith in the virtues and the abilities and capacities of Negroes. Not only Negroes, but all of the people too. In fact, I have so much faith in the virtues of Negroes that I do not even think those virtues are so frail that they will be corrupted by contact with other people.

Mr. X also indicated that Negroes imitate whites. It is true, we do, he is right. We fix our hair and try to straighten it; I don't do mine, I haven't had a conk in my life, I think they call it a process, now, etc. But this is a part of the culture of course. After the black culture was taken away from us, we had to adopt the culture that was here, adopt it, and adapt to it. But it is also true that white people try to imitate Negroes, with their jazz, with their hair curlers, you know, and their man-tans. I think, Mr. X, that perhaps the grass is always greener on the other side of the fence. Now when we create integration, perhaps it won't be so necessary for us to resort to these devices.

The black bourgeoisie—is it only the middle class that wants integration? Were the sit-in students black bourgeoisie? They didn't fit into the definition in E. Franklin Frazier's book on the black bourgeoisie. Quite to the contrary, these students were lower-class people. Many of them were workers working to stay in school. In the Freedom Rides, were they black bourgeoisie? No, we didn't have exceptions there, we had some people who were unemployed. These are not the black bourgeoisie who want integration. Quite to the contrary, very frequently, the middle class developed a vested interest in the maintenance of segregation. Because if they have a store, and if segregation is eliminated, then I'll be in open competition with the white stores. And thus it is most often true, as Frazier pointed out in his book, that the middle class tends to be opposed to desegregation. Now I would wonder also in the building of black businesses if we are not going to be building another black bourgeoisie? If Negroes may not perhaps be giving up one master for another, a white one for a black one? Are we going to build a new Negro middle class and say that no matter how tyrannical it may prove to be it is my own and, therefore, I like it?

Now we of course know that the Negro is sick, the white man is sick, we know that psychologically we have been twisted by all of these things; but still, Mr. X, you have not told us what the solution is except that it is separation, in your view. You have not spelled it out. Well, now, this sickness, as I tried to indicate in my first presentation, springs from segregation. It is segregation that produces prejudice, as much as prejudice produces segregation. In Detroit, at the time of the race riot, the only rioting, the only fighting, was in the all-Negro and all-white sections of the city, where separation was complete. In those several sections of the city where Negroes and whites lived together, next door to each other, there was no fighting because there the people were neighbors or friends. Now you propose separation as the solution to this problem, as the cure to the disease. Here we have a patient that is suffering from a disease caused by mosquitoes, and the physician proposes as a cure that the man go down and lie in a damp swamp and play with wiggletails.

Malcolm X *(Rebuttal):* I hadn't thought, or intended anyway, to get personal with Mr. Farmer in mentioning his white wife; I thought that perhaps it would probably have been better left unsaid, but it's better for him to say than for me to say it, because then you would think I was picking on him. I think you will find if you were to have gone into Harlem a few years back you would have found on the juke boxes records by Belafonte, Eartha Kitt, Pearl Bailey; all of these persons were very popular singers in the so-called Negro community a few years back. But since Belafonte divorced Marguerite and married a white woman it doesn't mean that Harlem is anti-white, but you can't find Belafonte's records there; or maybe he just hasn't produced a hit. All of these entertainers who have become involved in intermarriage, and I mean

Lena Horne, Eartha Kitt, Sammy Davis, Belafonte, they have a large white following, but you can't go into any Negro community across the nation and find records by these artists that are hits in the so-called Negro community. Because, subconsciously, today the so-called Negro withdraws himself from the entertainers who have crossed the line. And if the masses of black people won't let a Negro who is involved in an intermarriage play music for him, he can't speak for him.

The only way you can solve the race problem as it exists is to take into consideration the feelings of the masses, not the minority; the majority, not the minority. And it is proof that the masses of white people don't want Negroes forcing their way into their neighborhood and the masses of black people don't think it's any solution for us to force ourselves into the white neighborhood, so the only ones who want integration are the Negro minority, as I say, the bourgeoisie and the white minority, the so-called white liberals. And the same white liberal who professes to want integration whenever the Negro moves to his neighborhood, he is the first one to move out. And I was talking with one today who said he was a liberal and I asked him where did he live, and he lived in an all-white neighborhood and probably might for the rest of his life. This is conjecture, but I think it stands true. The Civil War was fought one hundred years ago, supposedly to solve this problem. After the Civil War was fought, the problem still existed. Along behind that, the Thirteenth and Fourteenth Amendments were brought about in the Constitution supposedly to solve the problem; after the Amendments, the problem was still right here with us.

Most Negroes think that the Civil War was fought to make them citizens; they think that it was fought to free them from slavery because the real purpose of the Civil War is clothed in hypocrisy. The real purpose of the Amendments is clothed in hypocrisy. The real purpose behind the Supreme Court Desegregation decision was clothed in hypocrisy. And any time integrationists, NAACP, CORE, Urban League, or what have you, will stand up and tell me to spell out how we are going to bring about separation, and here they are integrationists, a philosophy which is supposed to have the support of the Senate, Congress, President, and the Supreme Court, and still with all of that support and hypocritical agreeing, eight years after the desegregation decision, you still don't have what the Court decided on.

So we think this, that when whites talk integration they are being hypocrites, and we think that the Negroes who accept token integration are also being hypocrites, because they are the only ones who benefit from it, the handful of hand-picked, high-class, middle-class Uncle Tom

Negroes. They are hand-picked by whites and turned loose in a white community and they're satisfied. But if all of the black people went into the white community, overnight you would have a race war. If four or five little black students going to school in New Orleans bring about the riots that we saw down there, what do you think would happen if all of the black people tried to go to any school that they want, you would have a race war. So our approach to it, those of us who follow the honorable Elijah Muhammad, we feel that it is more sensible than running around here waiting for the whites to allow us inside their attic or inside their basement.

Anti-Discrimination Groups Discriminate

Every Negro group that we find in the Negro community that is integrated is controlled by the whites who belong to it, or it is led by the whites who belong to it. NAACP has had a white president for fifty-three years, it has been in existence for fifty-three years; Roy Wilkins is the executive secretary, but Spingarn, a white man, has been the president for the past twenty-three years, and before him, his brother, another white man, was president. They have never had a black president. Urban League, another so-called Negro organization, doesn't have a black president, it has a white president. Now this doesn't mean that that's racism, it only means that the same organizations that are accusing you of practicing discrimination, when it comes to the leadership they're practicing discrimination themselves.

The honorable Elijah Muhammad says, and points out to us that in this book *(Anti-Slavery)* written by a professor from the University of Michigan, Dwight Lowell Dumond, a person who is an authority on the race question or slave question, his findings were used by Thurgood Marshall in winning the Supreme Court Desegregation decision. And in the preface of this book, it says that second-class citizenship is only a modified form of slavery, which means the Civil War didn't end slavery and the Amendments didn't end slavery. They didn't do it because we still have to wrestle the Supreme Court and the Congress and the Senate to correct the hypocrisy that's been practiced against us by whites for the past umteen years.

And because this was done, the American white man today subconsciously still regards that black man as something below himself. And you will never get the American white man to accept the so-called Negro as an integrated part of his society until the image of the Negro the white man has is changed, and until the image that the Negro has of himself is also changed.

Collateral Reading

Breitman, George, ed., *Malcolm X Speaks.* New York, 1965.

Epps, Archie, *The Speeches of Malcolm X at Harvard.* New York, 1969.

————, *Freedom—When?* New York, 1966.

Essien-Udom, E. U., *Black Nationalism.* Chicago, 1962.

Warren, Robert Penn, *Who Speaks for the Negro?* New York, 1965.

Westin, Alan E., ed., *Freedom Now! The Civil Rights Struggle in America.* New York, 1964.

Study Questions and Problems

1. What is the basic issue of this debate?

2. What are the basic contentions of each speaker?

3. What evidence and arguments are used to support each contention?

4. Which speaker did the better job of refuting the arguments of his opponent?

5. Did you note any faulty reasoning?

6. Which speaker was more clearly organized?

7. Which speaker had more evidence? Also, which speaker had the better evidence? Whom do you think won the debate? Why?

Selected Bibliography

There are hundreds of books and articles dealing with the Negro in American society. See, for example, the *Dictionary Catalog of the Schomburg Collection of Negro Literature and History* (Boston, 1962). The most useful bibliography of speakers and speeches is Rogert Hite, "Racial Rhetoric: A Bibliography" and Patrick Kennicott, "The Black Revolution in America: A Selected Bibliography" in *Proceedings of the SAA Summer Conference V Theme: Research and Action* (New York, 1969).

Serious scholars of black history and black speaking should consult the collections located in various Negro history archives. The Schomburg Collection at the New York Public Library contains an excellent collection of historical materials on Negro history. Libraries located at Atlanta University, Fisk University, Howard University, Yale University, and Tuskegee Institute also contain valuable historical materials. The following bibliography will suggest some of the most scholarly and useful sources of black history and black oratory.

Historical Works

Three of the most cogently written general surveys containing excellent bibliographic material are John Hope Franklin, *From Slavery to Freedom,* 2nd ed. (New York, 1956); E. Franklin Frazer, *The Negro in the United States* (New York, 1957); and historians August Meier and Elliott M. Rudwick, *From Plantation to Ghetto* (New York, 1966). Gunner Myrdal, *An American Dilemma,* 2 vols. (New York, 1944) remains an informative sociological study of the Negro in America.

Journals devoted to historical and behavioral research of the American Negro include *Journal of Negro History* (Washington, D.C., 1916-), *Journal of Negro Education* (Washington, D.C., 1932-) and *Phylon* (Atlanta, 1940-).

The best collection of published documents is Herbert Aptheker (ed.), *A Documentary History of the Negro People in the United States,* 2 vols.

(New York, 1951). Aptheker's work includes edited segments of Negro convention speeches which should be consulted by persons interested in nineteenth-century Negro speaking. Another worthwhile collection of documents which includes many significant speeches is Francis L. Broderick and August Meier (eds.), *Negro Protest Thought in the Twentieth Century* (Indianapolis, 1965). Howard Brotz (ed.), *Negro Social and Political Thought 1850-1920* (New York, 1957) is also a good source of texts.

A number of books have analyzed Negro movements and civil rights organizations. The most nearly adequate account of the NAACP is Langston Hughes, *Fight for Freedom: The Story of the NAACP* (New York, 1962). Also read Warren D. St. James, *The NAACP: A Case Study in Pressure Groups* (New York, 1958). SNCC is thoughtfully analyzed in Howard Zinn, *SNCC: The New Abolitionists* (Boston, 1964). A not very satisfactory account (but the best available) of CORE is provided in James Peck, *Freedom Ride* (New York, 1962). Marcus Garvey's UNIA movement is satisfactorily treated by Edmund O. Cronan, *Black Moses: The Story of Marcus Garvey and the Universal Negro Improvement Association* (Madison, Wis., 1955). Black Nationalism is studied in depth by C. Eric Lincoln, *The Black Muslims in America* (Boston, 1961) and E. U. Essien-Udom, *Black Nationalism: The Search for Identity in America* (Chicago, 1962). Herbert Garfinkel, *When Negroes March* (Glencoe, Ill., 1949) is an excellent study of the March On Washington Movement. Also read Whitney M. Young, Jr., "The Urban League and Its Strategy," *The Annals of the American Academy of Political and Social Science* (January, 1965). Finally, Martin Luther King, Jr., *Stride Toward Freedom: The Montgomery Story* (New York, 1958) is an intimate account of the Montgomery bus boycott.

Among the best autobiographical works of significant speakers are Frederick Douglass, *The Life and Times of Frederick Douglass* (rev. ed., 1893); Booker T. Washington, *Up From Slavery* (New York, 1901); W. E. B. Du Bois, *Autobiography* (New York, 1968); James Weldon Johnson, *Along This Way* (New York, 1933); Malcolm X, *Autobiography of Malcolm X* (New York, 1965); and Eldridge Cleaver, *Soul on Ice* (New York, 1967).

In addition to life sketches located in various biographical directories, there are a number of perceptive biographies of black speakers. Among the best are Philip S. Foner (ed.), *The Life and Writings of Frederick Douglass,* 4 vols. (New York, 1950-1955); Francis L. Broderick, *W. E. B. Du Bois: Negro Leader in Time of Crisis* (Stanford, 1959); and Amy-Jacques Garvey (ed.), *Philosophy and Opinions of Marcus Garvey* (New York, 1923). Also read M. M. Brewer, "Henry Highland Garnet,"

Journal of Negro History (January, 1928); "Churches and James Forman," *Christian Today* (June 6, 1969); and Kathleen Cleaver, "On Eldridge Cleaver," *Ramparts* (June, 1969).

Finally, there are numerous black newspapers on the contemporary scene, but perhaps the newspaper of greatest historical importance is Frederick Douglass' *North Star.*

Rhetorical Works

Unfortunately, there is no completely adequate, comprehensive rhetorical analysis of black public speakers. However, individual black speakers have been critically analyzed in national and regional speech journals. *Southern States Speech Journal, Western Speech,* and the *Central States Speech Journal* contain several excellent rhetorical critiques of individual black speakers. Specifically, the reader should consult Robert C. Dick, "Negro Oratory in the Anti-Slavery Society 1830-1860," *Western Speech* (Winter, 1964); Elizabeth F. Phifer and Dencil R. Taylor, "Carmichael in Tallahassee," *Southern States Speech Journal* (Winter, 1967); Parke G. Burgess, "The Rhetoric of Black Power: A Moral Demand?" *Quarterly Journal of Speech* (April, 1968); Maxine S. Ferris, "The Speaking of Roy Wilkins," *Central States Speech Journal* (May, 1965), pp. 91-99; and Pat Jefferson, "The Magnificent Barbarian at Nashville," *Southern Speech Journal* (Winter, 1967), pp. 77-88.

The best collection of historically significant Negro speeches is Carter G. Woodson (ed.), *Negro Orators and Their Orations* (Washington, D.C., 1921). A less satisfactory collection of historically important orations is Roy Hill (ed.), *The Rhetoric of Racial Revolt* (Denver, 1964).

Good individual collections of speeches include Martin Luther King, Jr., *Where Do We Go From Here: Chaos or Community?* (New York, 1967); Archie Epps, *The Speeches of Malcolm X at Harvard* (New York, 1969); George Breitman, *The Last Year of Malcolm X: The Evolution of a Revolutionary* (New York, 1967); and E. D. Washington (ed.), *Selected Speeches of Booker T. Washington* (New York, 1932).

Among the best collections of contemporary black speeches are Haig Bosmajian and Hameda Bosmajian (eds.), *The Rhetoric of the Civil Rights Movement* (New York, 1969) and Arthur L. Smith (ed.), *Rhetoric of Black Revolution* (Boston, 1969). Robert C. Scott and Wayne Brockriede, *The Rhetoric of Black Power* (New York, 1969) contains speeches together with critical evaluations of some of the speeches. Some significant black speeches are available in Lester Thonssen, *Representative American Speeches* (New York, 1950).

Some good theses and dissertations on Negro oratory include Gary

L. Allen, "Anthology of Selected Civil Rights Speeches," unpublished Master's thesis, George Washington University, 1933; DeWitt C. Bennett, "A Survey of American Negro Oratory," unpublished Ph.D. dissertation, Florida State University, 1967; Patrick C. Kennicott, "Negro Antislavery Speakers in America," unpublished Ph.D. dissertation, University of Southern California, 1955; Lowell Moserberry, "An Historical Study of Negro Oratory in the United States to 1915," unpublished Ph.D. dissertation, University of Southern California, 1955; and Helen B. Whittaker, "The Negro in the Abolition Movement, 1830-1850," unpublished Master's thesis, Howard University, 1935.